SOCIAL AND CULTURAL DIVERSITY IN A SPORTING WORLD

RESEARCH IN THE SOCIOLOGY OF SPORT

Series Editor: Kevin Young

Recent Volumes:

RESEARCH IN THE SOCIOLOGY OF SPORT   VOLUME 5

SOCIAL AND CULTURAL DIVERSITY IN A SPORTING WORLD

EDITED BY

CHRIS HALLINAN
School of Human Movement,
Recreation & Performance, Victoria University, Australia

STEVEN JACKSON
School of Physical Education,
University of Otago, New Zealand

Emerald
JAI

United Kingdom – North America – Japan
India – Malaysia – China

JAI Press is an imprint of Emerald Group Publishing Limited
Howard House, Wagon Lane, Bingley BD16 1WA, UK

First edition 2008

British Library Cataloguing in Publication Data
A catalogue record for this book is available from the British Library

ISBN: 978-0-7623-1456-0
ISSN: 1476-2854 (Series)

Awarded in recognition of
Emerald's production
department's adherence to
quality systems and processes
when preparing scholarly
journals for print

INVESTOR IN PEOPLE

CONTENTS

AN OPEN LETTER FROM RUGBY BOYS IN
NO-VOICE-LAND: REFLECTIONS ON RUGBY AND
RACE BY SOUTH AFRICA'S 2007 SCHOOLBOY
PLAYERS

LIST OF CONTRIBUTORS

Michael Burke	School of Human Movement, Recreation and Performance, Victoria University, Melbourne, Australia
Cora Burnett	Department of Sport and Movement Studies, University of Johannesburg, South Africa
Tim Crabbe	Sheffield Hallam University, UK; The Substance Cooperative, UK
Andrew Grainger	Department of Kinesiology and Health, Miami University, Oxford, OH, USA
Chris Hallinan	Centre for Ageing, Rehabilitation, Exercise and Sport, and School of Human Movement, Recreation and Performance, Victoria University, Melbourne, Australia
Steven Jackson	School of Physical Education, University of Otago, Dunedin, New Zealand
Hiroshi Komuku	Ryukoku University, Seta, Otsu, Shiga, Japan
Roger LeBlanc	Ecole de Kinésiologie et de Récréologie, Université de Moncton, Moncton, NB, Canada
Jessica Macbeth	School of Sport, Tourism and the Outdoors, University of Central Lancashire, UK
Nalin Mehta	Visiting Fellow at Australian National University, Canberra
Boria Majumdar	Senior Research Fellow at La Trobe University, Melbourne

Brent McDonald   Centre for Ageing, Rehabilitation,
                         Exercise and Sport, and School of Human
                         Movement, Recreation and Performance,
                         Victoria University, Melbourne, Australia

Fabien Ohl   Université de Lausanne, ISSEP,
                         Faculté des SSP, Switzerland

Bente Ovèdie Skogvang Department of Sports Science, Hedmark
                         University College, Elverum, Norway

Brendon Tagg   School of Physical Education, University of
                         Otago, Dunedin, New Zealand

Marijke Taks   Faculty of Human Kinetics, University of
                         Windsor, Windsor, ON, Canada;
                         Katholieke Universiteit Leuven, Leuven,
                         Belgium

Lone Friis Thing   Department of Exercise and Sport Sciences,
                         University of Copenhagen, Denmark

THE DIFFERENCE WITHIN: DIVERSITY AS A KEY CONCEPTUAL FRAMEWORK

Chris Hallinan and Steven Jackson

An array of major global events of the last decade have drawn attention to issues of nations, nationalism and national borders in conjunction with issues of social and cultural diversities. Within the context of the post 9/11 era a complex and arguably contradictory and paradoxical set of conditions, practices and policies have emerged in relation to how we see, represent, understand and acknowledge the diversity of "Others." For example, Blokker (2008) has referred to Europe as "united in diversity" (p. 257). We suggest there are contradictions and paradoxes because on the one hand a paradigm of consumer capitalism driven by the global deregulation of international trade and other barriers is contributing to an increasing flow of not only ideas and products but also people. However, despite the discourse of free markets, seamless synergies and the free flow of goods and services we are witnessing evidence of increasingly tightened, restrictive and even closed national boundaries. Without doubt these official state security policies are impacting how we see the world and our place in it. Likewise, it is shaping how we negotiate a range of identities associated with social and cultural difference and diversity. Consider the way in which particular groups in society have been targeted and demonised by some sections of the mass media. In Australia as in many other countries, Muslim Australians have recently been the focus of a sustained vilification by certain commercial

Social and Cultural Diversity in a Sporting World
Research in the Sociology of Sport, Volume 5, 1–13
Copyright © 2008 by Emerald Group Publishing Limited
All rights of reproduction in any form reserved
ISSN: 1476-2854/doi:10.1016/S1476-2854(08)05001-2

media outlets. One of the upshots of this campaign is the generation of fear. Perhaps inevitably, this accumulation of fear and loathing resulted in a confrontation on Cronulla Beach in Sydney in 2005. Whilst Cronulla Beach lies within Sutherland Shire, a municipality among the lowest proportions of non-English-speaking-background residents in Australia, it is also the only beach along the Sydney shores which has a train station. It is thus a popular destination for youths from the western suburbs but they are less welcome than the self-described "locals." It appears that it is not just the sun that is being screened out at the beach these days.

This example points to a paradox with the concept of cultural diversity within a globalising world. Where democracy, human rights and the tolerance of difference are championed by a range of international organisations along with particular segments of society, the complexity, challenges and even validity of some programs are increasingly being scrutinised. This may be due in part to the very nature of the concept of diversity itself. As Levin and Rittel (1994) astutely note, there is a diversity of meanings associated with the concept of diversity or in their words "diversity is itself diverse" (http://epaa.asu.edu/epaa/v2n2.html). This is because aspects of its dominant meanings and representations often become essentialised thereby marginalising or, at times, masking alternative perspectives. Furthermore, diversity is not new, but our understanding of it and policy approaches to it have changed significantly. For example, there is increasing recognition that the "successful" response to diversity may actually lead to less diversity, not more (Levin & Rittel, 1994).

We assert that part of the challenge is that cultural diversity is an evolving, value-laden ideological concept that often articulates with other contested concepts such as difference, differentiation and multiculturalism. For example, consider the parallels between debates about cultural diversity and Todd Gitlin's (1995) critique of "multiculturalism,"

> The word is baggy, a melange of fact and value, current precisely because it is vague enough to serve so many interests. Partisans may use the term to defend the recognition of difference, or to resist policies or ideas imposed by conquerors, or to defend cosmopolitanism –the interests and pleasures that each may take in the profusion of humanity. The purists of identity politics use it to defend an endless fission, a heap of monocultures. On the other side, multiculturalism and its demonic twin, 'political correctness' serve conservatives as names for a potpourri of things they detest – including an irritating insistence on the rights of minorities. (p. 228)

Hence, cultural diversity, like multiculturalism is vulnerable to exploitation by a range of interest groups spanning the political spectrum. As a consequence some champion the possibility that "diversity furnishes the texture and variety of social life" (Boston, Callister, & Wolf, 2006, p. xi) representing a "quality of difference" ... strength, "cultural vitality, national pride and solidarity" (Boston et al., 2006, p. xi). However, diversity is also claimed to "generate social conflict, ethnic tension and political instability" (Boston et al., 2006, p. xi). In short it can be a focal point of both collective action and social celebration and conversely a site of protest and discord.

Consider some of the following examples which point to the complexity of the issue:

- In 2006 a Danish newspaper published a cartoon featuring the prophet Muhammad resulting in widespread Muslim protests and even death threats against the artist. Further highlighting the seriousness of such threats, in 2004 Dutch film maker Theo van Gogh was killed after he released a documentary about violence against Muslim women.
- Rap and hip musicians from all over the world are drawing upon an African American musical art form often to express their own discontent. However, in doing so they may be appropriating what rightfully belongs to others and perhaps more significantly may be reproducing elements of misogyny, violence and oppression against women and gays and lesbians that undermine any sense of cultural diversity.
- The 2006 season of the highly successful reality TV series "Survivor" featured tribes constructed around the most visible of cultural diversities: race. Tribes consisted of "White", "Black", "Asian" and "Hispanic" Americans arguably transforming diversity into an entertainment commodity.

And, what about sport? The world of sport is often promoted as sanctuary from the world-at-large. It is popularly considered to be a place where competition is conducted "on a level playing field." However, consider the following:

- Like all Bahraini athletes, Ruqaya Al Ghasara is supplied with clothing and footwear from Nike. Unlike many Muslim competitors, Al Ghasara adheres to traditional Islamic clothing standards for females when she races. That is, she wears long sleeves and pants, and a hijab. During the final of the 2006 Asian Games she again wore a hijab but on that occasion with a Nike swoosh on the left side of the hijab.
- One of the eight sections of the Hyundai A League's Code of Conduct for spectators reads as: "comply with the ban on bringing national and

political flags, banners or emblems into a venue (except for recognised Australian or New Zealand national or state flags);"

- Part of the mission of the CBC Radio Canada's regional stations is to "partner with organizations to support local cultural and sports events with the greatest potential for outreach and increased visibility in diverse communities."
- According to BBC Sports, the 2007–2008 Premier League season resulted in the least number of English players ever in the League. English players accounted for 34.1% of the total starters. The leading four clubs: Manchester United, Chelsea, Liverpool and Arsenal averaged 2.64 English starters per game during the 2007–2008 season.
- Baseball is romantically referred to as "The American Pastime." Yet, a quarter of the players in the United States-based Major League Baseball are from Puerto Rico and Latin American countries, especially the Dominican Republic, Venezuela, Cuba, Colombia and Mexico.
- Over the past decade a very influential social movement to eradicate the use of Native Indian mascots and other imagery in relation to sport teams in North America has emerged. This, despite the fact that a few, albeit a minority, of high schools and universities have been given permission by local tribes. Moreover, as Michael Robidoux (2006) notes in some cases native communities themselves proudly display these images (or various transformations).
- Gus Hiddink, the Dutch soccer coach who helped Korea to the semi-finals of the 2002 FIFA World Cup was awarded "honorary citizenship" a rare award in a country that continues to try and remain culturally homogenous that was only possible by passing special legislation.
- Oscar Pistorious, disabled South African runner renowned for his successful performances on his carbon constructed "Cheetah" prosthetics gained formal approval (on appeal) to compete against able-bodied athletes at the 2008 Beijing Olympics. The IAAF originally declined his application indicating that their undisclosed scientific tests indicated that his carbon feet would give him a performance advantage. Within the context of international sport where nation's reputations are at stake and millions of dollars in endorsements for athletes riding, the far-reaching implications of a disabled athlete having an advantage over able-bodied athletes should not be lost.
- Following the dismantling of apartheid in South Africa, the number of black male participants in road running events has increased noticeably. However, the trend was not evident in black women's participation (Paruk & de la Rey, 1993).

THE FRAMEWORK

We explore the dimensions of cultural diversity that relate to many of the aforementioned issues, as they are located within the broad context of sport. In doing so, we acknowledge that there are likely to be gaps. Worldwide, the response to diversity brought about by both the flow of people and concentration of some population groups has been varied. Not all of these frame diversity in the categorical variables of "ethnicity." Rather, the contributions are conceptually and theoretically varied. We sought to present a variety of contributions dealing with policy, inclusion, affirmative action legislations, identity and equity in all aspects of sports and sports organisations as well as related issues that have emerged within the context of social and cultural diversity. These topics include: the politics of identity and representation, theorising sport and inclusion practices, accommodation and resistance to diversity/equality, symbolic construction of sports communities, ethnocentrism and whiteness, ethnic identities and corporate managerialism, exploration of alternative leadership paradigms and affirmative action. Additionally, the chapters are constructed around themes including gender, race, ethnicity, indigeneity, sexuality, (dis)ability and religiosity.

FROM ASSIMILATION TO DIVERSITY

Much of the earlier research in sports studies was associated with the idea that sport could (and should) serve as an integrating mechanism – particularly for certain population groups. For example, Pooley's (1976) classic study of soccer football clubs in Milwaukee, USA was constructed around the implied desirability of structural assimilation. Indeed, Pooley's study used the Gordon (1964) model of structural assimilation. Part of Gordon's model included the comment "incorporating with them in a common culture" (p. 62). Pooley instigated the study of soccer football clubs on the assumption that not only was assimilation desirable "but their (the ethnic group) survival depends upon it" (p. 168). Pooley drew primarily upon the "structural assimilation" variable from Gordon's model. According to Gordon, "once structural assimilation has occurred, ... all other types of assimilation will follow" (p. 81). However, Allison's (1982) analysis of the data from several studies of ethnicity and sport in the USA led her to conclude that the implied assimilationist framework of these studies was inadequate. In fact, she discussed the benefits of diversity within sport. Likewise, Cheska's (1984) study of the American Southwest, led her to conclude that many groups conducted their sporting practice so as to maintain their distinction – a re-affirmation of one's own culture" (p. 253). Central to the exploration of social and cultural diversity are the contributions of social theorists. Much of the more recent research investigating elements of diversity and difference in sport has drawn upon the work of social theory. In the next sections we introduce several of the theorists. Whilst not a comprehensive review, we pay particular attention to those who form the basis of the contributions to this volume.

LOCATING CULTURE

Even though Homi Bhabha (1994) is not alone in theorising about culture and identity, his work reasonably captures the analysis we pursue in this work. Without doubt, globalisation has increased awareness of the implications and consequences of the flow of people, products and processes. Of course, one particular issue that has emerged as a result of the global–local nexus is that of social and cultural diversity which we consider to be broader than issues just related to globalisation such as multiculturalism and cosmopolitism. As Bhabha (1994) puts it: "A just measure of global progress requires that we first evaluate how globalising nations deal with "the difference within" – the problems of diversity and redistribution at the local level, and the rights and representations of minorities in the regional domain" (p. XV). Thus, social and cultural diversity becomes a key conceptual framework and lens through which to examine and understand a wide range of cultural issues related to: nationalism, gender, race, ethnicity, indigenous culture, sexuality, (dis)ability, religiosity and sport. For example, the legislative advances made in some societies have not necessarily transferred into the realm of sport. Australia is among the most multicultural nations in the world yet the men's national cricket team continues to be dominated by Anglophiles. As Christian Ryan editor of Wisden Cricketers' Almanack Australia (2004) wryly noted, "tot up every Aboriginal first-class (cricket) player in the past 153 years and you're left just shy of a 1st XI, never mind a whole squad." Yet, when the men's soccer football team was assembled for the 2006 World Cup, all of the players lived and played outside of Australia.

CONSTITUTIONAL PATRIOTISM

Following the substantial changes to the European political map in the last two decades, Habermas (1996) proposed the notion of constitutional patriotism. Habermas was primarily motivated by the unification of his native Germany and the desire for a workable collective identity for the "new" nation. Habermas' notion has been the subject of critique because it focusses too much on political legitimacy (Baumeister, 2007) and was too specifically German (Muller & Scheppelle, 2008). However, Muller & Scheppelle maintained that constitutional patriotism was a preferred option and that it was distinct from cosmopolitanism and nationalism in that it drew attachment to the norms and values of liberal democracy rather than a national culture. Many studies in sports identity have considered ethnocentric nationalism and its link to a desired national patriotism. Hallinan, Hughson, and Burke (2007) argued that the Hyundai League in Australia received government and mass media endorsement because it embraced the assimilationist policies of the (Howard) right wing national government. In England, there has been simmering tension during Test cricket series – none more so than when India is involved. The politics of sport spectating has been associated with the comments of conservative politician Norman Tebbit and the "test of Englishness" and former England captain Nasser Hussain (Fraser, 2005). Likewise, it was a test of "Australian-ness" with conservative Australian former politician Peter Costello arguing that cheering for the Socceroos was a measure of citizenship loyalty (Hallinan & Hughson, 2008). In this volume, Andrew Grainger contends that the contemporary framing of New Zealand as a Pacific-centred multicultural society is played out through the discourse surrounding the All Blacks. Nevertheless, like other Pacific rim nations (Australia and Canada) that have embraced multiculturalism, New Zealand also maintains a Eurocentric legacy. Grainger also draws upon Bhabha's (1994) notion of the paradoxes involved in the discursive engagement of diversity – the almost simultaneous processes of differentiation and concentration.

ACCESS, OPPORTUNITY AND POLICY

For a number of years, Tim Crabbe and colleagues have established a program focussing upon the use of sport as an engagement tool for youths in less-advantaged communities. The Substance Cooperative (www.substance.coop) is an endeavour which seeks to bridge the gap between the policy makers and those in the community yet to be engaged by the available programs – particularly youths. In this volume, Crabbe's chapter outlines the challenges associated with engaging youths in sport-based programs. Crabbe claims that the successful programs are difficult to describe in a categorical sense. He draws upon the work of Raymond Williams in cautioning the idea that successful engagement programs can be entirely and simply attributed to the progressive social inclusion perspective. Nevertheless, their success in retention is due to an acknowledgement that the pathways to success are usually uneven, disrupted and indirect. Crabbe draws on the work of Williams (1997) that the myriad cultural forces overlap and are not distinct and separate. The most successful programs provide access and opportunity and ultimately positive life options to those not currently involved.

Jessica MacBeth's chapter presents a study of partially sighted football in England. She discusses the social construction approach utilised in her research and introduces readers to the research issues associated with disability sport and football in particular the current "state of play" in partially sighted football at both the elite and grassroots level. MacBeth's main focus is with equality issues and the recruitment to the England squad, the relationship between elite and grassroots football, the format of small-sided football and the opportunities for players with poorer levels of sight. She concludes with some recommendations regarding the impact of change of format.

The profound and well-documented deconstruction of apartheid in South Africa came with much anticipation surrounding opportunity in the new South Africa for previously indentured citizens. One of the first major events to coincide with the re-entry of South Africa into international competition was the 1995 Rugby World Cup. Like no other sport, Rugby had been emblematic of South Africa's refusal to engage non-white participation. White-only rugby was deeply embedded into South African rugby. Government authorities were impatient for a change that would better represent the demographic profile of South Africa. The outcome of this policy implantation has been controversial and a simmering issue. Cora Burnett's chapter focuses upon this issue and the outcome of this policy on junior boys' rugby. She draws upon interview excerpts from the participants of two elite level tournaments. She refers to the players as "the boys from no-voice land." Notably, the data was drawn after South Africa had recently won the 2007 World Cup and two South African clubs had contested the 2007 final of the Super 14 competition comprising teams from Australia, New Zealand and South Africa.

FOUCAULT AND GOVERNANCE

While the incorporation of exercise prescription is not new, the research conducted by Lone Friis Thing examined the incorporation of exercise as prescription within a hospital clinic setting. More specifically, her study examined the effects on Danish immigrant women. The focus of the study is the use of exercise as a medicament, which is taken in measured doses under the guidance of exercise experts. Exercise prescription has been initiated as a preventive and treatment measure, despite the fact that relatively few studies have examined the effect hereof, and international studies show that marked improvements of the level of physical activity are not to be expected with the majority of patients, due to drop-out rates and lack of maintenance of an increased level of physical activity.

Friis Thing's chapter discusses the fundamental technologies of the "exercise prescription concept". Based on the evaluation of the interventions with different ethnic groups, she discusses the results of the evaluation against the backdrop of a critical analysis of exercise prescription.

She draws upon Foucault's ideas regarding "governing as governance" and critiques the practice which privileges a medical treatment model in engaging the participants into physical activity. In doing so, the treatment regime may promote a dependence upon expertise.

CONSPIRACY OF SILENCE AND GAY SPORT

With a view to addressing the void of knowledge regarding the silence and invisibility of gay men within mainstream team sports, Roger Le Blanc's chapter informs us of the meanings from the perspective gay athletes give to their experience of participating in mainstream sport and how these meanings create barriers and opportunities for their participation. The athlete's negotiation of fear emerged as they strategically reconciled all aspects of their identity into their sporting worlds in order to accommodate the ongoing resistance to diversity and equality in sport. A number of important sociological, political, moral and philosophical implications of the gay athlete's silence are addressed in this chapter and are all the more pertinent as gay rights and equality are currently manifested within social institutions other than mainstream sport.

BOURDIEU AND CAPITAL

Even though African footballers have plied their skills with European clubs for some time, their presence in some European countries has been quite recent. In her chapter on African footballers in Norway, Bente Skogvang draws upon Bourdieu's *field theory* and the concepts: "enonomic capital," "symbolic capital," "symbolic power," and "doxa" in her analysis. She discusses the complexity of transfer of football players from Africa and the situations of African footballers in Norway and draws upon the "The John Obi Mikel case" to highlight. The chapter is based upon observations undertaken at international fixtures, practices, meetings in three elite football clubs, interviews with players and coaches and a study of the media coverage of "the John Obi Mikel case" in two Norwegian newspapers during 2005 and 2006. The chapter focusses empowerment, discrimination, abuse and the complex contracts made for African footballers from Africa in European clubs. The informants in her study also reveal the extent to which cultural diversity variables such as gender, class and race, affect their wellbeing.

GENDER, MUSCULAR RELIGION
AND CULTURAL IDENTITY

Hargreaves (1997) contended that her research investigating cultural diversity and women's sport in South Africa was reliant upon observations and other original material collected during her visit because there was an absence of research in the specific area. Taylor and Toohey (2001) have made a substantial contribution to the study of cultural diversity and sport in Australia (Taylor, 2004; Taylor & Toohey, 2002). The authors have expressed their concern that most of the research investigating ethnicity and sport in Australia has focussed upon males. Further, most of the research concerning females and sport has focussed upon Anglos. Michael Burke and Chris Hallinan go some way towards addressing this shortcoming in their chapter and based the research on an ethnographic approach to investigate the increasing significance of basketball participation for junior women to the development of an athletic Jewish female identity in Melbourne, Australia. Informants, especially parents of the players, suggested that participation in basketball, allowed them to remodel adolescent Jewish female identity in positive and community-enriching ways. However, this positive, identity-affirming participation by Jewish girls sometimes resulted in violent opposition from players and parents from other clubs, possibly a by-product of the "wedge" politics that was a hallmark of the right wing Howard government and now part of the broader Australian community.

Notably, Burke and Hallinan also comment on the cultural significance of the Algerian Islamic female distance runner, Hassiba Boulmerka, at the Olympics. Walseth (2006) and Walseth and Fasting (2003) provide a substantial insight into the meanings attached to sport and physical activity by Muslim women. In her study of Egyptian women, Walseth echoed our point of emphasis regarding the consideration of diversity within. In this volume, Brendon Tagg identifies similar issues and discusses the problems generated by Western popular perceptions about Muslim women and sports participation. For example, Tagg argues that while Muslim women in Islamic countries may encounter access and opportunity barriers, Muslim women in Western countries are subject to discrimination and harassment.

THE CROSS-CULTURAL LIFE OF SPORTING GOODS

Despite a trend to a globalisation and standardisation of production and retail sporting goods, Ohl and Taks contend that the social uses of sporting goods are still the expressions of sub-cultures. The authors explore the meanings associated with this consumption as a way to understand cultures and particularly sporting sub-cultures. Additionally, Ohl and Taks seek to understand the meanings embedded in sporting goods and clarify the relations between sporting styles and goods. They ask questions such as: Does sporting goods consumption express a social class lifestyle? Are they signs of postmodern tribes? What kind of social and cultural diversity does the consumption of sporting goods express for a male youth culture, a particular class, local, female or "ethnic" sub-cultures? Ohl and Taks argue that the consumption of sporting goods is also a social and cultural experience which plays a central role bringing specific emotions and sensations that are central in sporting sub-cultures.

INTERNATIONALISM AND SPORT ENGAGEMENT

The development of Olympism in India was substantially influenced by men who had been educated in the West. Majumdar and Mahta thus argue that Indian Olympism was substantially influenced by the already globalised nature of the colonial Indian elite. That is, it was a westernised and male-dominated cohort. Some of the key figures in altering the outlook were Sir Dorabji J Tata, the Maharaja of Patiala and his trusted lieutenant G.D. Sondhi. Majumdar and Mahta contend that after establishing control over cricket, Patiala went on to establish himself as the standalone patriarch in India's sporting landscape. His control of Olympic sport embellished the idea that sport authority was a contour for the westernised cultural (male) elite.

Brent McDonald and Hiroshi Komuku' chapter examines the role of educational sport in producing and reproducing a particular version of Japanese identity. Despite the influences of globalisation on Japanese professional sport and the resultant increases in diversity both in terms of participants and of practice, Japanese educational sport remains a bastion of traditional values and the production house of the homogenising notion of "Japaneseness." Based on research conducted within sports at both high school and university, this chapter examines and makes sense of the apparent contradiction between the increasing diversity of the elite model of Japanese sport and subsequent resistance to this model at an educational level, which in turn reinforces the reproduction of a particular notion of Japanese identity.

CONCLUDING REMARKS

Within an increasingly globalised sporting world diversity has emerged as a touchstone of our times. Research related to social and cultural diversity and sport has been available in journal articles for some time. However, this book brings together the work of experts in the field into a single volume. Although it was not possible to include all expert contributions, the collection is comprehensive in content and draws on scholars from Australia, Canada, Switzerland, Denmark, England, Japan, New Zealand, Norway, South Africa and the United States. In our view this is only fitting given that social and cultural diversity issues and factors in sport concern participants and scholars across the world.

REFERENCES

Allison, M. T. (1982). Sport, ethnicity and assimilation. *Quest, 34*(2), 165–175.
Baumeister, A. (2007). Diversity and unity: The problem with 'Constitutional Patriotism'. *European Journal of Political Theory, 6*(4), 483–503.

Bhabha, H. (1994). *The location of culture.* London: Routledge.

Blokker, P. (2008). Europe' united in diversity': From central European identity to post-nationality. *European Journal of Social Theory, 11*(2), 257–274.

Boston, J., Callister, P., & Wolf, A. (2006). *The policy implications of diversity.* Wellington, NZ: Institute of Policy Studies.

Cheska, AT. (1984). Sport as ethnic boundary maintenance: A case of the American Indian. *International Review for the Sociology of Sport, 19*, 241–257.

Fraser, D. (2005). *Cricket and the law: The man in white is always right.* Abingdon, UK: Routledge.

Gitlin, T. (1995). Prime time ideology: The hegemonic process in television entertainment. In: H. Newcombe (Ed.), *Television: The critical view* (5th ed.). New York: Oxford University Press.

Gordon, M. (1964). *Assimilation in American life.* New York: Oxford University Press.

Habermas, J. (1996). Why Europe needs a new constitution. In: R. Rogowski & T. Charles (Eds), *The shape of the new Europe.* Cambridge: Cambridge University Press.

Hallinan, C., & Hughson, J. (2008). Hallinan, the beautiful game in Howard's 'Brutopia': Football, ethnicity and citizenship in Australia. *Soccer in Society* (in press).

Hargreaves, J. (1997). Women's sport, development, and cultural diversity: The South African experience. *Womens Studies International Forum, 20*(2), 191–209.

Levin, B., & Rittel, J. (1994). Dealing with diversity: Some propositions from Canadian education. *Education Policy Archives, 2*(2), ISSN 1068–2341. Available at http://epaa.asu.edu/epaa/v2n2.html

Muller, J.-W., & Scheppelle, K. L. (2008). Constitutional patriotism: An introduction. *International Journal of Constitutional Law, 6*(1), 67–71.

Paruk, Z., & de la Rey, C. (1993). Race and gender constraints in SA road running. *Agenda, 17*, 25–28.

Pooley, J. (1981). Ethnic soccer clubs in Milwaukee: A study in assimilation. In: J. Loy, G. Kenyon & B. McPherson (Eds), *Sport, culture and society: A reader in the sociology of sport* (pp. 168–178). Philadelphia: Lea & Febiger.

Robidoux, M. (2006). The nonsense of native American sport imagery: Reclaiming a past that never was. *International Review for the Sociology of Sport, 41*(2), 201–219.

Taylor, T. (2004). The rhetoric of exclusion: Perspectives of cultural diversity in Australian netball. *Journal of Sport and Social Issues, 28*, 453–476.

Taylor, T., & Toohey, K. (2001). Sport and cultural diversity: Why are the women being left out?. In: C. Gratton & P. Henry (Eds), *Sport in the city: The role of sport in economic & social regeneration* (pp. 204–213). London: Routledge.

Taylor, T., & Toohey, K. (2002). Behind the veil: Exploring the recreation needs of Muslim women. *Leisure/Loisir, 26*(1), 85–105.

Walseth, K. (2006). Sport and belonging. *International Review for the Sociology of Sport, 41*, 3–4447-464.

Walseth, K., & Fasting, K. (2003). Islam's view on physical activity and sport: Egyptian women interpreting Islam. *International Review for the Sociology of Sport, 38*(1), 45–60.

Williams, R. (1977). *Marxism and literature.* Oxford: Oxford University Press.

A GAME OF TWO HALVES: UNDERSTANDING SPORT-BASED SOCIAL INCLUSION

Tim Crabbe

PROLOGUE

A cold night in Stoke Newington

Stoke Newington is one of those increasingly omnipresent but incongruous districts of London. High levels of deprivation and street crime have led to the attraction of public investment, with central government believing the place to be in need of 're-generation', whilst increasing numbers of young professionals continue to move into the area attracted by the trendy bars and bistros of suddenly hip Church Street.

The new leisure centre across the road from Stoke Newington School brings the issues into stark focus. Funded by lottery money the building was several million pounds over budget when finally completed but its opening was heralded as marking a significant development in the rebuilding of a supposedly shattered community. Whilst the excellent sporting facilities the centre had to offer were beyond doubt community sports activists (and those more generally concerned with urban deprivation and its unequal consequences) remained concerned about the pricing mechanism that was put in place. Prices were regarded as too high for the areas more established residents. The suspicion was that the facility, rather than serving the needs of the borough's traditionally under-privileged population was a subsidised sports centre for the more affluent new arrivals.

On the 'other side of the tracks' it is on the new astro turf at Stoke Newington School-where the newer young professionals have been less inclined to send their children to be educated-that Leyton Orient Community Sports Programme (LOCSP) runs its training sessions for the Eastside team.

Social and Cultural Diversity in a Sporting World
Research in the Sociology of Sport, Volume 5, 15–31
Copyright © 2008 by Emerald Group Publishing Limited
All rights of reproduction in any form reserved
ISSN: 1476-2854/doi:10.1016/S1476-2854(08)05002-4

It's the middle of November, Tuesday night, 7 pm – heavy rain is falling diagonally, driven by a spiteful wind. It's cold. 'Stevo', the coach, parks the mini-bus close to the gate leading to the astro-turf. There are six of us in the bus; 'Stevo' has been regaling us with tales of his times as a pro in Norway. He stops the stories as we pull up:

'Right fellas, five minutes to change, and then I want you ready to go. Anybody late and they're going to be running for some time. You don't want to be running tonight'.

He opens the door and shouts the same instructions to those huddled in small groups around the car park. The pitch at Stoke Newington School is state of the art, protected by a five-metre high perimeter fence, it gleams electric green. The floodlights are on but the changing rooms are shut. Players make do in the back of cars or under the steps, anywhere that offers relief from the weather.

'I need to warm up man. This is too cold you know. I need to live somewhere where the sun shines'.

'Stevo' has a training session planned.

'I always have something planned, but one of the things that I've learned since starting this community work is that you've got to be flexible. You can have something all mapped out in your head but when you get to the session you might only get six kids when you were expecting twenty so you've got to change everything. You've got to be able to think on your feet'.

Despite the appalling conditions there is a good turn out tonight, only a couple of the regulars are missing. Those training compete for a place in Eastside, LOCSP's senior club side. Many have been associated with the programme for a considerable time. Some since the activity consisted of an evening kickabout on their housing estate. Things have moved on since then and they have become used to the rules that 'Stevo' and 'Sol' lay down. Those who miss training without any reasonable excuse know that the sanction involves exclusion from the selection process. Similarly those who arrive late are told to go home and forget about playing on Saturday.

'Stevo's' coaching qualifications set him aside from other team managers in the league in which Eastside compete. 'Stevo' insists,

'You go on these courses, and you have to prove this and that, all technical stuff. But when you train these guys it's all different. The things that I have learnt that have been most useful for this kind of work I learnt from 'Sol'. I have got my Level one and two coaching badges but a lot of that stuff isn't much use here'.

Nevertheless as an observer you cannot help but be impressed by the aura of professionalism, which surrounds tonight's training session.

'First five minutes sprinting then fifteen minutes fast-feet work, then we do twenty minutes cardio-vascular work. For the last hour we concentrate on a particular aspect of the game; heading, defending, corners. We do that in monthly cycles, it's defending this month'.

The training sessions have an etiquette which governs social relations. This is distinct from match days and more informal meetings between the squad and the coaches. Here there is a complete monopoly of power. What 'Stevo' says, the squad does. There is no arguing, bar a few groans when he tells them to do another lap of the pitch. There is no room for banter. There is an acceptance that this is hard work that has to be done, that it is all in everybody's best interests both at an individual and team level. 'Stevo' snaps out his instructions,

'Half-way line, SPRINT!'.

'Come on! I need more effort. You're young men, young should be fit'.

With ten minutes of the training session left 'Sol' arrives to look over the squad that he has been so instrumental in developing. He watches with a tutored look. When 'Stevo' calls an end to the session the spell of subservience is broken.

'Alright 'Sol' you coming to watch us on Saturday'.

'You call that running I seen my little two year old girl run faster than that'.

'Hey 'Sol' you should see this Hackney girl I'm seeing'.

'You seeing a girl? She can't be seeing you properly'.[1]

INTRODUCTION: IDENTIFYING A NEW APPROACH TO THE PRACTICE AND EVALUATION OF SPORTS-BASED SOCIAL POLICY

These opening passages are presented with a view to introducing what might be seen as a fresh approach towards the mobilisation of sport to achieve social ends. In contrast to much of the more conventional sports-based social policy, many of the initiatives that have informed this writing[2] are clear in their assertion that they are not concerned with 'diversionary' or even sports development work as traditionally understood and practiced. Rather, they have tended to adopt the ethos of the UK Home Office funded Positive Futures programme which describes itself as a 'relationship strategy'. Working in some of the most deprived neighbourhoods in England and Wales, this programme seeks to use sport and other activities as a basis for establishing relationships with young people who have otherwise become alienated and distanced from mainstream social policy agencies and 'authority' figures. Central to this approach is a commitment to a flexible, organic local development strategy and the role of community workers in establishing a platform of trust. Working from this position the intention is that participants talk about and begin to address issues affecting their lives. Through these means, Positive Futures aims to:

'have a positive influence on participants' drug use, physical activity and offending behaviour by widening horizons and access to lifestyle, educational and employment opportunities within a supportive and culturally familiar environment'. (Home Office, 2003, p. 6)

One of the things that has also marked Positive Futures out from other sport-based social inclusion initiatives is its commitment to the development of a comprehensive programme of research, monitoring and evaluation that combines both quantitative and qualitative assessments. This was borne of an early recognition of the failure of a succession of similar initiatives to demonstrate their achievements or provide definitive evidence of a direct causal relationship between involvement in sports and specific social outcomes (see Long & Sanderson, 2001). Part of the reason for this failure is precisely because other initiatives have too often focused on trying to establish a direct connection between involvement in sport and the social policy concerns of the day. Attempts to quantify such 'outputs' are inevitably problematic and the shortcomings of this approach are now increasingly being recognised. At best, this method can produce a numeric record of, for example, how many participants have not been arrested over a given period of time. However, the incomplete nature of this 'data' renders its usefulness limited. Such statistics are notoriously unreliable as, in the case of arrest figures, they ignore unreported crimes whilst the 'fact' that somebody has not been *arrested* gives no indication as to whether they have actually been involved in crime or not. Furthermore, any evidence of non-involvement in crime could never be directly attributed to the impact of a specific policy intervention.

In this sense, successive attempts to establish a relationship between sport and singular 'outcomes' can be seen as a rather crass effort to bang square pegs into round holes. Whilst politically expedient, this approach ultimately represents a staged attempt to validate the social benefits of sport rather than providing a more reliable and complete account of what is actually involved in the process. Increasingly then the move has been away from a focus on sport itself, or any particular key outcomes indicator, towards obtaining a more complete picture of the ways in which *projects* (rather than sports or other activities) influence participants' attitudes, engagement, interests, education, employment, peer groups and relationships. Furthermore, the programme's commitment to this research process was informed not only by a determination to generate evidence of projects' achievements but also by its desire to identify ways of learning from the diverse range of agencies, staff and contexts in which the work is delivered.

This represents an important step change. It breaks with the more common reliance upon the simple reporting of monitoring statistics, but also goes beyond more sophisticated attempts to quantify social interactions associated with social capital perspectives (see Putnam, 2000; Blackshaw & Long, 2005). What such quantitative approaches represent is a search for a certainty and finality which is absent from the lives of the young people with whom initiatives of this type work. If sport-based social interventions are to be regarded as 'relationship strategies', then the success of the relationships they create, just like our own private personal relations, cannot be 'measured' in a finite, quantifiable sense.

In what follows, drawing upon the findings from this emergent body of research and learning from the Positive Futures programme in particular, the core features of the most effective sports-based social inclusion work will be presented. These will be considered alongside a fresh consideration of the ways in which such initiatives contribute to social policy outcomes.

WHAT'S SPORT GOT TO DO WITH IT? EMPIRE, RISK AND ENGAGEMENT

Within a range of populist and political discourses, 'sports' are frequently regarded as wholesome pursuits for young people to be involved in, activities which are conferred with a whole series of positive attributes with the power to 'cure' the social ills facing society. Indeed, such perspectives follow the Victorian's attempts to influence attitudes within Britain's public schools and to service the needs of the 'Empire' through the concept of 'Muscular Christianity': A perspective which advocated the moral value of sports and games and set the tone for the missionary zeal with which 'modern' sports were developed over the course of the following century (Money, 1997). More pertinently, during this period, sports were argued to have played 'a major part ... in the creation of a healthy, moral and orderly workforce' and in shaping the values and behaviour of working class youth (Holt, 1989, p. 136).

It is this model which has since been revisited with the emergence of 'third way', supply side, approaches to social policy (Giddens, 1998) and concerns about the erosion of social and civic engagement (Putnam, 2000). Nostalgic evocations of sport have emerged in the context of the 'respectable fears' which associate a perceived moral decline with a loss of discipline and direction amongst contemporary youth (Pearson, 1983). In this context, sport has been held up as the embodiment of a social tradition which values discipline and personal responsibility. Equally it has been seen as a symbol of the identifications and processes of connection and belonging associated with 'community', itself the focus of renewed interest amongst academics, politicians and policy makers. 'Community', and by extension the notion of 'community sport', has then increasingly been wheeled out as both a lament to a more certain past and as an appeal and means to the achievement of a 'better' future.[3]

Such perspectives have typically been tied into a model of sport which sees it as capable of 'building character'. Indeed research tied to this model has focused on a whole range of issues associated with the relationship between sports participation and character, morality, delinquency, academic performance, status, political attitudes and social mobility. Yet, for a variety of reasons, very little evidence has been produced that sports participation does in fact make a consistent contribution in terms of 'character building', however narrowly defined. It *is* clear that when people live significant periods of their lives in and around sports, much like any other cultural environment, their characters and behaviours are to some extent influenced by that activity. However, it is not possible to make generalisations about specific patterns of character development or behaviour as a consequence of particular patterns of sports participation. More contemporary research then has tended to emphasise 'sports as *sites* for socialisation experiences, not *causes* of socialisation outcomes' (Coakley, 2003, p. 102).

In this context the assertion within the *Cul-de-sacs and gateways* strategy document that Positive Futures is 'not concerned with the celebration, development or promotion of sport as an end in itself' (Home Office, 2003, p. 8) is highly significant. This position is based upon recognition that the principal attraction of sport is its capacity to *engage* young people, rather than some intrinsic developmental quality within sport itself.

In some ways sports provide what Victor Turner has referred to as a 'liminal' space, which provides the individual with a 'spatial separation from the familiar and habitual' (Turner, 1973, p. 213). Sport can be experienced as a site of legitimised conflict, where 'normal' social rules are broken and subverted and participants undertake socially acceptable forms of 'risk taking'. Ironically though, it is this perspective which underpins the appeal of using sports as a 'diversionary' tool since it provides an alternative and less disruptive basis for young people to transgress convention than those associated with 'anti-social' behaviours such as 'joy riding', street drinking and harassment. Equally though, at the more 'extreme' end of sporting experience, such as white water rafting and rock climbing, researchers have identified that an emphasis is placed on a similarly exclusionary orientation which maintains that the skills involved are possessed by a select few who identify with one another on the basis of their perceived status (Lyng, 1990). The attractions are rooted in a similar desire to engage with risk and the public display of risky behaviour in the context of the secure, monotonous, repetition that more often characterises our contemporary social condition.

Nevertheless it can also be established that sport and related activities do offer something more. What is significant here is not the sport as such, but the context in which it occurs. As well as providing a space in which people can escape their wider troubles through an intense, un-self-conscious involvement with a physically rewarding activity, more generally, sport can provide spaces in which participants may:

- Enter unfamiliar locations and meet new people.
- Talk and reflect upon relationships and performances.
- Be encouraged by coaches and peers to take personal and mutual responsibility, thus refining their sense of both individual potentials and mutual dependencies.
- Experience strong and open inter-generational contact, thus fostering more respectful forms of interaction.
- Be encouraged to recognise the importance of partnership, consensus and reliance on others through their own experience.
- Feel able to freely submit to the 'rules of the game' and the time-limited disciplinary regimes of particular sports.

The point is however that the value of sport can *only* be realised when it is undertaken *within* a 'developmental approach'. In this sense it is the adoption of a personal and social development model which is 'sacred' to sport-based social inclusion programmes rather than 'sport' itself. It is this point of departure than enables wider distinctions to be made between a 'diversionary' *sports* approach and a 'developmental' sports-based *social inclusion* approach which might be characterised in the terms presented in Table 1.

Table 1. Diversionary vs. Developmental Approaches.

Diversionary Approach	Developmental Approach
Providing alternative 'beneficial' activity to anti-social behaviour, substance misuse, etc.	Using activity as a gateway to ongoing personal development
Fixed outcomes as targets (e.g., reduction in crime figures)	Open-ended outcomes (e.g., the 'distance travelled' of participants)
Mass participation as indicator of success	Quality of engagement as indicator of success
Belief in *intrinsic value* of the activity itself (e.g., sport, physical activity)	Focus on value of wider personal development which might be facilitated by the use of activity rather than a belief in the activities intrinsic value
Short- or fixed-term delivery	Ongoing, open-ended delivery
Structured schemes of work or programs of coaching	Flexible, organic, local development and readily adaptable activities
Authoritarian, based on discipline	Mutual respect, based on trust
Doing something program leaders think is worthwhile	Doing something participants think is worthwhile

Within this schematic, the community development principles of the sports-based social inclusion approach are implicitly represented as having more value and 'depth' than the short-term control imperatives of diversionary work. However, such distinctions are themselves inherently problematic since where good community work is practiced there will usually be elements of *both* diversionary and developmental work. Nearly all engagement work with young people could be regarded in the first instance as diversionary in that during its time of operation it offers an activity that may be a diversion from other forms of behaviour. It is from this base though that it becomes possible to build a more developmental approach.

ASSESSING THE IMPACT: SOCIAL CAPITAL, SOCIAL POLICY AND CRIME PREVENTION

In terms of success, what distinguishes a developmental approach built upon individual support and more diversionary approaches towards working with young people is the capacity they offer to generate useable and culturally appropriate 'social capital'. In recent years this concept, as espoused by Robert Putnam (2000) in *Bowling Alone*, has come to dominate theoretical thinking about the social potential of sport and leisure programmes (Nicholson & Hoye, 2008). Focusing on the sport of ten pin bowling, Putnam observes that the American leagues of his own youth, which were characterised by *teams* of players, are no longer the dominant form of participation and that people now increasingly 'bowl alone' with established friends and family. In support of his thesis he uses evidence to reveal a marked decline in social connectedness, or 'social capital', over the past half century. For his critics though, social capital cannot be understood in isolation since it is indelibly linked with social background and context. In Bourdieu's terms it has two decisive features: on the one hand it is a tangible resource derived from family, friendship or other kinds of social networks whilst on the other, it has a symbolic dimension, which contrives to hide networks of power associated with familiarity (1984). For Blackshaw and Long, 'in terms of sport and leisure policy, [this] ... has the effect of normalising the marginality of the poor' (2005) on the basis of their lack of access to or capacity to influence the networks that count.

What maybe significant about the more effective projects then is their efforts to engage disadvantaged participants through a *respect* for the cultural contexts in which they live, whilst also striving to open new avenues of opportunity and transition gateways. Whilst conventional policy 'speak' might 'translate' the ways of living and thinking of marginalised groups into its 'own' language, effective sports-based social inclusion projects operate as 'cultural intermediaries' which *understand* young people on their own terms, acting as a 'go-between' providing access to the 'mainstream' (Crabbe, 2007). They embody a kind of split personality which enables them to empathise with participants whilst having the gravitas and wherewithal to work with and introduce participants to those organisations and experiences to which they would normally be denied access. In this sense, at their best, they are able to open up possibilities, provide guidance and, crucially, demystify mainstream society rather than merely providing a fleeting cache of 'social capital'.

In the context of Putnam's distinction between bonding (ties between like people) and bridging (inter-group) forms of social capital, evidence of a project's capacity to open social gateways is provided by the wider commitment to driving participants' engagement forward in this way. For Positive Futures this is evidenced through the tracking of participants' movement through resistant, disconnected and self-constraining positions of 'disengagement' to self-directed and empowered positions of 'autonomy'. For the purposes of monitoring and reporting, proxy assessments are made of the programme's contribution to participants' bonding and bridging capital through the use of a tailored engagement matrix.[4] It is this which provides the evidence that, for those who remain engaged, as stronger connections are made with wider and wider circles of contacts, *breadth* and *depth* is built into project-related friendships, networks and opportunities rather than just access to 'more people'.

In terms of more specific social outcomes, and the crime prevention agenda in particular, sports-based social inclusion projects are also beginning to shift the terms of their claims to success. In the context of a succession of evidence to show how 'risk' and 'protective' factors influence outcomes for young people it is the layers of protection highlighted in Table 2 that are increasingly becoming significant.

Longitudinal studies tracking children's development have plotted some of the most significant predictors of future offending and found a cumulative effect, in that, on aggregate, the greater the number of risk factors to which a child is exposed, the greater the likelihood of future offending behaviour (Farrington, 2003). Over time, whilst the more progressive sports-based social policy initiatives have sought to distance themselves from claims of any direct causal relationship between activity

Table 2.   Engagement and Social Capital.

Engagement	Breadth of Contact	Depth of Contact
Disengagement	Participants	Fleeting, hostile
Curiosity	Participants, delivery staff	Transitory, interested
Involvement	Participants, delivery staff, volunteers & office staff	Ongoing, engaged
Achievement	Participants, delivery staff, volunteers, office staff, partners & funders	Celebrated, committed
Autonomy	Other projects, colleges & employers	Mutually rewarding, respectful

provision and crime reduction, the focus on 'protective factors' has come to be more central to the approach in terms of their capacity to:

- reduce the impact of, or exposure to, risk;
- reduce chain reactions to negative experience;
- promote self-esteem and achievement;
- provide positive relationships and new opportunities (McCarthy, Laing, & Walker, 2004)

Rather than reflecting a dichotomy between structural responses to the 'causes' of criminal behaviour on the one hand and a focus on the individual on the other, sports-based social policy initiatives appear to represent a key element within a 'layered' response that embraces both. Within most western industrial countries, at the broadest level sits the criminal justice system which provides the statutory legal framework directing responses to criminal behaviour. Outside of this framework lies the range of initiatives aimed at establishing a sense of social justice, social inclusion, collective efficacy and neighbourhood renewal which seek to create fresh opportunities within disadvantaged communities and to ameliorate underlying structural inequalities. Whilst often targeted at deprived neighbourhoods this 'layer' of intervention is essentially socially oriented in the sense that it seeks to impact upon entire localities rather than specific individuals or groups within them.

The type of sports-based social policy interventions highlighted here, whilst often adopting an open access approach towards participation, might be seen to contrast with this approach through their focus on participant engagement and progression. They are more concerned with providing *individual* support through the building of relationships and development

Table 3. Risk and Protective Factors.

Risk Factors	Protective Factors
Family	
Poor parental supervision and discipline	Surrogate supervision and discipline
Conflict	Supervised, ordered environments
History of criminal activity	Positive involvement of former offenders
Parental attitudes that condone anti-social and criminal behaviour	Intergenerational work, and peer mentoring
Low income	Free/low cost activity in locality
Poor housing	Alternative places to go
School	
Low achievement beginning in primary school	Alternative markers of achievement
Aggressive behaviour (including bullying)	Protection from and challenge to aggressive behaviour
Lack of commitment (including truancy)	Alternative education
School disorganization	Structured activities
Community	
Living in a disadvantaged neighbourhood	Investment of resources
Disorganisation and neglect	Active community development
Availability of drugs	Alternative sources of excitement
High population turnover, and lack of neighbourhood attachment	Reasons to stay
Personal	
Hyperactivity and impulsivity	Activity-based management of impulse
Low intelligence and cognitive impairment	Alternative sources of development
Alienation and lack of social commitment	Positive involvement
Attitudes that condone offending and drug misuse	Drug education and peer mentoring
Early involvement in crime and drug misuse	Early intervention
Friendships with peers involved in crime and drug misuse	Alternative peer networks

pathways which it is hoped will protect against the risk factors that are understood to impact most heavily on children living in the localities they target. This model is borne out by the extent to which the contribution of this type of provision can be mapped against the most common risk factors as revealed by the UK Youth Justice Board (Communities that Care, 2005) and presented in Table 3.

CONCLUSION

In their insightful thesis on community sports development Hylton and Totten (2001) invoke the work of Raymond Williams' (1977). According to Williams, at any given moment within a social formation, there is a 'dominant' culture, an 'emergent' culture, and one that has past, but still leaves its 'residual' marks on the current forms of culture. Looking at the field of community sports practice, within this framework it is possible to distinguish between:

- A 'dominant' approach characterised by sports development perspectives.
- A 'residual' approach, the legacy of which derives from the Victorian Rational Recreation and Muscular Christianity movements but which is now reflected in diversionary 'social control' perspectives.
- An emergent approach associated with the social inclusion and community development perspective.

Of course the whole point of Williams' work is that these cultural influences are not distinct and separate. Instead, the dominant, residual and emergent forces overlap; none having a final authority. In this sense, the categories cannot be applied to specific programmes or periods in the way that Hylton and Totten have suggested. Therefore, although it is appealing to represent the more progressive social inclusion perspective outlined here as an emergent influence which is likely to assume a dominant position within the field of community sport practice, this cannot be claimed in any complete or uniform sense.

However, it is those projects operating from this perspective that have most clearly and un-self-consciously demonstrated their success in retaining participants' engagement, thereby contributing to their personal development and impacting upon their wider patterns of behaviour. They are able to do so through their acceptance that the journeys young people make will typically be not only complex, but rhizomatic, or meandering and non-linear, rather than being rooted in the orderly social conditions more conventionally associated with the social category 'youth'.

Participants are likely then to engage, drift off and then perhaps re-engage. They do not necessarily follow prescribed routes, and, therefore, adaptability in working with them and longevity in trying to analyse or chart any progress is vital. It is often only with hindsight that real impacts are revealed, and the multifarious routes become apparent, complete with dead ends, bridges, blind alleys, and sudden gateways. 'Progress' is often complex and apparently contradictory and, in this sense, it could be argued that effective projects can engage young people in high-quality relationship building work and record developmental progressions whilst flashpoint incidents out of the realm of projects' influence continue to occur. Such fractured and inconsistent progression should not be seen as a 'failure' but rather as the inevitable context in which work with participants occurs. In such circumstances the continued involvement of participants throughout periods of disruption represents a success in and of itself.

Previous studies and commentaries within the field have struggled with this complexity, and developed *either* an ideologically informed critique of sports-based initiatives as capitalist social control mechanisms (see Hargreaves, 1986; Clarke & Critcher, 1985; Rigauer, 1969) or a more simplistic celebration of sport's assumed social worth (Labour Party, 1997). It is now becoming clear though that initiatives cannot be evaluated in such straightforward ways. When considered in terms of their role as personal and social development programmes, there are no fixed outcomes to be pursued. Rather, the focus on widening the horizons and aspirations of participants – and the associated evaluatory tools introduced to assess programme achievements – relates to a desire to help them achieve a sense of personal autonomy. This sense of autonomy must be regarded as the antithesis of social control, but does not lend itself to a simple celebration of sport's social worth.

Indeed, it would be foolish for sports-based social policy initiatives to make grand claims about their capacity to transform the social and economic conditions which contribute to the social problems of the areas in which they operate. Rather, where projects are at their most effective, they open access to social worlds and opportunities which are not currently accessible to the people with whom they work in order that those participants are in a stronger position to make positive life choices from a wider range of options.

EPILOGUE

A hot afternoon in Walthamstow

It's got to be the hottest day of the year. Scottish 'Doug' arrived at the office early. Scottish 'Doug' only comes to the office on a Tuesday and each Tuesday he arrives early. 'Anyone for a brew?', he asks as he switches on the kettle.

This is the usual Tuesday routine. Scottish 'Doug' has brought a friend with him, she has come before but she isn't as regular as him. She will come for a couple of Tuesdays on the trot and then we might not see her for a month or so. Scottish 'Doug' and his friend don't look like the regular kind of LOCSP 'client'. Certainly neither of them will celebrate their fortieth birthday again, but attempting to guess their age is difficult because they both have sallow complexions and haunted eyes that tell of hard living and premature ageing.

'Five minutes guys'.

'Sol' is talking to a new recruit to the rehabilitation programme which now takes referrals from London's only residential crack detox and a less regimented alcohol project in Hackney as well as those who established contact through LOCSP's football programmes. 'Alex' is about twenty, he has short-cropped hair, he is about six foot one with a lean well-toned frame. 'Alex' got out of prison two weeks ago; he had been there for two years. After revealing that he played for the prison football team 'Sol' tells him about Eastside, when they train, when they play.

We get into 'Sol's' car, the three 'clients' squeezing into the back. Scottish 'Doug' and his friend talk about a mutual acquaintance that has fallen off the wagon. 'Alex' points out a youth club and tells us that he used to box for their team.

When we arrive at the YMCA 'Zaidie', 'Gav', 'Tel' and a couple of others are waiting for us on the steps.

'Come on 'Sol' we've been waiting ten minutes'.

'Sol' looks at his mobile, unperturbed;

'The session starts at two o'clock. It's five-to two'.

'Sol' glides by 'Gav' and co and says hello to the woman at reception.

'It's a hot one today', she says familiarly and hands 'Sol' a set of keys.

It is a smaller turn-out than usual for the regular Tuesday afternoon gym session, but this really must be the hottest day of the year and even though the fan is on maximum speed I'm completely soaked in sweat before getting close to the exercise bike. Those who are missing had probably decided that there were better ways of spending a summer's afternoon. 'Sol' doesn't seem particularly fazed, the gym session has always been a fairly casual affair from his perspective; clients drop in and out on a regular basis, even if those on the residential programme are watched over by their supervisors. Sanctions do not follow absences in the way that they do with failure to make a football coaching session, it is as if this is an additional extra available to all those who want to make use of it.

'Tel' is sitting on the chest-press machine. He is huge. 'Sol' laughs and jokes in admiration, he talks about 'penitentiary muscles'. Just like Scottish 'Doug', 'Tel' is only to be seen on a Tuesday afternoon. He doesn't play football but he very rarely misses the gym session. 'Tel' trains by himself, he works through the machines methodically before moving on to the free-weights. He rarely speaks to anybody; he just gets on with his business, lifting improbably heavy pieces of metal, bulking-up an already considerable frame.

'Sol' leads 'Alex' through an induction, he explains authoritatively how to use the machines properly and safely. 'Alex' knows how to use the weights properly and safely, he learnt all of that in prison, and is gushing with enthusiasm. He needed something to do now that he was out. He loves the gym and he reckons that he will fit easily into the Eastside set-up.

'I've got good skills, I'm fast'. He is a lively and bouncy character.

We never saw 'Alex' again.

Scottish 'Doug' and his female friend take their time and chat gently about people and things that they have in common. The conversation is under-scored by a resigned sadness. It is about friends who did not make it to the other side, friends who did make it to the other side but who then turned back and drowned. Most of all it is talk of a new reality that was impoverished and nowhere near as much fun as the 'old times' – nevertheless one that had to be adhered to in order to survive.

Zaidie has just completed a set of leg exercises.

'Gotta build 'em up for speed on the pitch.

'Zaidie' has recently had trials with Northampton Town and feels that he is on the cusp of 'making it' as a pro. All that is needed is some fine-tuning. We move on to bench presses. Starting with a set of ten repetitions of 60 kg we increase the weight until a 'lift' is beyond an individual's capabilities.

Encouragement is shouted when someone begins to falter.

'Come on, strength. Go on you can do it. That's it – go on, go on!'

As we start to fall by the wayside 'Zaidie' goes past 100 kg. It is by any standards an incredible effort; at most he must be only five foot nine and no more than ten and a half stone. He is incredibly focused;

'I need more strength man. 'Sol' you gotta sort this out, one time a week isn't no good, I'm not gonna get any bigger'.

Some banter is shared about bigger muscles and sexual conquests but there is no mistaking why 'Zaidie' is here, he sees this as one of the last things that he needs to get right before he moves into the big time.

For the last ten minutes 'Sol' runs a sit-up session. It is the only time throughout the afternoon that there has been a structured, coach-led, exercise. Scottish 'Doug' and his friend leave to get changed;

'See ya 'Sol'',

'Tel' bends laden dumbells around his biceps. Everybody else attempts to keep up with 'Sol'. I give up after a couple of minutes, others keep on going, groaning out in pain;

'Enough 'Sol' man!'.

A burst of desperate laughter prompts 'Sol's' admonishment,

'If you're fit to laugh you're fit to work. Another ten.'

When everything is finished I resolve to do something else next time it is this hot.[5]

NOTES

1. Abridged excerpt from Crabbe and Slaughter, 2004, p. 87.

2. Over a 15-year period these have included the work of Leyton Orient Community Sports Programme, Football Unites – Racism Divides, Positive Futures, Standard Chartered Bank's Goal programme, the Football Foundation managed Kickz programme and a series of other projects working with the social research co-operative substance (www.substance.coop).

3. This trend is not unprecedented and was a feature of the thinking of the Wolfenden Committee on Sport (1960) and the Action Sport programme of the 1970s and 1980s

4. The SPRS participation and engagement matrix is based on learning from youth work progression models and the engagement matrix developed by Darts (see Hirst & Robertshaw, 2003).

5. Abridged excerpt from Crabbe and Slaughter, 2004, p. 89.

REFERENCES

Blackshaw, T., & Long, J. (2005). What's the big idea? A critical exploration of the concept of social capital and its incorporation into leisure policy discourse. *Leisure Studies*, *24*(3), 239–258.

Clarke, J., & Critcher, C. (1985). *The devil makes work: Leisure in capitalist Britain*. Basingstoke: Macmillan Press.

Coakley, J. (2003). *Sport in society: Issues and controversies* (8th ed.). Boston: McGraw Hill.

Communities that Care. (2005). *Risk and protective factors*. London: Youth Justice Board.

Crabbe, T. (2007). Reaching the 'hard to reach': engagement, relationship building and social control in sport based social inclusion work. *International Journal for Sport Management and Marketing*, *2*(1–2), 27–40.

Crabbe, T., & Slaughter, P. (2004). *On the eastside: Research report into the estate based social inclusion interventions of Leyton Orient community sports programme*. Unpublished research report: Sheffield Hallam University.

Farrington, D. P. (2003). Key results from the first 40 years of the Cambridge study in delinquent development. In: T. Thornberry & M. Krohn (Eds), *Taking stock of delinquency: An overview of findings from contemporary longitudinal studies* (pp. 137–183). New York: Kluwer Academic/Plenum.

Giddens, A. (1998). *The third way: The renewal of social democracy*. Cambridge: Policy Press.

Hargreaves, J. (1986). *Sport, power and culture*. Cambridge: Polity Press.

Hirst, E., & Robertshaw, D. (2003). *Breaking the cycle of failure – examining the impact of arts activity on attending pupil referral units in Doncaster*. Doncaster: Darts.

Holt, R. (1989). *Sport and the British*. Oxford: Oxford University Press.

Home Office. (2003). *Cul-de-sacs and gateways: Understanding the positive futures approach*. London: Home Office.

Hylton, K., & Totten, M. (2001). Community sports development. In: K. Hylton, P. Bramham, D. Jackson & M. Nesti (Eds), *Sports development: Policy, process and practice*. London: Routledge.

Labour Party. (1997). *Labour's sporting nation*. London: The Labour Party.

Long, J., & Sanderson, I. (2001). The social benefits of sport: Where's the proof?. In: C. Gratton & I. Henry (Eds), *Sport in the city: The role of sport in economic and social regeneration*. London: Routledge.

Lyng, S. (1990). Edgework: A social psychological analysis of voluntary risk taking. *American Journal of Sociology*, *95*(4), 851–886.

McCarthy, P., Laing, K., & Walker, J. (2004). *Offenders of the future? Assessing the risk of children and young people becoming involved in criminal and antisocial behaviour*. DfES Research Report No. 545. HMSO, London.

Money, T. (1997). *Manly and muscular diversions: Public schools and the nineteenth century sporting revival*. London: Duckworth.

Nicholson, M., & Hoye, R. (Eds). (2008). *Sport and social capital*. Oxford.

Pearson, G. (1983). *Hooligan: A history of respectable fears*. Basingstoke: Palgrave Macmillan.

Putnam, R. (2000). *Bowling alone: The collapse and revival of American community*. New York: Simon & Schuster.

Rigauer, B. (1969). In: A. Guttmann (Trans.), *Sport und Arbeit. Soziolgische Zusammenhänge und ideologishche Implikationen*. Frankfurt am Main: Suhrkamp. [*Sport and Work*, 1981.] New York: Colombia University Press.

Turner, V. (1973). The centre out there: Pilgrim's goal. *History of Religions, 12*(3), 191–230.
Williams, R. (1977). *Marxism and literature*. Oxford: Oxford University Press.
Wolfenden Committee on Sport. (1960). *Sport and community*. London: Central Council on Physical Education.

AFRICAN FOOTBALLERS IN EUROPE ☆

Bente Ovèdie Skogvang

INTRODUCTION

In this chapter I will discuss the complexity of transfer of football[1] players from Africa to Europe, and the situations of African footballers in Norway. Male African footballers will be in focus. I will apply a gender perspective as an analytical tool, and a short introduction about female African footballers will be given. '*The John Obi Mikel case*' which involved Norway, England and Nigeria, will be used to visualise the complexity. Why do players want to move from developing countries, and which reality do they meet and which experiences do they get when they come to a new and different country than their origins?

☆ I am aware of the debate about the variation in different countries and different cultures in use of concepts, and that you can stigmatise people through your use of concepts. For me who am a Sami, a 'minority group' and the aboriginal people of Norway, it is very important not to wound anybody in my use of concepts. They are meant as tools to understand the context football. 'African Footballers' or 'African football players' in this chapter refers to African football players who immigrate to Europe with the aim of playing professional football. I use the term "Norwegian Africans" for footballers who are brought up in Norway and have one or both of their biological parents with African background. Thanks to my colleagues Prisca Bruno Massao and Stein Egil Hervik for the discussion about these concepts and comments on this chapter.

Social and Cultural Diversity in a Sporting World
Research in the Sociology of Sport, Volume 5, 33–50
ISSN: 1476-2854/doi:10.1016/S1476-2854(08)05003-6

The theme came up through the project 'Elite Football – a *Field*[2] of Changes'[3] (2006a), where a field is defined by Pierre Bourdieu as: ' ... positions, including those of power, which have developed during history and which create structures between the positions of actors struggling for the field-specific capital and the fields' hegemony and the right to define its rules of function and change; and the habitus of the agents, their systems of dispositions which are based on objective material and social conditions as well as subjective preferences' (Bourdieu & Wacquant, 1992). In 'the field of football' there are struggles between actors about the types of capital which give positions (of power) in the field. A privileged position in society is based on the language and '*symbolic power*' which confers to the right to define the concept of sport, where language and definition rights are developed by the group or the groups in power (Bourdieu, 1991). Bourdieu refers to the general forms of capital such as economic, cultural and social, as well as symbolic and field-specific capital. Further the structure of a field is defined by the distribution (amount and composition) of capital, which is based on the results of previous struggles, and which direct future struggles (Bourdieu, 1993b; Bourdieu & Wacquant, 1992).

In this study observations were done in international championships (World Cup for men in France 1998, European Championship for men 2000 (EURO, 2000), The Olympics 2000 and European Championship for women 2001). Observations were also done in practices, meetings and matches in three Norwegian elite football clubs, combined with in-depth interviews with 22 players (11 of each sex) and eight coaches. In addition to that, a study of the media coverage of 'the John Obi Mikel case' in two Norwegian tabloid newspapers (Dagbladet and VG) was done during 2005 and 2006 (Skogvang, 2006b).

ABOUT 'THE JOHN OBI MIKEL CASE'

John Obi Mikel came from Nigeria to Norway in 2004 when he was 17 years old. He was head hunted by agents during the under-17 World Cup in 2003. He started to play football for FC Lyn's junior team in Oslo. After attaining the age of 18 (in April 22nd, 2005), he was allowed to play professional football. The same day three clubs and many football agents started a competition to get the rights to this talented player; FC Lyn in Oslo, Chelsea FC and Manchester United in England. Football agents from Norway, Nigeria and England were involved. Big clubs as Chelsea FC and

Manchester United both wanted to sign Mikel, and huge amounts of money was involved. One week after his 18th birthday, he signed a contract with Manchester United for about 11.9 million USD/8.8 million Euro. FC Lyn Oslo should get a percentage of this money, and the deal between the clubs was that Mikel should play for FC Lyn Oslo until December 31st, 2005. At the same time different agents from Chelsea claimed that Mikel had signed for them already in 2003, but at that time he was too young to sign such contracts according to the FIFA's rules. Chelsea wanted to pay more money than Manchester United. Mikel's wages per year in United should be 3.4 million USD/2.5 million Euro. Chelsea also said that it was Chelsea's agents who brought Mikel to Norway and that they had paid his wages and education in Norway so far (Skogvang, 2005).

An enormous media attention suddenly changed the life for this young, very talented Nigerian player. Because of high pressure from agents, clubs and all the media attention, Mikel went abroad together with one of his agents, John Shittu from Nigeria. FC Lyn Oslo sent the 'John Obi Mikel case' to FIFA for a final decision. Mikel did not want to return to Oslo and FC Lyn Oslo before FIFA had made their decision about which club he belongs to. On August 12th 2005, FIFA decided that Mikel belongs to FC Lyn Oslo. In October 2005 Mikel returned to Oslo and FC Lyn with hundreds of journalists running after him. He played a few matches for FC Lyn Oslo, but he did not manage to perform as good as expected. The pressure on him was tremendous, so the last part of the Norwegian football season Mikel only practiced. He did not want to play matches anymore, because of all the focus and all the conflicts around him. Both FC Lyn Oslo and Mikel and his agents brought the case to the Norwegian court. Mikel won the case in the second court. In the period from September 2005 until June 2006, Mikel did continue to play on the Nigerian National team, but he could not play club football when the case was running in the court system and in FIFA. He was exposed for a tremendous pressure through all the media attention. One of the largest Norwegian newspapers, 'VG', wrote for instance *more than 500 cases* about the 'John Obi Mikel case' during the 1.5 years long period it was running. Dagbladet wrote nearly 400 cases, and FC Lyn Oslo's fans discussed it in 6,600 cases on 320,000 web pages (www.dagbladet.no, 2005, 2006; www.lyn.no, 2006; www.vg.no, 2005, 2006).

June 1st, 2006 an agreement was made between Chelsea FC, FC Lyn Oslo and Manchester United. John Obi Mikel transfer to Chelsea and Chelsea pays about 7.7 million USD/5.6 million Euro to FC Lyn Oslo, and about 23.5 million USD/17.1 million Euro to Manchester United in so-called compensation. The player's salary is not known, but one agent got 25 percent of the transfer fee. At the same time Mikel could start to play club football again and all the cases brought to court were stopped. A part of the agreement was also that two other Nigerian players (Edu and Zeki) should continue to play for FC Lyn Oslo. During this 1.5 years long process, a young, very talented football player was mentally threatened in his life, he had to move between different countries, and he was nearly 'destroyed' by media attention, conflicts about agents, money, contracts and so on. In this way many players from, for instance, countries in Africa are abused and pressed to sign complicated contracts with their agents and clubs in Europe. Most of the conflicts are because of the huge amount of money involved (Poli, 2005; Skogvang, 2006a).

One hundred and five players from foreign countries played in the men's top league in Norway in 2005, of whom seventeen were from different African countries (Gammelsæter & Jakobsen, 2006). Beside John Obi Mikel, Edu and Zeki, four other players from Nigeria have visited FC Lyn Oslo to show their skills in 2006. Mikel was lucky who could sign a good contract with a Premier League club in England, and is earning a lot of money. All over Europe there are plenty of African players who play at lower level, have a dream about being a professional player, and are kept in clubs on 'low-cost contracts' just in case they improve their skills (Bennhold, 2006; NRK, 2004; Solberg, 2007). An argument is that the players at the same time shall get education through the training academies, and some of them do. Another argument is that many of the players live under better conditions in these clubs than, for instance, in the slum areas where some of them are recruited from, and some of them can send money back to their families. However, the most questionable ethical dilemma is when a second part, like agents and club owners themselves do earn a lot of money on selling players (human beings) from club to club all over the world and at the same time control the player's lives. Solberg (2007) says that the transfer market have many similarities linked to the slavery history. And even if some of the successes are visible, it is important to address all the others, both women and men, who experience discrimination, like Poli (2005) states: 'If some African players have an upward mobility which allows them to reach the top European clubs, we should not neglect the examples of downward mobility of a great number of players, who are very often victims of the speculation system based on players' transfers.'

The Mikel-story is one example of the '*Dance around the golden calf*' (Wahlstrøm, Sæbø, & Kvam Hojem, 2005), which involved Sir Alex Fergusson, Manchester Uniteds' manager, Chelsea-manager Josè

Mourinho, the Russian multi-millionaire and Chelsea-owner Roman Abramovitsj, FC Lyn-Oslo's club owner Atle Brynestad, FC Lyn-Oslo's director Morgan Andersen, football agents like Daniel Fletcher, John Shittu and Rune Hauge, several lawyers and a lot of others. At the end Chelsea won 'the golden calf', but both the agents and the clubs got their millions of Euros and Mikel earns a lot of money in Chelsea today. A part of the Mikel story is that the director of FC Lyn Oslo; Morgan Andersen, at an early stage of the case in May 2005 called the Nigerian agent John Shittu a liar, and said: 'As club we could not close our eyes and leave John Obi Mikel to the agents whom now are the active ones, to let them totally control his life and his economy. We think we have been conscious our responsibility with giving John Obi Mikel the help he asked for in relation to make it possible for him to resolve his own life and to play football for the club he wanted himself'(Andersen, 2005). In October 2007, two years after Mikel went to Chelsea, the public prosecutor in the Norwegian Court brought a charge against Morgan Andersen for forgery of documents through writing Mikel's signature on the transfer contract in 2005. Morgan Andersen was convicted by the Oslo City Court, first level court, on March 26th 2008. He appealed, but later he withdrew the appeal. The Oslo City Court's judgment is therefore binding. The club owner and Norwegian businessman Atle Brynestad has sold back all the shares he controlled in FC Lyn-Oslo, for a symbolic NOK 1 after a 10-year relationship, caused by the John Obi Mikel case (www.aftenposten.no, 2008; www.dn.no, 2008). At the beginning of August 2008 the case is still running for instance between the Norwegian FA and the club, with the agent Rune Hauge, and between FC Lyn-Oslo and Morgan Andersen (www.vg.no, 2008; www.aftenposten.no, 2008; www.fotball.no, 2008). In the media the focus on 'the bad Nigerian agent' had suddenly changed to focus on 'the bad Norwegian club director/club owner/agent'. After the prosecution was raised against Morgan Andersen, he was released from his job as a director in another Norwegian elite club; Fredrikstad FK (www.dagbladet.no, 2007, 2008; www.vg.no, 2007). After the decision in the Norwegian Court, Andersen is unwanted inside Norwegian football, and the other cases continue in the Norwegian court and in the decision-making bodies inside football (www.fotball.no, 2008).[4]

PIONEERS

Transfer of African football players to Europe has a long history, but it is not till quite recently that African footballers have become really visible in some European countries. Arthur Wharton was the world's first black professional footballer in the end of 1800s and the beginning of 1900. He came from a wealthy Gold Coast/Ghanaian family, enjoyed national celebrity in England as an all-round athlete. Vasli (1998) describe Wharton as an eminent sportsman with a turbulent personal and professional life. At the same time the author gives insight into the onset of professionalism in British sport, the class divide and the beginnings of institutionalised racism. According to Andreff (2006) France had its first recruitment drive in its North African colonies in the 1930s and in West Africa in the 1950s. According to Poli (2005) Belgium was claim to be a starting point for African players in Europe and still nowadays play an important role in the transfer market 'game'.

Many Africans have played in European football since Arthur Wharton, and since Wharton there have been many pioneers, who have been important for African players both in Europe and in Africa. In Norway it is taken for granted (doxic), according to Bourdieu's use of the concept 'doxa' (Bourdieu & Wacquant, 1992) that a professional football player is a man, even if female players are professional, but with less income than their male colleagues (Skogvang, 2006a). In the same way it is taken for granted that Norwegian (and European) footballers are white, and most of the professional players still are, even though a lot of footballers at different levels in Norway have other ethnic backgrounds. Poli (2005) presents Nauchâtel Xamax, the first African player to be chosen a captain of a Swiss team. Another example is the great 'Norwegian African' player John Carew. He is born in Norway, and grew up in Lørenskog, a small place nearby the capital Oslo. Carews' mother is Norwegian, and his father is from Ghana. Carew was the first player at the Norwegian national men's team which had origins in Africa ('Norwegian Africans'). Today he is a big star and a role model for many young football players in Norway. Mette Andersson (2008) discusses the footballers as multicultural players between national and global elite sport. Players like John Carew and Pa Modou Kah are described as examples on role models inside men's professional football. Carew and Kah are two of the first professional players in Norwegian football, brought up in Norway with African origins. At the moment Carew plays both at the Norwegian national team and at Aston Villa in Premier League in England. Kah is a former national team player of Norway, plays for AIK in the Swedish professional league today, and in his interviews to Andersson (2008) he says he was proud and that it was a great moment when he entered the Norwegian national team. He experiences himself as an important role model for Norwegian people regardless of ethnic background. He has also been an important profile in the 'Give Racism Red card' project in Norwegian football.

On the women's side; Charmaine Hooper, often called 'the black star' in Norwegian newspapers in the 1990s, was another 'first' with great success. She was born in Georgetown in Guyana, moved to Canada, and played her first international match for Canada against USA in 1986 (Norway Cup Exhibition). From 1994–1997 she played professional for teams in Norway, Italy and Japan (http://www.CharmaineHooper.com, 2007). However, on the Norwegian women's national A-team there has never been a none-white player. Nasra Abdullah (Team Strømmen), who is born in Kenya, plays at the women's under-23 national team, and is the first black women at this level in Norway. She is also a front figure in the two projects; 'Kicking Aids out' and 'Give Racism Red Card'. Another profile is one of the top goal scorers in women's Premier League in Norway in 2007; Una Obiose Kriston Nwajei. She plays for Amazon Grimstad, the club which have had much significance in forwarding the cause for women's football in Norway (Skogvang, 2007). Nwajei is born in Nigeria and has her citizenship in Great Britain, and she has played international matches for England. Both Nasra Abdullah and Una Nwajei have been important players in the Norwegian premier league the last season.

MEN'S AND (WOMEN'S) FOOTBALL IN AFRICA

Even if more research has been done on women's football since the millennium change, most studies in the field of football are on men. Although research about women's football in USA and Europe has increased in the last decade, there is very little research about other parts of the world, and even less is known about female African footballers.[5] Saavedra (2004) presents the development of the women's football in Senegal, Nigeria and South Africa, and states: 'With regard to football, the immense popularity and weighty social meaning for men's game in Africa, has made it that much harder for a women's game to develop.' When Williams (2003) states that 25 of 41 of the CAF[6] member football associations includes women's football, Saavedra (2004) writes that women are playing organised football in at least 30 African countries and probably more. Prisca Bruno Massao has done research on sport in Tanzania (Massao & Fasting, 2003; Massao, 2001), and her new project is on Norwegian athletes with African background (Massao & Fasting, 2006).

Anyway, there is still a need for more documentation and research in women's football in Africa and female African footballers in Europe.

During the last years many researchers have addressed global sport in relation to identities and societies, and several studies put focus on sport and men's football in Africa from different theoretical angles.[7] The focus on the economics of sport globally in relation to developing countries is crucial here (Andreff, 2006; Andreff & Szymanski, 2006; Massao & Fasting, 2006). According to Darby, Johnes, and Mellor (2005) the lack of money in the African football clubs result in that the best players leave home to play in Europe. Talent scouts from the richest European clubs who are searching for the cheapest players, is one of the reasons for the strong mobility that characterises the careers of professional football players, especially Africans, in the European labour market (Poli, 2005). One example of the victims of trafficking in the global players market is, for instance, the Cameroonian player Bodo Njiki who was a victim of "neo-colonial exploitation" both in France and Belgium, according to Bale and Cronin (2003). Another factor is the complex relationship between the migrants and the people they leave behind, something Carling (2007) addresses when he develop a model for understanding variation and change in 'trans-national ties'. He concludes that people who migrate from one country often sustain strong links to their country of origin, for instance by sending money, going for holidays, and facilitating the migration of others. Carling states that these trans-national ties can play an important role in the development process in migrants' country of origin, if the countries of destination not adopt progressively more restrictive immigration policies.

Football and other sports play an important role in peoples' lives. Through examples from Tanzanian sport Sendeu Titus Tenga (2000) illustrates the connections which sport has with other major social institutions in society such as family, education, economy, religion and politics. Tenga concludes that there is a need for a redefinition of the role of sport in 'a globalisation perspective', and states: 'The overall developmental policy for the country is also crucial in the redefinition of the role of Olympic sport in Tanzania. This is because the country's socio-economic realities not only hinder the genuine development of sports, but also make it insignificant. Compared to other crucial social services such as education and health, sport in general and Olympic sport in particular are considered a luxury' (Tenga, 2000).

As it is for other immigrants there are many 'push'- and 'pull' factors involved in a migration process (Carling, 2007). The push factors are circumstances in their home countries which 'push' people to migrate, such as poverty, lack of human rights and war. The pull factors are incentives in other countries which attract migrants looking for a better life. The situation of sports and sports organisations in developing countries, for instance in Africa, has to be taken into consideration in this context. No widespread physical education, low numbers of participants in sport, lack of money, and low ability of sport teachers, coaches and both the numbers and quality of sport facilities are often the shortcomings (Andreff, 2006; Bale & Cronin, 2003; Darby et al., 2005). This situation inside the country is often 'push-factors' when male African footballers want to move to Europe. 'One major consequence of sports underdevelopment and lower sports performance in developing countries is the so-called 'muscle drain' of talented Third world athletes (players) to developed countries' (Andreff, 2006). 'Pull-factors' like promises of education and money and employment as professional football players in Europe are both presented through media, and through talent scouts and satellite training schools, which some European clubs have set up in Africa. Examples are the Dutch club Feyenoord Rotterdam with football academies both in Africa and Latin America, Ajax Amsterdam in South Africa, Belgian clubs in corporation with Manchester United (Royal Antwerp), Chelsea (Westerlo) and Arsenal (Beveren) on for instance the Ivory Coast and other places in Africa. Manchester United writes that they are ' ... establishing a world-wide scouting network aimed at trawling the best teenage talents on the planet and bringing them to United' (www.manchesteronline.co.uk, 2007). The restrictive immigration law for people from Africa to Europe has opened up for middlemen like players' agents to influence the increasing 'sophisticated human trade', as Solberg (2007) calls it. This shows the 'big clubs' symbolic power[8] which is one of the consequences of the close relationship between sport, media and elite football (Gammelsæter & Ohr 2002; Morrow, 1999; Skogvang, 2006a) and how this influence African footballers in Europe and football clubs in Africa. Andreff (2006) argue that the increasing inflow of money poured into the Third world by foreign and multinational sponsors, media and bookmakers unfortunately is being accompanied by increased corruption. 'Clubs and federations are run without a strong economic rationale or even a clear managerial strategy, and circumventing them proves to be an easy game for talent-seeking player's agents and professional clubs based in developed countries' (Andreff, 2006). The symbolic capital[9] including the physical capital which African footballers have, is sought-after, but the 'big clubs' in Europe want to spend as little economic capital on them as possible.

TRANSFER MARKETS IN PROFESSIONAL FOOTBALL AND THE INFLUENCE OF 'THE BOSMAN CASE'

The transfer market's long history is illustrated by the story about Arhtur Wharton (Vasli, 1998). Most of the football leagues operating under the jurisdiction of the governing bodies of football in Europe (UEFA) and of world football (FIFA) have a transfer system (Morrow, 1999). One of the objectives for the transfer system was to prevent players club-hopping. The transfer system has been important for the clubs in helping them to build teams that will achieve success in sporting results. The players are bought and sold, often under the control of the manager of the club, with the intention of increasing playing strength and improving a team's performance and thus achieving football success. In a small country like Norway, I found that a few 'big clubs' according to their economic capital, numbers of spectators and amount of media attention have the symbolic power in 'the Norwegian football field' (Skogvang, 2006a). In a global perspective the constellation of the "G14"-group[10] in Europe shows how the concentration of both the economic power and the symbolic power is concentrated in these 18 clubs from 7 European countries. 'The more or less hidden agenda of the "G14" lobby is to organise a European Super League, which could widen the existing gap in the European football economy. The "G14" lobby tries to impose its influence also on FIFA, by demanding financial compensation when players are selected to represent national teams' (Poli, 2005).

The Belgian footballer *Jean-Marc Bosman* brought his case to court, and the decision in *'the Bosman case'*[11] was crucial for the development of transfers of football players all over the world. Until the decision in the European Court in 1995, a player who has signed for a particular club, to a certain extent he or she was tied to that particular club, through the retention element of the transfer system. The top clubs both in Norway (Gammelsæter & Ohr, 2002; Skogvang, 2006a) and other countries (Morrow, 1999; Poli, 2005) try to protect themselves against the Bosman ruling when they tie up players on longer term contracts, and a lot of clubs recruit young players before they are 18 years old and make agreements about their future football carrier. FIFA tried in 2001 to tighten the rules with requiring FIFA certification of the players' agents, and Article 38 of FIFA rules states that the professional clubs must release players selected for national teams. One example of the effect on African football is that all the key players for Nigeria's national team plays abroad: Obafemi Matins (Newcastle, England), John Obi Mikel (Chelsea, England), Joseph Yobo

(Everton, England) and Stephen Makinwa (Lazio, Italy). Andreff (2006) describe how the European professional clubs in international championships do not release football players from Africa for selection to their domestic national teams and writes: 'The African Cup is nicknamed "cattle fair" because a number of well-known European club managers, coaches and players' agents attend it with the objective of recruiting talented new players.' In the global football field with close relationships between sport, media and market, the existence of discrimination in terms of salary for black players is a fact (Poli, 2005). The minimum wage in Europe is well above the average income of a Third world player in his home country, and the wage gap between the African and the European labour markets for footballers is between 1:10 and 1:20 (Andreff, 2006; Poli, 2005).

Bennhold (2006) in *International Herald Tribune* has interviewed the former Cameroonian national team player Jean-Claude Mbvoumin. Today he is the founder of the 'Culture Foot Solidaire' in Paris, which is a non-governmental organisation that supports African youths, who are brought to France ostensibly to play football but are abandoned on arrival. The organisation estimates there are 600 such cases in Paris area alone and more than 7,000 youths across France and 70 percent of them are younger than 18 years old. Earlier it was more common to recruit underage Brazilians to European clubs, but more recent research shows that the recruitment from Africa to France has exploded after the decision in the 'Bosman case' in 1995 (Poli & Ravenel, 2006, 2007). The number of African players in the top division clubs of 11 major European football nations has doubled to 316 the last 10 years (*op. cit.*). Bennhold (2006) writes: 'Far from the festive atmosphere of the World Cup, the race for cheap muscle and talent in Europe's lucrative soccer industry has created yet another wrinkle in the immigration debate: Every year thousands of school-age boys from Africa and Latin America are lured to Europe by dubious agents hawking dreams of glory and wealth. After paying large sums for their passage to Europe, some are groomed in a succession of clubs. A very few rise to stardom and the millions of euros that come with it. Far more end up on the street, as illegal residents of a new country.'

On the other side and for others involved in professional football, the consequence of the Bosman case has been increases in the clubs wage costs, and today we see the 'Bosman as football's cost driver' as Morrow (1999) states. A global players market became more pronounced and was accompanied by an increase in financial rewards for players, coaches and directors and agents. The media, television and especially satellite television has been the most important contributory factor in the new economics of football, and for the increase in players' salaries, the Bosman decision has been the main driving force. Professional male footballers in Norway have got better finances, but at the same time both players, coaches, and, volunteers in Norwegian elite clubs are disappointed about the amount of and the symbolic power that money makes to the investors, players' agents and club owners. What seems to be very important for the salaries in Norwegian elite football is first of all if you are male or female, second how well you perform, then how long a contract you will make with the club and how long you have played (Skogvang, 2006a). In Norway as in other countries male players earn much more than female players and good players have a greater income than average players. Players who sign long contracts and who change clubs for free at the end of the contract period get more money. There is also a difference in income between players recruited internally from the club and the players who come from other clubs. Because not all players will receive this new wealth, male elite players like 'Biera' says: 'I think that it has gone totally out of control ("over stokk og stein") with these transfer money and money in general inside professional football especially after the Bosman case. I am very happy because I earn a lot of money, but at the same time I mean it is out of control now. It is players and agents which put all the money in their own pockets, while the clubs which have developed the players get nothing back to develop other young players' (Skogvang, 2006a).

Some clubs have started to impose an upper limit on the total that they can spend on player's salaries (salary caps), and in Norway there was a period at the end of the 1990s and in the beginning of the new millennium with salary caps in men's premier league, but now the wages seems to increase again. One of the reasons is the Norwegian FA's huge increase in income from sale of television rights from 2006. The new media agreement between the Norwegian FA and TV2/Channel Digital from 2006 until 2009 gives about 170 million USD to the Norwegian FA, who distributes the most of it to the male elite clubs. This seems to influence the salaries both for players, coaches and other employees in the male elite clubs. Football has turned to be entertainment and business, and the commercial value of a 'football product', like a club or a player, is decided from how many minutes this product is shown in television or how many centimetres it is written about it in the newspapers. This symbiotic relationship between professional football, media and market or '*the Sport/Media Complex*' (Boyle & Haynes, 2000; Rowe, 1999) is seen as positive for professional football because it brings a lot of money into the game and give full-time playing opportunities and better playing and training facilities, but at the same time it challenges traditional values in Norwegian sport, and one example is the agents and the media's role in the so-called 'John Obi Mikel case' (Skogvang, 2005).

PROFESSIONAL FOOTBALL: A FIELD OF EMPOWERMENT AND/OR DISCRIMINATION?

In 'the field of elite football' players experience both empowerment and discrimination. Male clubs are split in "big" and "small" clubs because of their economical situation, numbers of spectators and media attention through a symbiotic relationship between the field of professional football, the field of media and the field of market. The best clubs have money to buy the best players and by that they get an advantage in the field all over the world. Because of that the competition on the pitch is experienced as unfair, or in Bourdieu's terms the autonomy in the football field is threatened, when agents, sponsors and the media get more power inside the football field. Black elite players, female elite players and male elite players in so-called 'small' male clubs feel that they are being discriminated against because of the lack of media attention and lack of economic capital. John Carew, John Obi Mikel, Pa Modou Kah, Nasra Abdullah, Charmaine Hooper and Una Obiose Kriston Nwajei have experienced empowerment through professional football in Norway and in other countries. At the same time I have showed some of the negative parts within the transferring process in professional football. The 'Give Racism Red Card' is an important campaign against racism, which in Norway has had role models like Nasra Abdullah and Pa Modou Kah as frontiers. Also in UEFA there is a partner network with 'Football Against Racism in Europe' (FARE) and a letter from UEFA President Michel Platini to all UEFA match officials of November 23rd, 2007 underlines that: 'UEFA policy is clear: zero tolerance of violence, racism or discrimination.' Such campaigns and information from governing bodies in football hopefully will help other black players in the future, but the conflicts and challenges in the field are more complex than that. A lot of money is involved and a lot of illegal agents are operating in 'our times slavery trade market' as Mbvoumin calls it (Bennhold, 2006). Here the concept of 'institutionalised racism' from Vasli (1998) can be used.

In this chapter I have put focus on abuse and so-called slave contracts for male footballers from Africa in European clubs. Some of the players gain success and end up with contracts in, for instance, Premier League in

England, like Mikel did. A lot of others arrive in European countries on tourist visa of three months for a trial in a club and often end up on the streets without visa, with no money or job, or they get lower paid then their European colleagues. Poli (2005) describes how the African players, ' ... at the beginning of their career lend themselves perfectly to the role of a flexible and easily exploitable labour force, of which European clubs and players' agents do not hesitate to take advantage.' My conclusion is that the symbolic power in the global football field belongs to the white, males and the big clubs in Europe, which are included in the "G14" group. They define what kind of capitals are needed to be defined as a good footballer, and from that they influence on the players' wages, their economic capital and their lives.

NOTES

1. Through out this chapter, the term football is used to refer to soccer or association football (as it is officially known in England).

2. See also Bourdieu (1993a, 1993b), Bourdieu and Wacquant (1992) and Bourdieu (1995).

3. In Skogvang (2006a), I use Bourdieu's concept of field to describe the symbiotic relationship between 'the field of elite football', 'the field of media' and 'the field of market' and how this effect professional football for men and women.

4. A recent deal between FC Lyn-Oslo and Atle Brynestad ends Brynestad's 10-year relationship with the club, which landed in international controversy a few years ago over its attempts to lay claim to young Nigerian soccer player John Obi Mikel. Lyn tried to profit on a sale of Obi Mikel to Manchester United, only to see its former club manager Morgan Andersen wind up in a court battle after top London club Chelsea also claimed rights to Obi Mikel (www.aftenposten.no, 2008). Also thanks for the help with the juridical concepts and the last facts about the decision in the John Obi Mikel case to my sister Susann Funderud Skogvang, who is a lawyer.

5. For further examples see for instance Bjertnes (2005), Caudwell (2007), Fasting (2004), Fasting, Scraton, Pfister, and Bunuel (1999), Hong and Mangan (2004), Hovden (2000), Lippe (2001), Macbeth (2007), Magee, Caudwell, Liston, and Scraton (2007), Newsham (2005), Prudhomme-Poncet (2005, 2007), Ratna (2007), Skogvang (2006a, 2007), Saavedra (2004), Williams (2003, 2004) and Woodhouse (2001).

6. CAF, Confèdeèration Africaine de Football (African Football Confederation).

7. Some examples from about the millennium change until now are: Andreff and Szymanski (2006), Archetti (2003), Armstrong and Giulianotti (2001), Armstrong and Giulianotti (2004), Bjertnes (2005), Boyle and Haynes (2000, 2004), Dunning (2002), Finn and Giulianotti (2000), Gammelsæter and Jakobsen (2006), Gammelsæter and Ohr (2002), Giulianotti (1999, 2004, 2005), Goksøyr and Olstad (2002), Helland (2003), Hognestad (2004, 2005), Larsen (2003), Lippe (2001), Maguire (1999), Morrow (1999), Murphy, Reilly, and Spinks (2002), Poli (2005), Rowe

(1999), Skogvang (2006a, 2006b), Sugden and Tomlinson (1998), Taylor (2007), Tenga (2000), Vasli (1998), Vertinsky and Bale (2004) and Whannel (2002).
8. See Bourdieu (1991).
9. See Bourdieu, *Ibid.*
10. 'G14' is a lobby group, which has clubs from England, Italy, Spain, Germany, France, Portugal and the Netherlands.
11. For more about 'The Bosman case', see for instance Morrow (1999) or Boyes (2005).

REFERENCES

Andersen, M. (2005). Redegjørelse om Mikel-saken. Available at www.lyn.no, the web site of FC Lyn Oslo.

Andersson, M. (2008). *Flerfarget idrett. nasjonalitet, migrasjon og minoritet.* Oslo: Fagbokforlaget.

Andreff, W. (2006). Sport in developing countries. In: W. Andreff & S. Szymanski (Eds), *Handbook on the economics of sport* (pp. 308–315). Cheltenham: Edward Elgar Publishing.

Andreff, W., & Szymanski, S. (2006). *Handbook on the economics of sport.* Cheltenham: Edward Elgar Publishing.

Archetti, E. P. (2003). Playing football and dancing tango: Embodying Argentina in movement, style and identity. In: N. Dyck & E. P. Archetti (Eds), *Sport, dance and embodied identities.* New York: Berg.

Armstrong, G., & Giulianotti, R. (2001). *Fear and loathing in world football.* Oxford: Berg.

Armstrong, G., & Giulianotti, R. (2004). *Football in Africa: Conflict, conciliation, and community.* New York: Palgrave Macmillan.

Bale, J., & Cronin, M. (2003). *Sport and postcolonialism.* Oxford: Berg.

Bennhold, K. (2006). Soccer dreams and reality. *International Herald Tribune* (www.iht.com), Paris.

Bjertnes, H. M. (2005). *Medieomtaler av mannlige og kvinnelige norske fotballspillere. En kvalitativ innholdsanalyse av Dagbladets tekster fra fotball-VM i et kjønnsperspektiv.* Oslo: Norges idrettshøgskole/The Norwegian University of Sport and Physical Education.

Bourdieu, P. (1991). *Language and symbolic power.* Cambridge: Polity Press.

Bourdieu, P. (1993a). *The field of cultural production.* Cambrigde: Polity Press.

Bourdieu, P. (1993b). *Sociology in question.* London: Sage Publishers.

Bourdieu, P. (1995). Pugs at work: Bodily capital and bodily labour among professional boxers. *Body & Society, 1*(1), 65–93.

Bourdieu, P., & Wacquant, L. J. D. (1992). *An invitation to reflexive sociology.* Cambridge: Polity Press.

Boyes, S. (2005). Law, regulation and the 'Europeanization' of a global game. In: J. Magee, A. Bairner & A. Tomlinson (Eds), *The bountiful game? Football identities and finances.* Oxford: Meyer & Meyer Sport.

Boyle, R., & Haynes, R. (2000). *Power, play: Sport, media and popular culture.* Essex: Longman, Harlow.

Boyle, R., & Haynes, R. (2004). *Football in the new media age.* London: Routledge.

Carling, J. (2007). *Transnationalism in the context of restrictive immigration policy.* Doctoral dissertation, University of Oslo, Oslo.

Caudwell, J. (2007). Hackney women's football club: Lesbian united? In: J. Magee, J. Caudwell, K. Liston & S. Scraton (Eds), *Women, football and Europe: Histories, equity and experiences*. Oxford: Meyer & Meyer Sport.

Darby, P., Johnes, M., & Mellor, G. (Eds). (2005). *Soccer and disaster: International perspectives*. New York: Routledge.

Dunning, E. (2002). *Fighting fans: Football hooliganism as a world phenomenon*. Dublin: University College Dublin Press.

Fasting, K. (2004). Small country-big results: Women's football in Norway. In: F. Hong & J. A. Mangan (Eds), *Soccer, women, sexual liberation. Kicking off a new era*. London: Frank Cass.

Fasting, K., Scraton, S., Pfister, G., & Bunuel, A. (1999). *The experience and meaning of sport and exercise in the lives of women in some European countries*. Oslo: International Olympic Committee and Norwegian University of Sport and Physical Education.

Finn, G. P. T., & Giulianotti, R. (2000). *Football culture: Local contests, global visions*. London: Frank Cass.

Gammelsæter, H., & Jakobsen, S.-E. (2006). Utlendinger og spillerutvikling i norsk football. Available at www.idrottsforum.org.

Gammelsæter, H., & Ohr, F. (2002). Kampen uten ball. Om penger, ledelse og identitet i norsk fotball, Abstrakt Forlag, Oslo.

Giulianotti, R. (1999). *Football: A sociology of the global game*. Oxford: Polity Press, Blackwell Publishers.

Giulianotti, R. (2004). *Sport and modern social theorists*. Basingstoke: Palgrave Macmillan.

Giulianotti, R. (2005). *Sport: A critical sociology*. Cambridge: Polity Press.

Goksøyr, M., & Olstad, F. (2002). *Fotball! norges fotballforbund 100 år*. Oslo: Norges Fotballforbund.

Helland, K. (2003). *Sport, medier og journalistikk: Med fotballandslaget til EM*. Bergen: Fagbokforlaget.

Hognestad, H. (2004). *Norway between Bergen and Middlesbrough: Football identities in motion*. Oslo: Norwegian university of Sport and Physical Education.

Hognestad, H. (2005). Fan and scientist-a schizophrenetic combination? Notes on sports research methodologies. *Moving Bodies* (Vol. 3, No. 1), Norwegian University of Sport and Physical Education, Oslo.

Hong, F., & Mangan, J. A. (Eds). (2004). *Soccer, women, sexual liberation. Kicking off a new era*. London: Frank Cass.

Hovden, J. (2000). Makt, motstand og ambivalens : betydningar av kjønn i idretten, Institutt for sosiologi, Det samfunnsvitenskapelige fakultet, Universitetet i Tromsø, Tromsø.

Larsen, Ø. (2003). The influence of coaches and textbooks in Norwegian football 1960–2002: From a one-dimensional to a multi-dimensional understanding of football. *Moving Bodies, 1*(1) 116–132, (Football History and Culture).

Lippe, vonder G. (2001). *Idrett som kulturelle drama. Møteplasser i idrettssosiologi og idrettshistorie*. Oslo: Cappelen Akademisk Forlag.

Macbeth, J. (2007). Women's football in Scotland: A historical overview. In: J. Magee, J. Caudwell, K. Liston & S. Scraton (Eds), *Women, football and Europe: Histories, equity and experiences*. Oxford: Meyer & Meyer Sport.

Magee, J., Caudwell, J., Liston, K., & Scraton, S. (Eds). (2007). *Women, football and Europe, Histories, equity and experiences*. Oxford: Meyer & Meyer Sport.

Maguire, J. (1999). *Global sport. Identities, societies and civilizations.* Cambridge: Polity Press.

Massao, P. B., & Fasting, K. (2003). Women and sport in Tanzania. In: I. Hartmann & G. Pfister (Eds), *Sport and women: Social issues in international perspective.* London: Routledge.

Massao, P. B., & Fasting, K. (2006). Racism in sport from a black feminism perspective. In: IV ISA World Congress of Sociology 2006: 'The Quality of Social Existence in a Global World', Durban, South Africa.

Massao, P. B. (2001). *Women in sport: Feminist analysis of the sport development policy of Tanzania.* Oslo: Norwegian University of Sport and Physical Education.

Morrow, S. (1999). *The new business of football. Accountability and finance in football.* Edinburgh: Heriott-Watt University, Palgrave Macmillan.

Murphy, A., Reilly, T., & Spinks, W. (2002). *Science and football IV.* London: Routledge.

Newsham, G. J. (2005). Focus: Dick Kerr Ladies. Paper presented at Women, Football and Europe (Keynote speaker), University of Central Lancashire, Preston.

NRK. (2004). *Fotballboblen som sprakk. NRK1-TV. Brennpunkt.* Oslo: Norsk rikskringkastning.

Poli, R. (2005). *Football players' migration in Europe: A geo-economic approach to African' mobility.* Oxford: Meyer & Meyer Sport.

Poli, R., & Ravenel, L. (2006). Annual review of the European football players' labour market, CIES; CERSOT, Neuchatel.

Poli, R., & Ravenel, L. (2007). Annual review of the European football players' labour market, CIES; CERSOT, Neuchatel.

Prudhomme-Poncet, L. (2005). Women of the ball-A history of French women's football. Paper presented at 'Women, Football and Europe', University of Central Lancashire, Preston.

Prudhomme-Poncet, L. (2007). Les Femmes, balle au Pied-A history of French women's football. In: J. Magee, J. Caudwell, K. Liston & S. Scraton (Eds), *Women, football and Europe: Histories, equity and experiences.* Oxford: Meyer & Meyer Sport.

Ratna, Aa. (2007). A 'fair game'? British-Asian females' experiences of racism in women's football. In: J. Magee, J. Caudwell, K. Liston & S. Scraton (Eds), *Women, football and Europe: Histories, equity and experiences.* Oxford: Meyer & Meyer Sport.

Rowe, D. (1999). *Sport, culture and the media. The unruly trinity.* Buckingham: Open University Press.

Skogvang, B. O. (2005). The sport/media complex' within Norwegian and international football. Paper presented at the International Sociology of Sport Association World Conference, ISSA, Buenos Aires, Argentine.

Skogvang, B. O. (2006a). Toppfotball-et felt i forandring ('Elite football-a field of changes'). Doctoral dissertation/Doktoravhandling, Norges idrettshøgskole/The Norwegian University of Sport and Physical Education, Oslo.

Skogvang, B. O. (2006b). Transfer of African football players to Europe and the media. Paper presented at the ISA World Congress 2006, Durban, South Africa.

Skogvang, B. O. (2007). The historical development of women's football in Norway: From 'show games' to international successes. In: J. Magee, J. Caudwell, K. Liston & S. Scraton (Eds), *Women, football and Europe: Histories, equity and experiences.* Oxford: Meyer & Meyer Sport.

Solberg, E. (2007). Et spill med mennesker. Available at www.NyTid.no, Oslo.

Sugden, J., Tomlinson, A. (Eds.), & Fédération internationale de football association. (1998). FIFA and the contest for world football: Who rules the people's game? Cambridge: Polity Press.

Saavedra, M. (2004). Football feminine-development of the African game: Senegal, Nigeria and South Africa. In: F. Hong & J. A. Mangan (Eds), *Soccer, women, sexual liberation. Kicking off a new era*. London: Frank Cass.

Taylor, M. (2007). Football, migration and globalization: The perspective of history. Available at www.idrottsforum.org

Tenga, S. T. M. (2000). *Globalisation and Olympic sport in Tanzania: A developmental approach*. Doctoral dissertation, Norwegian University of Sport and Physical Education, Oslo.

Vasli, P. (1998). *The first Black footballer, Arthur Wharton, 1985–1930: An absence of memory*. London: Routledge.

Vertinsky, P., & Bale, J. (2004). *Sites of sport: space, place, experience*. London: Routledge.

Wahlstrøm, R., Sæbø, T., & Kvam Hojem, L. (2005). Dansen rundt gullkalven. Available at www.dagbladet.no, the web site of the Norwegian newspaper Dagbladet.

Whannel, G. (2002). *Media sport stars. Masculinities and moralities*. London: Routledge.

Williams, J. (2003). *A game for rough girls? A history of women's football in Britain*. London: Routledge.

Williams, J. (2004). The fastest growing sport? Women's football in England. In: F. Hong & J. A. Mangan (Eds), *Soccer, women, sexual liberation. Kicking off a new era*. London: Frank Cass.

Woodhouse, D. (2001). The post war development of football for females: A cross cultural and comparative study of England, the USA and Norway, October 2001 Edition. University of Leicester, Leicester.

www.aftenposten.no/english/sports/article2553722.ece (2008). July 22, 2008, Oslo.

www.CharmaineHooper.com. (2007). Charmaine Hooper's web site.

www.dagbladet.no (2005). The Norwegian newspaper Dagbladet's web site about "Obi Mikel-saken" and "Morgan Andersen-saken".

www.dagbladet.no (2006). The Norwegian newspaper Dagbladet's web site about "Obi Mikel-saken" and "Morgan Andersen-saken".

www.dagbladet.no (2007). The Norwegian newspaper Dagbladet's web site about "Obi Mikel-saken" and "Morgan Andersen-saken".

www.dagbladet.no (2008). The Norwegian newspaper Dagbladet's web site about "Obi Mikel-saken" and "Morgan Andersen-saken".

www.dn.no/forsiden/naringsliv/article1442402.ece (2008). July 11, 2008, Oslo.

www.fotball.no (2008). The Norwegian Football Association's web site. March 26, May 14, June 9, and July 7, 2008, Oslo.

www.lyn.no. (2006). The web site of FC Lyn Oslo. FC Lyn Oslo, Norway.

www.manchesteronline.co.uk. (2007). Manchester United's web site.

www.vg.no (2005). The Norwegian newspaper VG's web site "VG NETT" about "Obi Mikel-saken" and "Morgan-saken".

www.vg.no (2006). The Norwegian newspaper VG's web site "VG NETT" about "Obi Mikel-saken" and "Morgan-saken".

www.vg.no (2007). The Norwegian newspaper VG's web site "VG NETT" about "Obi Mikel-saken" and "Morgan-saken".

www.vg.no (2008). The Norwegian newspaper VG's web site "VG NETT" about "Obi Mikel-saken" and "Morgan-saken".

RELIGION AND ATHLETIC BODIES: WESTERN REPRESENTATIONS OF ISLAMIC VEILS AND MUSLIM ATHLETES

Brendon Tagg

Though most Muslim societies do allow women to play sport, it is usually on the proviso that they obey their religion's insistence on modesty. That can mean training in an exclusively female environment, with female-only coaching or tuition, and often wearing the traditional Islamic hijab. (Bee, 2004, n.p.)

While welcoming Afghan women's newfound freedom to throw off the burka, several readers cautioned that the celebration should not veil other limits on women's liberty. "You said, nowhere in the Muslim world are women treated as equals," observes a Californian woman. "Excuse me but nowhere in the whole wide world are women treated as equals". (Letters to the Editor, 2001, p. 4)

She is a real Iranian fighter, fierce and focused on taking down an opponent. At 20 years old, tae kwon do champion Sara Khoshjamal is taking her fight to Beijing. This summer she'll travel from her home on the outskirts of Tehran to the heights of the Olympic stage. (Setrakian, 2008, n.p.)

The quotes above illustrate some of the ways that Islamic veils, from simple *hejab* (headscarf) to all-enclosing *burka*, are "[s]ituated at the intersection of dress, body and culture" (El Guindi, 1999, p. xvi). On the one hand, liberal Muslim writers argue the veil is only tenuously linked to Islamic theology; subsequently, some Muslim athletes such as Indian tennis

Social and Cultural Diversity in a Sporting World
Research in the Sociology of Sport, Volume 5, 51–63
Copyright © 2008 by Emerald Group Publishing Limited
All rights of reproduction in any form reserved
ISSN: 1476-2854/doi:10.1016/S1476-2854(08)05004-8

player Sania Mirza ignore criticism from conservative Islamic groups and do not veil when competing (Chaube, 2005). Alternatively, veiled Muslim athletes represent a small but growing presence within competitive sporting events. While many from conservative Islamic countries do find it difficult to access competitive sport, others from many Western countries face discrimination due to their religious identity.

Furthermore, even when female Muslim athletes find sports compatible with veiling, they may face criticism and discrimination. Iranian Laleh Seddigh gained international media coverage when she became the first woman to win her country's national rally car championship, yet even her privileged background and supportive parents could not prevent her from being unfairly (and illegally) excluded from at least one race. Subsequently, she sought a fatwa, or religious ruling, to defend her right to compete against men (Tait, 2006). The story of American high school Muslim athlete Juashaunna Kelly reflects the discrimination that veiled Muslim athletes often experience in Western nations, as well as the obvious difficulties associated with competing whilst wearing additional layers of clothing (Goldenbach, 2008).

Given the wide cultural diversity associated with Muslim women's participation in sport, it is useful to consider the cultural and historical relationship between Islamic veils and the Western imagination. First, according to Moroccan sociologist Fatima Mernissi (1991) the status of women in Islamic societies encompasses many complex issues, most crucial of which surround access to education and economic welfare. And while veils are sometimes forced on Muslim women, many freely embrace veiling because it is often perceived as a positive and even liberating institution (El Guindi, 1999, p. 172). Even in nations where women's freedom of dress has only recently been reinstated, for example Afghanistan, not all women simply abandoned the *burka*. Indeed, BBC news reporting around the time of the new Afghan parliament in June 2002 revealed both heavily and relatively lightly veiled women interacting with many men.

Also, according to some readings of the Qur'an, regulations surrounding birth, death, marriage, sex, warfare, fragmentation, eating, alcohol and prayer appear more important to the purity of the Islamic body than veiling. Qur'an 24:31, for example, demands women "wear their head-coverings over their bosoms" (see, e.g., Shakir, 1989), thereby clarifying which parts of the body are the most crucial to cover. Meanwhile no respected *hadith* outline penalties for unveiling. In this sense, Islamic veiling can be interpreted as a means to protect women, not to hide their bodies or restrict their physical activity. Finally, veiling has at times also been a popular cultural tradition within Judaism and Christianity, yet the meanings associated with Christian veils, in particular, now seem quite different to those associated with Islamic veils (El Guindi, 1999, p. 151). Considering many Muslims do not perceive the tradition of veiling as either archaic or perfidious, it is crucial to understand how veiling has come to virtually constitute many Westerners' understanding of Islamic women's bodies as symbolically oppressed.

IMPERIALISM, FEMINISM AND EARLY DISCOURSES OF THE VEIL

Leila Ahmed suggests the debates surrounding the veil have complex historical roots. According to Ahmed (1992, p. 145), *Women's Liberation* (a book written by French-educated Egyptian jurist Quassim Amin in the 1880s) reflects the imperialist agenda behind the push for socio-political reform within Islam; abolishing the veil is described as a symbolic, yet critical step "to bringing about the desired general social transformation" of colonial rule and economic development.

Since the opening of the Suez Canal in 1869, Egypt has been a prominent site of imperialism within the Muslim world. While Western capitalism brought educational and economic benefits to some middle class Egyptians, the majority, and particularly the very poorest, ended up much worse off. And while British influence was quickly associated with the increased social tension between the elite and the desperately poor masses (El Guindi, 1999, p. 174), it became particularly noticeable with regard to 'body culture' because many who profited from Western influence also abandoned their traditional lifestyle. While in many cases the three-piece suit replaced traditional Arab garb, debate emerged regarding to the future of Egyptian culture:

> The colonial presence and the coloniser's economic and political agenda, plus the role that cultural training and affiliation played in widening the gap between classes, provided ample ground for the emergence at this moment of the issue of culture as fraught and controversial. (Ahmed, 1992, p. 149)

Although the early debate surrounding the British role in Egypt focussed on political and economic issues rather than religious or cultural practice, rapid colonisation encouraged lower class Muslim Egyptians to cling to their cultural heritage and religious values. Conversely, the Egyptian elite typically embraced Western traditions; in 1843 Reverend Olin noted that

"Englishmen of distinction and influence" brought prostitution to Gheneh, Egypt (quoted in Mabro, 1996, pp. 235–236).

Conflict between Western and Islamic body politics, and specifically the issue of veiling, was also rooted in the tensions between Islam and Christianity. Until the seventeenth century, Westerners' attitudes toward and representations of Islam were exclusively based upon Christian explorers, missionaries and crusaders. Lady Mary Montagu, an eighteenth century writer and traveller, argued that many early misapprehensions about Islam arose from poor translations of the Qur'an made by "Greek Priests, who would not fail to falsify it with the extremity of Malice" (cited in Ahmed, 1992, p. 50). Furthermore, until the twentieth century, the few travellers who ventured to the Middle East had only superficial encounters with Muslim women (Parker, 1999). Thus, the popular belief emerged that a 'civilised Islam' could only be achieved if all Muslims abandoned their 'archaic practices'. The veil was seen as the most obvious target because of the way it marks Muslim women's bodies as different (and therefore inferior) to the 'true pinnacle' of social evolution: Victorian England (El Guindi, 1999, p. 106).

It seems the British, whether ruling Egypt from within or from back home, never *really* saw Egyptians' welfare as a central concern. For example, Lord Cromer's attitudes were important because of his influence over Egyptian social policy and lived culture. But while he was a staunch advocate for unveiling Egyptian women, in England he founded and sometimes presided over the 'Men's League for *Opposing* Women's Suffrage', and apparently believed that while Western feminism should be suppressed, when "directed against the cultures of colonised peoples, it ... admirably served and furthered the project of the dominance of the white man" (Ahmed, 1992, p. 153). Rather than expand the national education programme in response to Egyptians' increasing desire for a basic Western education, he raised fees and restricted access. And while criticising restrictions women faced in Islamic society, he fought to *remove* medical training for women (conservative Islamic law almost always requires women doctors to examine female patients). Given the prestige and social power associated with the medical profession, it provides an important site for women's liberty (Malti-Douglas, 1991, pp. 130, 133).

Cromer's policies reflected sexist Europeans' attitudes. Travelling through Egypt in 1886, an anonymous Westerner (cited in Mabro, 1996, pp. 161–162) described female doctors as "a great evil in Egypt, as they frequently, I am led to believe, attempt operations upon women, the perpetration of which in England if found out, means penal servitude for life!" And while many people joined in the battle to 'liberate' Muslim women, by undermining Egyptian culture and identity, these practices only furthered oppression:

> Whether such proselytisers from the West were colonial patriarchs ... or missionaries or feminists, all essentially insisted that Muslims had to give up their native religion, customs, and dress, or at least reform their religion and habits along the recommended lines, and for all of them the veil and customs regarding women were the prime matters requiring reform. (Ahmed, 1992, p. 154)

Although unveiling women was often a means to further imperialism rather than liberate women, this was not the way it was portrayed publicly. While Amin criticised seclusion and veiling of 12 to 14 year-old girls because this period is crucial for social and intellectual development, his position was rather incompatible "with his earlier statement that anything beyond a primary-school education was 'unnecessary' for girls" (Ahmed, 1992, p. 160).

According to Ahmed, the French feminist Eugenie Le Brun naïvely encouraged Muslim women to accept the Western conception of the veil as symbolic imprisonment. Aside from the feminist rationale, the case for unveiling also assumed the superiority of Western culture. While recognising that the three main Abrahamic faiths (Jewish, Christian and Islamic) share a history of veiling and secluding women, Amin suggested that the virtual abandonment of these traditions, with the notable exception of Christian nuns, facilitated Western cultural superiority:

> Do Egyptians imagine that the men of Europe, who have attained such completeness of intellect and feeling that they were able to discover the force of steam and electricity ... could possibly fail to know the means of safeguarding women and preserving her purity? (Amin quoted in Ahmed, 1992, pp. 160–161)

Under the guise of women's liberation, the thoroughly patriarchal Amin was simply advocating the substitution of Western for Islamic patriarchy, followed, crucially, by Western economic exploitation.

Challenging the legitimacy of the Muslim body by undermining the veil was crucial to justifying political domination of Islamic nations, although the popularity of discourse surrounding the veiling of women was by no means for political purposes only. In her anthology of eighteenth to twentieth century travel notes, Judy Mabro (1996) finds a rather disturbing sexual interest in Muslim women's bodies, described below.

'OH, THE PRETTY LITTLE SAVAGE!'

Tales about the beauty of Arabian women, epitomised and instigated by English-language versions of *The One Thousand and One Nights*, are central to Western discourses of Other women. Many early European travellers composed elaborate descriptions of encounters with exotically beautiful 'Mohammedan' women; others desperately searched the lands for them. Judy Mabro (see, Mabro, 1996, pp. 66–67) collected writings from eighteenth and early nineteenth century European travellers; an incredibly valuable source of material for a study wishing to outline Westerners' attitudes during this period. Three broad themes run through her collation: the fantasy (childlike beauty of flirtatious harem girls), the disappointment (unattractive Muslim women that should be covered) and the frustration (all-enclosing *burka*, and conservative Islam).

A common story relates to the fantasy of releasing beautiful young girls from the clutches of the 'wretched Muslim jackal', for the purposes of sexual liaison. The Frenchman Paul Fagault made no effort to hide his intentions for an Algerian girl he saw at a Bedouin camp. Although it is unclear whether he ever talked to her, he conversed extensively with an accompanying man, who spoke French. Fagault said he took an immediate liking to this man, this is until he realised that the two were married:

> Yes I *had* understood, my gazelle belonged to this jackal ... she was his wife. Then I saw that I hadn't looked very closely at him at first, for now I found him hideous with his large teeth and dirty burnous [cloak] ... When I departed I shook his hand; oh! If only I could have crushed it! (Fagault cited in Mabro, 1996, pp. 102–103)

Such stereotypical clichés of animal imagery were often used to describe Muslim women, with the intention of creating a vivid impression of tremendous beauty and deficient intellect (the quintessential Victorian ideal). But the irony of the stereotypically beautiful Arabian women is that Western men could rarely meet local Muslim women: there was much resentment of seclusion and veiling *because* it impeded Western travellers' self-asserted 'right' to scrutinise the world's peoples. In response, for example, the Hon. Lewis Wingfield apparently "barged into a house, took a good look at the women's dress, and then ran out describing the women [who confronted him] as 'very questionable society'" (Mabro, 1996, p. 223).

Similarly, when William Bromfield, received "an expression of impatience from the women, if we indulge in a stare of curiosity or speculation" (see Mabro, 1996, p. 231), he may have misunderstood notions of 'sacred privacy' in an Islamic context (for a description of this, see, El Guindi, 1999, pp. 77, 81–82, 96). And while studying anthropometrics and cultural traditions was an explicitly stated objective of many travellers in North Africa and the Middle East, it was considered intolerable for the locals to reciprocate. For example, Syrian culture fascinated Gertrude Bell but she found the townsfolk's curiosity of her totally intolerable. Bell attributed their behaviour to cultural inferiority: "no better way of spending [the afternoon] ... occurred to them than to assemble to the number of many hundreds around my tents and observe every movement of every member of the camp" (cited in Mabro, 1996, p. 232).

In 1907 Eustache de Lorey (who was apparently with the French Legation in Teheran) and Douglas Sladen (who had never visited Iran but had lived in other Muslim nations), drew upon Christian religious rhetoric to insult Persian women's distinctive clothing. They called them "black phantoms; they were true daughters of Eve ... no torturing of my imagination could poetise creatures as void of form as the earth on the day of its creation"(cited in Mabro, 1996, p. 53). In 1858 Reverend E. Davies believed heavily veiled women who failed to subscribe to Victorian standards of beauty lacked religious morality and therefore true humanity:

> Were it not for the beautiful eyes whose sparkle cannot be veiled, [Mauresques] might be mistaken for ghosts passing to and fro silently and mysteriously *among the human crowd*, but taking no part in its affairs. (cited in Mabro, 1996, p. 52, italics added)

Some European travellers' explicit fascination with employing animal imagery to represent the bodies of Other women reached the point where sometimes it was even used to justify the veiling of *non-Muslims*. Such narratives, particularly those from Algeria and Tunisia, propose precisely the opposite argument: the apparent 'ugliness' of these nations' women denoted the degenerate nature of the African soul. The 'devout Christian', Mrs Albert Rodgers seemed to be caught between her detestation of Islamic faith and repulsion at Algerian women's bodies, she resigned herself to advocating that women "adopt the Moslem fashion, and hide their repulsive features, [because] it would save one many a shock" (cited in Mabro, 1996, p. 257). Despite Lott's assertions, these comments suggest it was the Christian, not the Muslim women, who demonstrated no coherent code of morals, indicative of an "unmistakable mark of want of intelligence."

Christians' depictions of Muslim bodies suggest at least one legitimate reason for veiling women; to protect them from unwanted sexual attention and public derision. Indeed, according to Mernissi (1991, p. 180), the prophet Muhammad veiled his wives precisely because the open society he was trying to create left his wives vulnerable to harassment. And indeed,

Christian travellers who chose not to veil often felt the power of the veil. In 1937 French author Lucie Margueritte employed what we might now label as 'Foucaultian' terms to describe how she felt when surrounded by Muslim women; "beside these women wrapped up from head to toe, whose eyes cannot always be seen, but are always seeing, I have the feeling of being naked" (Mabro, 1996, p. 50).

On the other hand, even a *burka* cannot protect women from all forms of harassment. In 1906, Douglas Sladen criticised heavily veiled women for their immodesty; "she covers her face so jealously, [yet] she thinks nothing of showing her skinny legs as high as her knees, and the effect of the incongruity is heightened, if she is a country woman, by huge silver anklets" (cited in Mabro, 1996, p. 62). Similarly, in 1911, London-based journalist John Fraser casually mocked Tunisian women because they did not subscribe to his ideals of beauty:

> Real fat, podgy, waddling, wobbling women-not ladies just inclined to stoutness ... The Tunisian woman is Humpty-Dumpty and Daniel Lambert reincarnated as one person. No scraggy, angular Gothic-framed females for the Tunisian! (Fraser, cited in Mabro, 1996, p. 58)

Paula Cooey (1994, p. 21) notes that despite the belief that Western culture has been purged of such outdated 'irrationalities', many of our attitudes and practices regarding femininity and masculinity reflect continuities with these assumptions. Indeed, Mernissi (2001, pp. 208–220) highlighted the absurdity of the Euro-centric gender and beauty norms referred to above by describing the impossibility for 'abnormal' women such as herself to fit into a size-six dress (what she calls the 'size-six harem'). She subsequently suggests that this is no less oppressive than veiling and segregation.

Mernissi also argued that, based on her own childhood experiences, harems are often far less oppressive than Western males' fantasies might suggest and that much of what Westerners understand about harem women is fantasy. While the opening sentence of one of Mernissi's books reads "I was born in a harem" (see Mernissi, 1995), she was amazed that Westerners associate them with an "orgiastic feast where men benefited from a true miracle: receiving sexual pleasure without resistance or trouble from the women they had reduced to slaves" (Mernissi, 1991, p. 14). While Western artists like Picasso, Maltisse and Ingres reduce both harem and Western women to their physical embodiment; nude and vulnerable:

> Muslim painters imagine harem women as riding fast horses, armed with bows and arrows, and dressed in heavy coats. Muslim men portray harem women as

uncontrollable sexual partners. ... The tragic dimension so present in Muslim harems-fear of women and male self-doubt-is missing in the Western harem. (Mernissi, 1991, pp. 15–16)

In fact, like so many Western representations of Islam, attitudes toward the harem reveal more about Western fantasy than Islamic reality. Although the tales of *The One Thousand and One Nights* are often sexually explicit, the broad moral and intellectual frameworks in which they were originally told portrays women as strong and independent, and even as brave heroines. Westerners' translations of the stories privileged male heroes such as Sinbad, Aladdin and Ali Baba "apparently because the Westerners were interested in only two things: adventure and sex" (Mernissi, 1991, p. 62). Reflecting on Immanuel Kant's *Observations on the Feeling of the Beautiful and Sublime*, Mernissi was amazed by the suggestion that because women are intended to be beautiful and men sublime (to think) no intelligent woman, irrespective of the shape of her body, can be considered attractive:

> Kant's book is as cutting as that of a Muslim Imam. The only difference between an Imam and Kant ... is that the philosopher's frontier does not concern the division of the space into private (women) and public (men) realms, but into beauty (women) and intelligence (men). (Mernissi, 1991, p. 91)

Essentially, while one of the most important minds of the Western Enlightenment ignored women's capacity to think, even tyrannical Muslim caliphs such as Harun Ar-Rachid paid well to enjoy harem girls' sharp-witted entertainment (Mernissi, 1991, pp. 92–93).

RESOLUTION: ALTERNATIVE VEILS NOT ALTERNATIVES TO VEIL

Because much of Western depiction of the Muslim woman and the veil has been a result of religious misogyny and cultural dogmatism, it might prove useful to end this chapter by reconsidering the place of the veil with regard Muslim identity and athletic female bodies. Some Westerners are surprised to see Islamic women defy stereotypical media representations, and are baffled to find liberal and powerful Muslim women playing competitive sport when they expect to see conservative and oppressed women cowering from public view. Interestingly, despite the stereotypes, many Muslims are somewhat unrecognisable from their physical appearance; in 2001, the Maldivian woman Ayesha Verrall was elected president of the Otago University Students' Association and very few people were aware of her religious background. Clearly, the physical embodiment of Muslim women is not always simply the stereotypical image of veiled, oppressed and politically invisible.

In contemporary Islam, the most common meaning Muslims give to their veil is that of a *shelter from the intruding gaze of men*. This is a meaning to which many Western women such as Lady Montagu (discussed earlier) can quite clearly relate. Muslims wearing the veil consider it an empowering device because it provides varying degrees of anonymity and protection, and because it is believed to promote modesty at a time when Western bodies are increasingly being used to market products. As people are becoming more 'body conscious' in the West, veiling reduces Muslims' concern about their physical appearance. For example, it allows women to feel as if they are being assessed on their intellectual skills rather than being viewed simply as an object of sexual desire (El Guindi, 1999, p. xvii). Of course, the veil also provides shelter from the physical environment.

A *symbol of personal etiquette* is a second unambiguous meaning of the veil; it openly affirms one's religious affiliation as a Muslim and leaves little ambiguity as to one's personal beliefs and morals. Perhaps in this sense Islamic and Christian (nuns') veils serve similar purposes (El Guindi, 1999, p. 145). However, while many Muslims living in the West act in similar ways to non-Muslim Westerners, there are certainly some social settings in which veiled women might seem somewhat out of place. Sometimes the cultural values associated with veiling are at odds with, or perhaps more likely, misunderstood within, the dominant social ideology. Examples of mistaken cultural values are the widespread assumption that veil equals Muslim equals socially oppressed, and the belief that veiling implies support for Islamic terrorist organisations. It does, however, often reaffirm "an Islamic identity and morality that rejects Western materialism, consumerism, commercialism, and values" (El Guindi, 1999, p. 145).

Despite these political connotations the veil is first an item of clothing, and as such can, in theory, be invested with any number of *alternative political connotations*. There is no reason why Muslims sympathetic to the West cannot reinvest the veil with fresh meanings, or that *hejab* is incompatible with Western conceptions of fashion. A newspaper article 'Muslim women blend fashion, faith into expression of style' embodies this argument (Mortimer, 2000). This article suggests that at certain times traditional Islamic dress etiquette can be seen to complement, and even encourage Muslim women to acquire Western values such as individuality and plurality, although in other contexts restrictions on religious plurality and freedom are still being hotly contested; in 1994 some French schools expelled veil-wearing girls under the pretence that it incites fundamentalist Islam (see Taylor, 1994). For many Muslims living in the developing world, it may not be feasible to purchase expensive clothing. However a simple and inexpensive scarf folded into *hejab* is an affordable way to personalise one's image and to protect one's modesty.

A Muslim customer who came into a store where I was working epitomises the potential for alternative political connotations. This young Muslim woman had obviously decided to purchase some new material for *hejab*; however, perhaps torn between a love of her religion and empathy for the plight of the post 11 September New Yorker, the material she chose was in the pattern of the American flag. Although veiling may draw undue attention in the West, removing one's veil as a result of social pressure is sometimes read as an implicit denial of one's faith. Therefore this veil is a superb way to deflect criticism from anxious Westerners, support New Yorkers affected by terrorism, and yet still stay true to one's religious values.

The veil is undoubtedly an important *symbol of cultural independence* from Western imperialism, a marker of political ideology (especially in Turkey, see El Guindi, 1999, p. 130) and to reflect a "renewal of cultural identity" (El Guindi, 1999, p. 145). Indeed this was the most common defence for the banning of the veil in French schools. Nevertheless, at a period in history in which many Muslims living outside the Middle East may feel alienated from their religion, it might be important for Muslims to retain their veil as a reminder of their religious beliefs, even if the contemporary political climate makes this fraught with difficulty.

From a theoretical perspective it is also interesting to compare perceptions of *hejab* as a symbolic form of imprisonment with Foucault's concept of panopticon and its relevance as a metaphor for Western objectifying and sexualising of the female body (Foucault, 1995). Margaret Duncan's analysis of *Shape*, a popular fitness magazine, demonstrates how under certain circumstances displaying the body can be inherently oppressive (Duncan, 1994). Yet, mainstream feminist theory has also taught us that covering the body in a veil is also deeply oppressive, even though Goldschmidt compares forced unveiling of Iranian women to what "Westerners would experience if women of all ages were forced to go topless in public" (Goldschmidt, cited in El Guindi, 1999, p. 130).

From the incongruity about whether Muslim women should veil or unveil, emerges an interesting contention; that the parameters for 'empowerment' and 'repression' are simply a function of cultural values. Therefore, because a number of Muslim women have the veil forced upon them, it is important to promote the idea of the veil as a *matter of personal choice*; there is scope for this within liberal Islamic thought and it is a reality for Muslim women in many Islamic and Western countries (El Guindi, 1999, p. 172). This is crucial for women, because it has the potential to give women control over their own destiny, and over their own sexuality (El-Moslimany, cited in Sanders, 2001).

Cases of the 'invisible veil', i.e. non-veiled Muslims, are interesting because they make it impossible to determine the individual's faith. Irrespective of the legitimacy of their reasons, given that Westerners feel more comfortable around unveiled Muslims, if some women decide not to veil, then they can more subtly further the case of liberal Islam. Such an argument would also likely apply to many competitive Muslim athletes. Also, at a time in which anti-Islamic sentiment is increasing in the West, the ability of unveiled Muslims to defend their religion without the initial stigma undoubtedly provides a valuable means of reaching narrow-minded Westerners.

CONCLUSION

This chapter has discussed some theological, historical and political issues surrounding Western stereotypes of Islamic veils, and these issues are relevant to a sociological analysis of Muslim women in sport. Whilst women throughout the Islamic world have been encouraged to veil, unveil and re-veil under the guise of women's rights since at least the early nineteenth century, popular Western thought has often paid little attention to Muslim women's own views on the matter. Indeed, there are actually plethora complex meanings that Muslim women may associate with their veils; they may see it as an opportunity for shelter from the male gaze, an embodied cultural and religious symbol, a signifier of personal etiquette, a canvas to be imbrued with alternative meanings, and finally (and ironically given the stereotypes), as an opportunity to demonstrate personal choice, as many Muslim women choose not to veil. Subsequently, the view that Islam is not a monolithic anti-Western entity, and that it, like modern Christianity, allows for multiple interpretations, should be kept in mind when considering Muslim women's participation in physical activity and organised sport. Although Muslim women in Islamic countries may have difficulty accessing competitive athletic opportunities, Muslim women in Western countries also sometimes face harassment and discrimination whilst playing sport.

REFERENCES

Ahmed, L. (1992). *Women and gender in Islam: Historical roots of a modern debate*. New Haven: Yale University Press.

Bee, P. (2004). The veil is slowly lifting for Muslim women athletes: Peta Bee on the battle to compete but not to offend. *The Guardian* website, October 11. Available at http://www.guardian.co.uk/sport/2004/oct/11/petabee

Chaube, K. (2005). Sania Mirza will not change dress – ready to face Islamic threats. *India Daily* website, September 16. Available at http://www.indiadaily.com/editorial/4607.asp

Cooey, P. (1994). *Religious imagination and the body: A feminist analysis*. New York: Oxford University Press.

Duncan, M. (1994). The politics of women's body images and practices: Foucault, the panopticon and Shape magazine. *Journal of Sport and Social Issues*, *18*(1), 48–65.

El Guindi, F. (1999). *Veil: Modesty, privacy and resistance*. Oxford: Berg.

Foucault, M. (1995). *Discipline and punish: The birth of the prison*. New York: Vintage Books.

Goldenbach, A. (2008). When the rules run up against faith: Prep athlete wearing Muslim clothing disqualified from track meet. Washington Post website, January 16. Available at http://www.washingtonpost.com/wp-dyn/content/article/2008/01/15/AR2008011503356.html

Letters to the Editor. (2001), *Time Magazine* New Zealand edition, 24 December, p. 4.

Mabro, J. (1996). *Veiled half-truths: Western travellers' perceptions of Middle Eastern women*. New York: I.B. Taurus.

Malti-Douglas, F. (1991). *Woman's body, woman's word: Gender and discourse in Arabo-Islamic writing*. Princeton: Princeton University Press.

Mernissi, F. (1991). *The veil and the male elite: A feminist interpretation of women's rights in Islam*. Longman: Addison Wesley.

Mernissi, F. (1995). *Dreams of trespass: Tales of a harem girlhood*. Cambridge, MA: Perseus.

Mernissi, F. (2001). *Scheherazade goes west: Different cultures, different harems*. New York: Washington Square Press.

Mortimer, J. (2000). Muslim women blend fashion, faith into expression of style: Western couture ignites desire for individuality, search for Islamic chic. *Detroit News*, 17 September.

Parker, K. (1999). *Early modern tales of orient: A critical anthology*. London: Routledge.

Sanders, E. (2001). Interpreting veils: Meanings have changed with politics, history. *Seattle Times*, 5(October).

Setrakian, L. (2008), Iran's girl fighter goes for gold: Tae kwon do champion trains for Beijing summer Olympics. ABC News website, March 13. Available at http://abcnews.go.com/International/Story?id = 4445066&page = 1

Shakir, M. (1989). *The Qur'an*. New York: Tahrike Tarsile Quran Inc.

Tait, R. (2006). Iran's female racing champion barred from defending title. The Guardian website, 4 October. Available at http://www.guardian.co.uk/world/2006/oct/04/gender.motorracing

Taylor, P. (1994). Hijab battles around the world. *Islamic Horizons Magazine*, November–December.

EQUALITY ISSUES WITHIN PARTIALLY SIGHTED FOOTBALL IN ENGLAND

Jessica Macbeth

INTRODUCTION

Disability football in England has, in recent years, undergone a range of developments from grassroots to elite level (Macbeth & Magee, 2006). Competitive football opportunities for partially sighted individuals were first provided in 1980 through the establishment of a competitive national league by the British Football Association for the Visually Impaired (BFAVI). The BFAVI operated independently until 1997 when it joined forces with British Blind Sport (BBS), a charity founded in 1975 to provide sporting opportunities for the blind and visually impaired, to establish the nationwide British Blind Sport Visually Impaired Football League (BBSVIFL). In 1999, the English Football Association (FA) became increasingly involved in the development of disability football, including partially sighted football. The FA's involvement in disability football over the last decade has been beneficial in many ways, including the development of pan-disability opportunities at grassroots level, support of eight national disability squads at elite level, and the development of *The FA Football Development Programme – Disability Football Strategy 2004–2006*.

Social and Cultural Diversity in a Sporting World
Research in the Sociology of Sport, Volume 5, 65–80
ISSN: 1476-2854/doi:10.1016/S1476-2854(08)05005-X

In terms of partially sighted football, the FA supports the national squad "through provision of Technical Advisors, kit, equipment and from 2003, with financial assistance, to help squads travel to their respective championships" (The Football Association, 2004, p. 3). It is BBS however, who have almost exclusive responsibility for running partially sighted football at the grassroots level, in particular through the BBSVIFL. As a result of these recent developments in the organization of partially sighted football, there exist a number of equality issues and significant challenges to the two key stakeholders (BBS and the FA) responsible for developing the sport from grassroots to elite level.

A particularly pertinent issue is the relatively diverse and segregated experiences of players at the grassroots and elite levels. Previous research focusing on the career paths of elite partially sighted footballers highlighted that few of the England Squad at the Partially Sighted World Championships (PSWC) 2004 actually participated in the BBSVIFL and had effectively been fast-tracked to the elite level (Macbeth & Magee, 2006). This finding raised several questions including: why do England players generally not compete in the BBSVIFL? Why are players who participate regularly in the BBSVIFL under-represented at the elite level? What is the nature of the relationship between grassroots and elite level? What equality issues exist within partially sighted football? And, most importantly, what are the experiences and views of the players involved?

This chapter draws on research with players at both grassroots and elite levels (which, with the exception of one player, are two separate groups) in order to address these questions. It prioritizes players' perspectives so as to gain an understanding of their experiences and perceptions of each other, the stakeholders involved, and the tensions that exist between these two levels of participation in England. The underlying aims of the chapter are to (1) provide a brief background to recent developments in partially sighted football at grassroots and elite levels; (2) analyse players' views on a range of equality issues within partially sighted football; and (3) discuss critically the implications for the future of partially sighted football in England.

DISABILITY THEORY AND SPORT

Developments in disability theory have been reviewed relatively extensively. It is outside the scope of this chapter to offer a thorough review (see Oliver, 1996; Barnes & Mercer, 1997) but in line with recent disability studies this research takes a social construction approach, conceptualising disability using the social model which:

> does not deny the problem of disability but locates it squarely within society. It is not individual limitations, of whatever kind, which are the cause of the problem but society's failure to provide appropriate services and adequately ensure the needs of disabled people are taken into account in its social organization. (Oliver, 1996, p. 32)

It was advocated that a reconceptualization of disability using the social model, as opposed to the medical model, was required in order to recognize and address the range of oppression experienced by people with various impairments and to bring about equal rights (Oliver, 1996). The adoption of the social model of disability, has led research within the field of disability studies to become more critical and "emancipatory" in nature (Barnes & Mercer, 1997, p. 4). Barnes (2003, p. 6) argues that "the integrating theme running through social model thinking and emancipatory disability research is its transformative aim: namely, barrier removal and the promotion of disabled people's individual and collective empowerment". In negotiating the extent to which it is emancipatory in nature, this research adopts a stance similar to Brittain (2004a) in his research on the sporting lives of elite disabled athletes. Brittain (2004a, p. 434) admits that, on its own, his research is not likely to lead to a "more just and fairer society", but it is "more an attempt at consciousness raising or 'cognitive emancipation'". This research is similarly an attempt at cognitive emancipation regarding key equality issues within partially sighted football in England. With the potential to inform and influence those responsible for providing opportunities for disability football this research also has a transformative aim similar to that expressed by Barnes (2003).

Research into disability sport has focused largely on access and provision issues (French & Hainsworth, 2001; Tregaskisk, 2003; Sport England, 2001, 2002), social inclusion factors (Hums, Moorman, & Wolff, 2003; Smith & Thomas, 2005; Sport England, 2001, 2002), empowerment, conceptions and perceptions (Blinde & Taub, 1999; Hargreaves, 2002; Taub & Greer, 2000; Groff & Kleiber, 2001; Page, O'Conner, & Peterson, 2001; Kristen, Patriksson, & Fridlund, 2002; Kristen, Patriksson, & Fridlund, 2003; Brittain, 2004a, 2004b), participation experiences (Devas, 2003; Sport England, 2001, 2002), and politics of the Paralympics (Howe, McDonald, & Hargreaves, 2005). That which is framed by disability theory tends to adopt the social model of disability.

Given that association football is the world's most popular sport, it is of note that research on disability football is under-developed. Atherton, Russell, and Turner (2000) have however been pioneers in this field and provided the most extensive study through their historical account of football for deaf people in Britain (see also Atherton, Turner, & Russell, 2001). The role of football in the British deaf community and the experiences of deaf footballer players were dominant themes to emerge. Similarly, but on a smaller scale, Stead and Waddington (1999) conducted research at the 1998 World Cup for Players with Learning Disabilities and featured, among other issues, the significance of football in the lives of people with learning disabilities.

Despite the emergence of these two studies, the development of a body of research on disability football, which is framed by wider disability theory, is warranted. Macbeth and Magee (2006) have begun to address this relative neglect, adopting a social construction approach in order to highlight that visual impairment does not necessarily disable individuals from accessing football opportunities. Instead, a range of social and political, as opposed to medical or individual factors, combine to disable individuals from participating, or at least from having a normalized experience, in partially sighted football. Although the growing body of research on disability sport and disability football has contributed significantly to an understanding of the equality issues that people with disabilities experience in comparison to non-disabled sports participants, the research has not yet explored to a significant extent equality issues within disability sport. This chapter seeks to make a further contribution to knowledge in this area by developing a more introspective analysis of equality issues within partially sighted football. These equality issues emerge from a range of social and political, rather than medical, factors and have varying effects on the experiences of current players at grassroots and elite levels.

The chapter will draw on qualitative data generated through a range of research methods including desk research (BBS documents and archives, BBSVIFL meeting minutes, FA strategies), focus groups with the Partially Sighted England Squad in December 2004 (Players A–H), and interviews with a sample of players competing in the BBSVIFL during 2005 and 2006 (Players H–L). It is important to point out that Player H was the only player participating at both grassroots and elite levels during both stages of the research.

CURRENT STATE OF PLAY IN PARTIALLY SIGHTED FOOTBALL

Developments in disability football in England have been outlined by Macbeth and Magee (2006). A number of changes have since occurred within partially sighted football and these warrant further attention. *The FA Football Development Programme – Disability Football Strategy 2004–2006*, launched in 2004, recognized the need to work in partnership with the relevant National Disability Sports Organizations (NDSO) to develop disability football across six impairment groups (amputee, blind, partially sighted, deaf, cerebral palsy, learning disabilities). In terms of partially sighted football the FA and BBS are in the relatively early stages of developing a working partnership.

The BBSVIFL is an established indoor five-a-side league based around monthly tournaments. BBS has a team of Sports Development Officers but, as they are responsible for all sports, the day-to-day running of the BBSVIFL is largely undertaken by the BBSVI Football Committee, which works in a voluntary capacity. The BBS and FA are joint stakeholders responsible for developing football for the partially sighted, with BBS focusing primarily on grassroots developments and the FA concentrating primarily on the elite level. However, the FA is beginning to gain more control over the BBSVIFL and has contributed financially to the running of the league. The Treasurer Report presented at the 2006 BBSVI Football Committee Annual General Meeting (AGM) showed an FA contribution of £2,300 to cover some of the basic costs for a league which between May 2005 and June 2006 cost approximately £7,300 to run (BBSVI Football Committee AGM Minutes, 2006, pp. 14–19).

In terms of the elite level, BBS supported a Great Britain squad at European and World Championships throughout the 1990s but the FA took over responsibility and has supported a partially sighted England Squad since 2000. The FAs of the other Home Nations have responsibility for developing disability football and representative squads in their own countries. The development of elite level disability football also involved the FA seeking to host major disability football tournaments and they agreed to host the Partially Sighted World Championships (PSWC) 2004 in Manchester as a non-profit event, underwriting the financial cost of the tournament through the local association (Manchester FA), organizing training weekends, hosting a warm-up tournament, and providing coaches, kit and equipment for the England squad.

The England squad finished in sixth place at the PSWC 2004 behind France (5th), Ukraine (4th), Spain (3rd), Russia (2nd), and Belarus (World Champions). At the 2007, IBSA Futsal European Championships the squad finished in fifth place behind Ukraine (4th), Spain (3rd), Russia (2nd), and Belarus (European Champions). Following the PSWC 2004, the England squad suggested that the superiority of particular nations was due to their experience of playing Futsal, the FIFA recognized format of small-sided football played at both European and World Championships, and also the traditional format played domestically by the majority of nations who compete. An over-riding view from England players and staff was that being exposed to regular Futsal, rather than five-a-side, is fundamental to bringing success at the elite level. However, as will be discussed later, there are some concerns about the appropriateness of Futsal for players with poorer levels of sight in the BBSVIFL.

EQUALITY ISSUES WITHIN PARTIALLY SIGHTED FOOTBALL

Partially sighted football is clearly in a phase if transition and the involvement of the FA as a key stakeholder within the last 10 years has resulted in greater support for players at the elite level. The desire for international success is also influencing developments at the grassroots level. With partially sighted football in a relatively fragmented state, perspectives on how the sport should develop are somewhat divided. A number of equality issues already exist within the sport, and proposed future developments raise further concerns among players at grassroots and elite levels. This section analyses several pertinent issues which were highlighted as of particular concern by the players themselves during the research.

Links between BBS and the FA

Despite the recognized need for a co-ordinated approach to developing partially sighted football from grassroots to elite level, all players interviewed alluded to very poor links between the two key stakeholders. Indeed some players considered both organizations to have relatively divorced objectives, as Player H expresses:

> BBS is all about participation, the FA's all about exceeding expectations within elite level ... the FA are looking after what they want to do, BBS are looking after what they want to do and it's not football, it's mainly the other sports.

This also suggests that, with responsibility for developing opportunities for the blind and partially sighted in a number of sports, BBS do not prioritize football. This is potentially as a result of recent FA involvement. It is perceived by players in the BBSVIFL that the running of the league is undertaken by the voluntary BBSVIFL Committee, as Player L comments, "I feel there is almost no correlation between the work the FA are doing at national level and the hard work being done by those individuals who run our clubs to encourage and develop those with a real visual impairment". This also hints at issues surrounding opportunities for players with more severe visual impairment and this will be discussed further in later sections. Player H has participated at both grassroots and elite levels for a number of years and is relatively pessimistic about the development of links between BBS and the FA:

> I've been involved in visually impaired football since '85 and at international level since '96 and I still don't see any improvement at all in opportunities ... you've got your elite level and then you've got your league, it's a big gulf, there's no join ... and I don't see anything improving at all.

The recent contribution that the FA has made in terms of funding the league might be interpreted as an attempt to forge better links with BBS. However, players in the BBSVIFL suggest that their financial contribution and attendance at BBSVIFL meetings is more of a token gesture, as Player L expresses, "they come to the AGM and then they lose interest for the next 12 months, they make a token gesture of coming to the AGM...I mean they don't give us huge amounts, I think it's only a couple of thousand a year, so it's...a tiny token gesture". There is also the suggestion that funding the BBSVIFL has enabled the FA to gain more power and control over key aspects, in particular the format of small-sided football that is played. This will be discussed in more detail later. Since the research took place, no FA representative attended the 2006 or 2007 BBSVIFL AGM, although reports on International Football were provided in advance. The relatively divorced relationship between the FA and BBS is further exemplified in the process of recruiting players to represent England at the elite level.

Recruitment to the England Squad

A salient issue to emerge from research with the England Squad was that five out of the eight players had minimal experience of participating in partially sighted football prior to their recruitment. The three players who had experience of participating in partially sighted football prior to their recruitment to the England Squad had all participated at grassroots level in the BBSVIFL league and at elite level for Great Britain prior to the FA's involvement. The FA was responsible for the recruitment of the 'new'

England players who all had minimal, or no, experience of participating in partially sighted football prior to being recruited to the England Squad. Macbeth and Magee (2006, p. 456) argue that this "is certainly unique within sport where recruitment to the international level precedes a process of introduction to the sport at the participation level and can be criticized for circumventing the traditional developmental route".

These players revealed how they were still able to compete in fully sighted football, and preferred to do so, rather than become involved in the BBSVIFL. The reasons for this are explored later. Despite all having participated in the BBSVIFL at some point, players acknowledged that it is not necessary to participate in the BBSVIFL in order to be recruited to the England Squad. As Player A expressed:

> I think if you're partially sighted and you're able to play fully sighted 11-a-side football and someone turns around to you ... and says 'look, come and play partially sighted football for your country' ... if that's not enough of an incentive and a goal for you to go and wear a shirt with the three lions on it I think there's got to be a few question marks on you.

For the England players, the opportunity to participate for their country is clearly one that they are keen to embrace. However, the way in which they have been selected to represent their country and their lack of involvement in the BBSVIFL is of concern to players who compete at grassroots level. Player H identifies flaws in the scouting process as a particular concern, stressing that:

> There's no professional link there through the FA, they don't turn up at the tournaments ... the only time they can be seen to pick up players it's on recommendation rather than picking out and scouting ... I think what they've done, they've gone to visually impaired tournaments, they've found out the standard is probably not what they want so they've got to find players from somewhere else.

Players in the BBSVIFL are quite adamant that FA representation at league fixtures is severely lacking. There is also a desire for a change in the selection of players for international sides so that "all England players should be taken from League players" (Player I). The potentially exclusionary process by which players are recruited to the England squad and their lack of involvement in the BBSVIFL has led to resentment within the BBSVIFL. As Player I stresses, "I don't see the players that are participating in the England side now actually playing for any of the league clubs ... there's a certain amount of resentment that exists either rightly or wrongly between the league that I participate in [BBSVIFL] and the elitist FA or England squad". There are tensions between the two sets of players and this warrants further examination of their relationship and perceptions of each other.

Player Perceptions of Elite and Grassroots Levels

Players are conscious of a gulf existing between those participating at the grassroots and elite levels. Player H quite explicitly asserts that "it's bad enough saying there's no link between BBS and the FA, but there's no link between the league players and domestic [elite] players". The choice of most England players not to compete in the league and the potential implications this has for the motivations of players in the BBSVIFL represents one of the most common grievances among players in the BBSVIFL:

> I don't think it does the game any good when you've got a league that's running week in, week out, the FA support that league financially, and I think one of their players' plays in the league ... You've got a load of players playing league ... they don't even know who these top players are...they should be the ones that can say he's a good player, you know, I've played against him, he plays for England. (Player J)

Greater representation of England players in the BBSVIFL is identified as an important factor that could raise awareness of the existence of elite opportunities and provide players with motivation to participate, otherwise, as Player H stresses, "how do they expect everybody else to aspire to what they're doing?" Despite the resentment expressed by BBSVIFL players, they do offer explanations for why there is minimal representation of England players participating in the BBSVIFL.

> People say well you play in the visually impaired league it detracts you, you know, you're not competing at the same levels ... they've either grouped together and thought 'what's the point in playing in that' or someone's suggested it to them, 'don't be playing at that level, go and play at this level'. (Player H)

The perceived poor standard of the BBSVIFL is also considered as an explanation for the FA's limited scouting of league players for the England Squad. As Player J argues, "they're not interested in the players from that league because they've got some notion that maybe they're not good". Similarly, Player L considers that "the message is quite clear that if you want to get into the England squad you have to be playing football outside of the VI league, they don't really look at anybody that's just playing in the VI league".

Experiences of England players confirm such attitudes and also the potential influence of the FA in encouraging players to avoid participation in the BBSVIFL in favour of competing in fully sighted Futsal teams. When asked at the end of the PSWC 2004 whether the next step was to participate in the BBSVIFL or to play fully sighted Futsal, Player C commented that "it depends what the manager tells us in the next meeting". Player D reiterated the negative attitudes towards the quality of the BBSVIFL and that participating in it may have a detrimental effect on England players, "[Player F] had it pin-pointed really, he just said 'you're playing in that league and them guys are bringing you down', and they are because they're crap".

Player A described in detail his first experience of playing in the BBSVIFL:

> When I first went up to my first tournament I didn't know what to expect ... no disrespect to them but they're just absolutely awful, you know, and they really are bad footballers. But that's the only exposure they get to playing football and I've got so much respect for them because they travel from all over the country to go and play this game because they're not going to get a game of football anywhere else.

Player B identified that the BBSVIFL was essentially about enjoyment stressing that "many of those lads do enjoy it, that's why they're there", with Player E adding that "there's nothing wrong with the VI League for that ... it's nothing to do with this [elite level]" effectively divorcing the BBSVIFL from the elite level. Player E takes this point further by suggesting that for the England squad to improve it is necessary to find new players from sources other than the BBSVIFL, ideally those who are able to participate in fully sighted football:

> We're not going to find younger, better players in the VI League. The only younger, better players we've got are playing fully sighted football ... maybe a bit controversial but if you're able to play fully sighted football do you have a need to go and play VI football?"

Overall, from the elite players' point of view, the BBSVIFL serves no function in terms of providing a pool of players that are of a high enough standard to participate at the elite level. Those players who are of a high enough standard are likely to be participating in fully sighted football and this is something that seems to be encouraged in order to gain success at in international competition. None of the 'new' England players identified any merit in improving links with the BBSVIFL in order to develop it as a potential source of future England players. However, the BBSVIFL players were more open to the prospect of trying to improve links between the BBSVIFL and the elite level, in order to serve both those players who strive to participate at the elite level and those who participate primarily for fun and enjoyment. As Player L asserts, the BBSVIFL should serve two key functions:

> We don't want to discourage those people who haven't got any chance of playing international football who want to participate because it's fun and basically enjoy playing, but we also want to encourage those players that are looking for international honours to stay within the league, otherwise the league itself becomes devalued and completely pointless.

With the perceived attitudes of the FA and the views of England players in mind, encouraging elite players to participate in the BBSVIFL is clearly going to be a challenge.

Format of Small-Sided Football

The BBSVIFL has played indoor five-a-side football since it was established in 1980. This is the traditional format of small-sided football played in England but is different in many ways to Futsal, the format of small-sided football recognized internationally by FIFA. There are two key differences between the two formats that have a particular relevance to partially sighted players. First, while five-a-side allows the ball to be played off surrounding walls, Futsal has distinct pitch boundaries and second, the ball is not allowed to be played above head height in five-a-side football whereas this is allowed in Futsal. The position of sixth place at the PSWC 2004 was largely attributed to players' lack of exposure to Futsal, for example, Player B revealed that "the first time I kick a ball [competitively] is with an England shirt on playing Futsal, I'd never even heard of the game". There is a clear need for England players to be participating regularly and competitively in Futsal in order to improve their chances of success in international competitions.

At the time of research the FA had proposed that the format of football in the BBSVIFL be changed from five-a-side to Futsal. Views on a change to Futsal are divided within the league. Those players who would prefer to continue playing five-a-side consider it to be "much more inclusive for people with lower abilities and vision" whereas Futsal "lends itself more to people who have got (a) better ability and (b) more sight" (Player I). Player L anticipates that "the worse team would struggle far more" particularly "those players who just can't cope with the ball up in the air". Player I considers that in Futsal, "playing with a ball that's going in the air is actually dangerous if you think of people with detached retinas, if they're going in for challenges with heads". Such concerns about Futsal are strong enough for Player L to predict that "there's definitely one club that would leave tomorrow if we changed the rules".

However, those supportive of Futsal consider it to be a more technical and skilful format than five-a-side, as Player J expresses, "I think it would improve the quality of play greatly, and I think long term that would be good for the top end of the England game". Player H is similarly supportive of but acknowledges that opinion within the BBSVIFL is "very divided". He recognizes that the "main clubs, your teams pushing for titles ... want to play Futsal" and considers that opposition to Futsal relates "to the resentment side of things really ... but because they've never tried Futsal they don't know how good it is" (Player H).

The proposed change to Futsal signifies the growing influence of the FA over the BBSVIFL and this is of particular concern to some players at grassroots level. Player I considers that "there's quite a wide gulf ... between elitism and grassroots, but that gulf's getting bigger and elitist sport is forcing conditions on grassroots, which is going to make the gap even wider". Player H similarly acknowledges that the BBSVIFL is under pressure to change to Futsal due to the FA's financial contribution to the league, stressing that "there's the threat of, if we don't go to Futsal and if we don't meet [their] suggested criteria that [the FA] is going to pull the funding" (Player H). As a result, and despite the concerns mentioned and practicalities of finding appropriate facilities, it was decided provisionally at the BBSVI Football Committee EGM in 2006 that "if we can get the right facilities where both divisions can be played together ... then we'll go to Futsal. But that will ultimately be decided at the AGM" (Player H). Since the research was conducted the BBSVIFL has changed to Futsal and the impact of this on players' experiences within the league, particularly players with lower levels of sight, warrants further research.

Opportunities for Players with Poorer Levels of Sight

The previous section alludes to concerns about opportunities for players with poorer levels of sight if the format of small-sided football in the BBSVIFL changes from five-a-side to Futsal. Those who participate in partially sighted football are either classified as B2 or B3 (with B1 being the classification for individuals who are totally blind). There is a significant degree of diversity across, and within, each of these classifications in terms of type and severity of visual impairment. Regardless of the changes in the format of football there is evidence to suggest that within the BBSVIFL players with poorer levels of sight are generally relegated to the lower standard teams. As Player J explains, "a low level B2 won't get in my team, that's the way it is, that's how the league works, it's competitive league, if you start bringing lower level B2s in then you're going to lose games". Player I suggests that the players "who fall between a good partial and totally blind are being squeezed out". This is clearly a concern for the BBSVIFL since, as Player L argues, there is a risk the league will struggle to serve those players it was originally set up for:

> It's the people that come to the league and come to play football because they can't play anywhere else because they feel they're not good enough because they can't see, because it's dangerous for them to play, it's those people that the league has always been there for, and it's those people that the league can't afford to leave behind otherwise it just becomes another branch of the FA to be honest ... it leaves its grass roots behind if you like.

Based on views in the previous section, the concern for players who have poorer levels of sight is heightened with the prospect of a change to the Futsal format. This relative exclusion of such players at the grassroots level is similarly mirrored at elite level. It is widely acknowledged among players in the BBSVIFL that there is limited opportunity for those with poorer levels of sight at international level, as Player J asserts "all the current England team players have very good levels of sight, there is no opportunity for lower level B2 players at international level". It is argued by Player L that due to the broad spectrum of visual impairment across B2 players, the grouping of B2 and B3 players together at the international level "is fundamentally discriminatory with virtually no opportunities for those with a great deal of talent but with poor vision not low enough to qualify for B1 status" (Player L). In terms of potential solutions, Player L argues for:

> greater efforts by the FA to acknowledge players who really need it. Yes it's great to find a player who JUST qualifies to play VI football and if he can be persuaded to play international VI football then England may be successful, but this kind of policy has alienated many dedicated VI players who rely on the BBSVI league to play competitive sport.

Player J suggests that players with poorer levels of sight could be provided with opportunities at elite level by either "sorting the classification system out or whether we get them an opportunity that would be a B2 classified squad". Unless these issues are addressed by both BBS and the FA then B2 players with poorer levels of sight are likely to continue to be relatively excluded at both grassroots and elite levels.

CONCLUSION

This chapter has explored a range of issues that have implications for players' experiences of partially sighted football from grassroots to the elite level in England. Based on the experiences of members of the England squad, Macbeth and Magee (2006) highlighted social and political factors that can act as barriers to accessing football opportunities. By examining the experiences and views of players at both grassroots and elite levels, this chapter has focused more introspectively on a range of equality issues within partially sighted football. The key issues to emerge from the analysis are that, despite the importance of working in partnership, players perceive the key stakeholders to have relatively divorced objectives and weak links with each other. This has a range of implications for players at both the grassroots and elite levels, particularly regarding the process of recruitment to the England squad.

Partially sighted football is in a phase of transition, with the FA gaining more influence over the BBSVIFL. This may be beneficial in terms of solidifying the links between grassroots and elite level. The FA's growing control has also influenced a change to Futsal in the BBSVIFL. However, there is strong concern among players at grassroots level of the impact of this change on B2 players with poorer levels of sight, especially since this particular group of players are considered to be relatively excluded within the BBSVIFL and at elite level. Further research is warranted to assess the impact of this change on player experiences in the BBSVIFL. The extent to which the change to Futsal will help to bring about international success and bridge the gap between grassroots and elite level, remains to be seen.

Partially sighted footballers are clearly not a homogenous group and there is a broad diversity of visual impairment between those who participate at, and within, both grassroots and elite levels. The social model of disability argues that the cause of disability is the way in which society is organized, rather than any medical or individual factors. This chapter has provided evidence that the current organization of partially sighted football in England could be considered to disable participants to some extent. More concerning is that recent developments in the game could have the potential to further disable players with poorer levels of sight at both grassroots and elite level. These issues present significant challenges to the key stakeholders responsible for developing partially sighted football in England in a manner that provides appropriate services and opportunities and adequately ensures "the needs of disabled people are taken into account" (Oliver, 1996, p. 32).

REFERENCES

Atherton, M., Russell, D., & Turner, G. H. (2000). *Deaf united: A history of football in the British deaf community*. Gloucestershire: Douglas McLean.

Atherton, M., Turner, G. H., & Russell, D. (2001). More than a match: The role of football in Britain's deaf community. *Soccer and Society, 2*(3), 22–43.

Barnes, C. (2003). What a difference a decade makes: Reflections on doing 'emancipatory' disability research. *Disability and Society, 18*(1), 3–17.

Barnes, C., & Mercer, G. (1997). Breaking the mould? An introduction to doing disability research. In: C. Barnes & G. Mercer (Eds), *Doing Disability Research* (pp. 1–14). Leeds: The Disability Press.

Blinde, E. M., & Taub, D. E. (1999). Personal empowerment through sport and physical fitness activity: Perspectives from male college students with physical and sensory disabilities. *Journal of Sport Behavior, 22*(2), 181–202.

British Blind Sport Visually Impaired (BBSVI) Football Committee. (2006). Minutes of the BBSVI Football Committee Annual General Meeting, Saturday 15 July.

Brittain, I. (2004a). Perceptions of disability and their impact upon involvement in sport for people with disabilities at all levels. *Journal of Sport and Social Issues, 28*(4), 429–452.

Brittain, I. (2004b). The role of schools in constructing self-perceptions of sport and physical education in relation to people with disabilities. *Sport, Education and Society, 9*(1), 75–94.

Devas, M. (2003). Support and access in sports and leisure provision. *Disability and Society, 18*(2), 231–245.

French, D., & Hainsworth, J. (2001). There aren't any buses and the swimming pool is always cold!: Obstacles and opportunities in the provision of sport for disabled people. *Managing Leisure, 6*, 35–49.

Groff, D. G., & Kleiber, D. A. (2001). Exploring the identity formation of youth involved in an adapted sports program. *Therapeutic Recreation Journal, 35*(4), 318–332.

Hargreaves, J. (2002). *Heroines of sport: The politics of difference and identity*. London: Routledge.

Howe, D., McDonald, I., & Hargreaves, J. (2005). *The politics of the paralympic games*. London: Routledge.

Hums, M. A., Moorman, A. M., & Wolff, E. A. (2003). The inclusion of the paralympics in the olympic and amateur sports act: Legal and policy implications for integration of athletes with disabilities into the united states olympic committee and national governing bodies. *Journal of Sport and Social Issues, 27*(3), 261–275.

Kristen, L., Patriksson, G., & Fridlund, B. (2002). Conceptions of children and adolescents with physical disabilities about their participation in a sports programme. *European Physical Education Review, 8*(2), 139–156.

Kristen, L., Patriksson, G., & Fridlund, B. (2003). Parents' conceptions of the influence of participation in a sports programme on their children and adolescents with physical disabilities. *European Physical Education Review, 9*(1), 23–41.

Macbeth, J., & Magee, J. (2006). Captain England? Maybe one day I will: Career paths of elite partially sighted footballers. *Sport in Society, 9*(3), 444–462.

Oliver, M. (1996). *Understanding disability: From theory to practice*. Hampshire: Macmillan Press Ltd.

Page, S. J., O'Conner, E., & Peterson, K. (2001). Leaving the disability ghetto: A qualitative study of factors underlying achievement motivation among athletes with disabilities. *Journal of Sport and Social Issues, 25*(1), 40–55.

Smith, A., & Thomas, N. (2005). The 'inclusion' of elite athletes with disabilities in the 2002 Manchester Commonwealth games: An exploratory analysis of British newspaper coverage. *Sport, Education and Society, 10*(1), 49–67.

Sport England. (2001). *Disability Survey 2000: Young people with a disability and sport*. Sport England, London, Available at: www.sportengland.org/disability_young_people.pdf. Accessed on 16 April 2008.

Sport England. (2002). *Adults with a disability and sport: national survey 2000–2001*. Sport England, London. Available at: www.sportengland.org/adult_disability_full_report.pdf. Accessed 16 April 2008.

Stead, A., & Waddington, I. (1999). Leicester 98: Football's other World Cup. *Singer and Friedlander Review, 1998–1999 Season, 5*, 33–36.

Taub, D. E., & Greer, K. R. (2000). Physical activity as a normalizing experience for school-age children with physical disabilities: Implications for legitimation of social identity and enhancement of social ties. *Journal of Sport and Social Issues, 24*(4), 395–414.

The Football Association (FA). (2004). *The FA football development programme: Disability football strategy 2004–2006*. London: The Football Association.

Tregaskisk, C. (2003). Towards inclusive practice: An insider perspective on leisure provision for disabled people. *Managing Leisure, 8*, 28–40.

THE SUM OF ALL FEARS: RECONCILING SPORT AND SEXUALITY

Roger LeBlanc

There are a lot of gay athletes in the world who are too scared to come out of the closet ... because society and the sports world won't let them.
                                        –Dennis Rodman (Rodman & Silver, 1997)

INTRODUCTION

It is often argued that sport is the one cultural arena that transcends social divisions associated with class, gender, race, religion, and sexualities, and on one level, there is no question that there has been a widespread integration of minorities in sport. However, there is considerable evidence that sport not only fails to break down, but also actually reinforces stereotypes associated with class, gender, race, religion, and sexualities (Andrews, 2000; Birrell & McDonald, 2000; Cahn, 1994; Genasci, Genasci, & Griffin, 1994; Griffin, 1998; Grossman, 1995; Krane, 1997; LeBlanc & Jackson, 2007; Lenskyj, 2003; Pronger, 1990b; Rhoads, 1995; Woods, 1992; McKay, 1991). For all its rhetoric and grandiose emancipatory possibilities, sport remains a social institution and cultural site that maintains the position of the power elite (Coakley, 1979). This is particularly true for most gay athletes today for whom a life of honesty and openness within mainstream team sport

Social and Cultural Diversity in a Sporting World
Research in the Sociology of Sport, Volume 5, 81–95
Copyright © 2008 by Emerald Group Publishing Limited
All rights of reproduction in any form reserved
ISSN: 1476-2854/doi:10.1016/S1476-2854(08)05006-1

organisations seems impossible. Indeed, the fate of the contemporary gay male athlete may be the most striking example of the exclusionary nature of contemporary sport.

Nevertheless, for many gay athletes the context of sport may also be a site where one finds a sense of emancipation. This article seeks to demonstrate the pervasive power of sport to both exclude gay athletes but also foster their inclusion. Moreover, it leads to a number of important sociological, political, moral, and philosophical questions.

The findings of this study present what may be suggested as starting and guiding points for both gay men and their allies to take action and create social change. Such actions would not only affect the gay rugby players in Aotearoa/New Zealand, but all athletes for they are the very people who can disprove the demeaning stereotypes, such as the belief that gay men are only 'hairdressers, fashion designers, and interior decorators?' It is individuals, such as gay rugby players and others, whose amateur and professional careers are seen as wholly undistinguished who are the ones heterosexuals encounter in the media everyday who will help end the absurd pretence of universal heterosexuality in general and in sport in particular.

METHODOLOGY

Throughout this research, the social phenomenology methodology was used to explain the *Conspiracy of Silence phenomenon* surrounding gay male athletes within mainstream team sport organisations and more importantly to gain an insight (knowledge) and understanding of how gay men think and feel about their 'life-world' (their world of experience) in the sport of rugby union. Arguably, its usage has made a significant contribution to the knowledge and understanding within the broad field of sport-related research by learning more about the gay male's perspective of his experience in sport. Phenomenology has given us an "insider's view" into the phenomenon.

Fifteen athletes (rugby players) were recruited and questioned using in-depth open-ended interviews. Initially, the recruitment of rugby players rested upon their interest as volunteers in this study. Finding individuals, some of whom are still living in silence, was not an easy task. Access to most of the fifteen participants was gained through an elaborate formation of a national gay and lesbian athletes' network, Gay Sport New Zealand Inc. (GSNZ) initiated in 1996. Initial participants for the study originated from the Krazy Nights Gay Rugby Team in Wellington, New Zealand. They were contacted using the GSNZ network of athletes. Additional interviewees were referred by word of mouth from other participants, one of whom is a former professional player. This is known as the "snowballing" technique (Woods, 1992). This proved to be most beneficial in contacting the elite and competitive rugby players who remain most silent within their mainstream rugby organisations. Two other participants made contacted directly after this research study was discussed on Queer Nation (QN), a nationally televised programme in Aotearoa/New Zealand. Many e-mail messages (45) from other gay rugby players across the nation giving personal experiences were also collected after the research topic was televised.

Once all the interviews were transcribed verbatim, participants were asked to read over the transcripts and reflect on the meaning they made of their experience as gay athletes in team sport organisations. Participants edited their interviews by further detailing their accounts and gave additional insight to some of my interpretations. This proved to be quite helpful as several additional detailed comments were provided. Their ability to reply to my transcriptions insured the fairness and trustworthiness of the interpretations and enriched the value of the data collected. Gathering detailed information on the lived experiences of these players was an important epistemological foundation of this thesis for constructing knowledge.

The underlying purpose of the data analysis was not to make generalisations about the experience of gay male athletes. Rather, the goal was to present a thick description (in the actual words of the participants) in order to make connections between the experiences of the participants within the context of sport and our own experiences. Phenomenological researchers search for the commonalities across individuals rather than only focusing on what is unique to a single individual (Johnson & Christensen, 2004). Using the actual words of the participants instead of paraphrasing communicates more directly the meaning they made of their experience. Therefore many direct quotes were used in this research. Presenting this data in this form is especially critical in understanding the phenomenon of silence (invisibility) that surrounds gay men's presence in mainstream team sport organisations. Direct quotes came from voices that have not previously been heard or that may be would never have been heard without this avenue of communication.

The participants in this study had all played a competitive level of rugby in the past, either in their formative school years or at the club level within mainstream structures (heterosexual organisations). They revealed and expressed their love of rugby and have well over 200 years of combined experience in this sport alone. They all identified themselves as being gay.

At the time of the study, most worked in professional fields (one lawyer, one physiotherapist, four educators, three public servants), three came from the private sector (one chef, one photographer, one banker), one rugby field groundsman, one garbage collector and finally Player X who is under contract, as a professional rugby player, with a professional team to make up the total of 15 rugby players. Besides all identifying themselves as current recreational players, 10 had played competitive first 15 high school rugby of which five had gone on to play colts level and senior premier representative rugby in New Zealand. Five of the participants still played on mainstream senior competitive teams and the same five also coached or assisted with minor (youth) teams. The average experience of years played was 20.

Most "came out" at the age of 27, the youngest at 19 and the oldest at 63. One has yet to come out publicly. Only one was married and two of the participants have children. Eight are in relationships that have lasted an average of seven years.

RESULTS

Results are consistent with the existing literature. However, while these findings were expected, they are not the sole bases of this research. The objective of doing phenomenological research is to explore and find new and different themes than those assumed and which are pertinent to the lived experiences of these players. For the purpose of this chapter, the theme of reconciliation that had emerged and that was not present in the current literature surrounding the silence of gay athletes is revealed and discussed. This theme is, however, consistent within the lived experiences of gay men who are out; meaning that they are visible. Visibility, in the context of this research refers to stages 4–6 of Griffin's (1991) identity management continuum where most men know or assume everyone knows they are gay. At this point in the lives of these men, silence, as it has been understood in this study, is absent.

The findings in this study indicate several defining identities within the gay athletes' lived experience. Notably, they are (a) his sporting identity; which reflects his sporting experiences and interactions as an athlete in the context of sport, (b) his sexual identity as a gay man and (c) his visible or known social identity traits as an individual which encompasses his gender, race, religion, marital status, etc. The three identities were at some point separated from each other or masked by others at particular points in time depending on which stages gay athletes are situated in their coming out process. That is, one part of their identity was experienced and lived in different contexts from the others.

Fig. 1 illustrates the separation of the participants' identities during the coming out stages of the men in this study. For example when gay men are

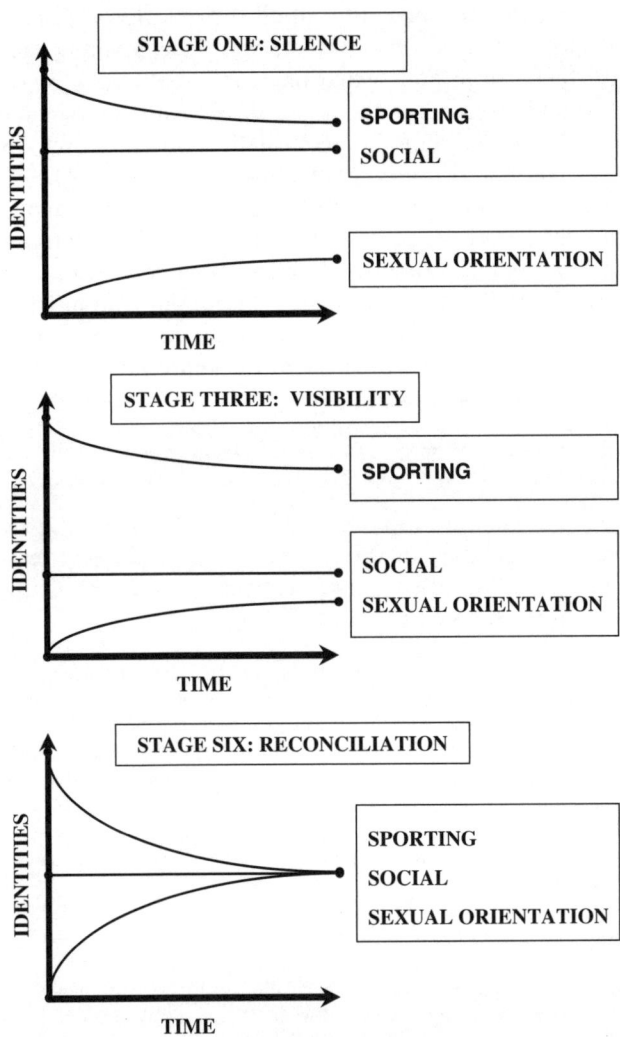

Fig. 1. Reconciliation of Identities.

totally silenced in the initial stage of their coming out process, their sexual identity is separated from their sporting and social ones. During the middle of their coming out process when they are visible to others, they separate and exclude their sporting identity from their social and sexual ones. Only when they are in the last stage of their coming out experience do they combine and identify all three identities into one. This is when all identities have merged and that reconciliation of all their worlds is produced. When gay men in sport attain a certain satisfaction in combining their sporting identity with their social and sexual ones, they have fulfilled the ultimate objective of what is considered the point of reconciliation of their total self.

One notable quote relevant to reconciliation was given by, one of three people who attempted to overcome the hijackers of flight 93 on September 11, 2001. Mark Bingham was one of them and sent his gay rugby team an e-mail a few weeks before his passing. He wrote it when he learned that their gay rugby team, the San Francisco Fog had been accepted as a permanent member of the Northern California Rugby Football Union. Its relevance is noteworthy in the understanding of the trials and tribulations gay men experience because of silence as well as for the appreciation visibility imparts on the freedom to be themselves.

> As we worked and sweated and ran and talked together this year, I finally felt accepted as a gay man and a rugby player. My two irreconcilable worlds came together. (Bingham, 2001)

However, for some men in this study and for most gay men in rugby today, the reconciliation of sport and sexuality remain impossible to attain because of the fear gay men harbour.

> #10 Marc: I experimented with both girls and guys when I was in primary school, but by late primary school I knew I was really interested in guys. In secondary school, apart from the obligatory girlfriend, I was really mostly interested in guys. I didn't tell anyone I was gay until I was in my forties, and that came out at a party to a friend when I'd had one drink too many. It was never mentioned again, but I was comforted by the fact that it didn't affect our relationship. However, it still didn't encourage me to come out to anyone else. *I've always led a double life* in a sense-my family, working, sporting, and social life on the one hand and my sexual life on the other. It's really been a case of 'never the twain shall meet'.

Art comments, somewhat more ruefully.

> #1 Art: [Sport in] New Zealand needs [reconciliation], we are a sporting nation, we are a rugby nation, we're also a gay nation and we need to reconcile them and there are so many, I think there are so many gay men out there that are just crying for this. They just need this opportunity to reconcile. [Playing gay rugby against a mainstream team] was

fantastic. It had all the aspects of mainstream sport I look for but with a gay skew. In the gay team of course it's all there for you. You're fully involved and it feels cool, yeah. And I think the most important thing for the gay sport was the reconciliation of different aspects of [one's] life; a mainstream sport [identity] being reconciled with being gay. And not just by yourself but with other people sharing that same experience. People with a similar interest, gay [and heterosexual] people with similar interest, you know. Yeah it means when you're with gay people doing sport all the barriers are down. You don't have to put defence mechanisms for anything and you can just be yourself. And that's really important I think. Because I mean being gay and playing rugby are two of the most important priorities in my life and it hurts when they don't match up. It's like trying to put a triangle through the circle slot in one of those kiddie toys, you know, and now I can say that they can [be joined]. It can work!

Val and Ron also talk about the significance of reconciliation and the empowerment it produces to bring about change in the lives of gay men in particular and possibly in sport in general. At this stage of their coming out process, Val, Ron, and others in this study realised the social significance of gay men participating in mainstream sport in New Zealand. Their pleasure and excitement of exercising their right to participate in mainstream sport are undeniable.

#2 Val: I mean I love playing rugby but I love getting hard and teaching these people as well so I'm sort of the coach as well but I want to play. You know it's a risk cause my knee has been a bit sore and I've pulled a couple of hamstrings. But [when I had heard about the gay rugby team being formed], I said: 'Put my name down.' I got the letter and thought: 'Hmmmm yes, you've got to make positive bloody moves.' So, since then it's been full on. Since then, I've talked about it ... to a lot of people who are friends of mine. I think it was just brilliant. Now I really realise a bit more the significance out of it [being publicly gay in sport]. There's a few people that made some interesting [negative] comments but I sort of told them to fuck off. I don't know what [others] talk about behind my back but I don't give a stuff about that. I have some good friends down there [at the rugby club] and it doesn't really matter [anymore].

#3 Ron: For whatever reason New Zealand's a sporting nation and if you're not interested in it you can't avoid it. I think there's an element of that in this [gay] rugby team. People finally learning what [playing rugby] is all about and they never did it when they were kids cause they were gay or whatever and they didn't feel they could contribute or play. So now finally they've been given an opportunity with this [gay rugby team]. Everybody spends so much time watching and talking about rugby and that's great, that's just great.

For others, such as Pete and Jeep, fear gives way to a sense of peace and comfort when they were finally able to openly identify as gay men in mainstream sport. They explain how important it was for them to reconcile all of their identities at this point in their lives.

#5 Pete: I have a lot of sense of finally being in peace; there's a vibrancy there. I'm so glad it's happening now because I would hate to think that I would only be starting to discover [the enjoyment of rugby] 10 years on from now. This is why sport has become quite important. This has become quite an important facet to [my life] because I'm discovering a new part of myself, a new joy, a new area of being healthy of being gay and you know, getting into healthy areas, like gay sports. That's just been a big positive thing for me; taking more risks. Because before, it was always incredibly threatening. Before, sport threatened my total identity. I'm glad I've got the confidence to be back. Because I'm with people who understand, it takes away the threat. It takes away a lot of that fear. Sport for me acted as a double-edged sword. It's because I'm gay that I got out of sports and it's because I'm gay that I got back into it.

#6 Jeep: I just think the gay rugby team members are great. I just really rate them. It's just so positive there's no crap when you're playing. I really take my hat off to the guys cause they're playing rugby for the first time, a lot of them, and they're giving it a go because they haven't had the opportunity to have played before, because most of them have felt uncomfortable amongst rugby circles and they had never ever thought about it as a possibility.

Henri explains his aversion to sport as a child as a result of his prejudices to the sport and the culture of rugby. His experience with rugby was that of a macho world of bigoted men. It is clear from his perspective that rugby has more to offer to gay men than first thought. For Henri and others, the context of rugby can be very positive and rewarding to all.

#11 Henri: I went along [to rugby practice] and I quite liked the team and I liked the training sessions, so I started going regularly. I think it overcame some prejudices I had. The school I went to, rugby was very much a macho thing and that was how you scored the girls and all the rest of it, more of which was pretty alien and obnoxious to me so in a way I'm overcoming my prejudices about rugby, rugby as it was in Southland. I'm really surprised to hear myself say that I like rugby. Wow! After all these years of hating it.

Finally, Jake best sums up the results of his reconciliation in sport as having the best of both gay and mainstream worlds.

#13 Jake: I've never stopped playing any sport because I'm gay, but I have thought about it. I've stood the test of time really and I guess now that I'm out, I'll play until someone tells me I can't instead of always thinking that someone will. Playing straight sport and gay sport is really having the best of both worlds.

At this point of the coming out process of gay men, fear of exclusion from sport is minimal. While the emerging theme of reconciliation shows that it is possible for silence to be replaced by visibility, it is important to understand and question the amount of personal torment and empowerment needed to overcome the fear that fuels the silence of gay men in mainstream sport organisations.

The reconciliation of the identities of gay men within mainstream sport transforms their sense of fear into a sense of contribution, accomplishment and/or fulfilment. At this stage of their coming out process, they have overcome their need to be militant and politicised. They do not simply see their participation in sport as a mere physical activity or political act. For many, openly participating in mainstream sport at this stage serves as a significant personal contribution to the gay community and society in general. It becomes an act of altruism. That is, caring and feeling responsible for the welfare of others because they know and understand the pain and suffering that may arise from being gay athletes. They recognised something beyond just the physical act itself, or the importance of it. They purposefully play the role of big brother to other gay men in their community who have not yet reached the visible stage of the coming out process. Jeep's quote best explains the significance and importance of developing a sense of altruism within the gay community.

> #6 Jeep: Over the last 3 or 4 years I haven't taken sport seriously, so this has been an opportunity to pass on my experience, my tackle kind of experience through rugby on to the guys like teaching them how to maul, how to fall, how to run lines and things like that. I think having gay sport and visible gays in [mainstream] sport will help younger people who are about to come out still want to get involved in sport. There are going to be people there who have been through what they've been through or maybe others who haven't been through what they've been through but can still add value to that person's life by being supportive. They will be able to develop a network of friends and feel comfortable about themselves within their teams in the sporting environment.

In the following quote, Bernie describes his intentions when he plays rugby as a self-identifying gay man. By reconciling his sexuality with the sport of rugby, he has developed a greater sense of altruism.

> #4 Bernie: But, I'm learning about different things that the gay community is trying to do and I want to be a part of it or do something for it, which is why I joined the rugby team, the Krazy Knights. When I heard that someone was going to start up the gay rugby team in Wellington, I was interested firstly because it was a rugby team, secondly because it was gay and perhaps I could help or do something for the gay community cause I've never done anything. I've never been on a gay float, never been in a gay dragon boating team or just you know just haven't done anything to give back to the community.

Pete also presents a sense of altruism. Yet not as overt as Bernie and Jeep's contribution, Pete's participation is nonetheless important and significant.

> #5 Pete: I think my only contribution to sport is that of having been a gay male who stood up to be counted for in rugby in New Zealand and I think in so far as I did that

I made a personal contribution to the struggle of the gay community. To be counted as a normal, healthy sector of the nation, to stand up and be seen and be accepted, to be no more and no less than anybody else was really a revelation for me.

Finally, Jake's participation within the gay community reflects his sense of altruism. It also reflects the positive results of eradicating the silence of gay men within rugby organisations. However, this should not be construed as the sole responsibility of the gay community. The moral consciousness towards the mental and physical health of gay men remains the responsibility of all stakeholders in sport: all players, all administrators, and all organisations, gay or straight.

#13 Jake: I like organizing gay stuff, like gay workshops and gay sport festivals, cause it gives me a sense of satisfaction knowing that my life contributes to making someone else's better. You know, if you question life enough it'll answer just at the right time.

Altruistic people give of themselves simply because they want to, not out of a sense of debt or because they want something in return. They have no ulterior motives, no guilt feelings, just a desire to give for the sake of giving. Feeling good about themselves is the one ulterior motive that the gay men in this study see as being acceptable.

Additional results also show that most men who come out within rugby organisations express feelings of enjoyment, altruism and of reconciliation of their social, sexual, and sporting identities. Yet, being gay can lead to overachievement and hypermasculinity and can also impede one's performance. By sharing their experiences, gay male rugby players were at the same time describing the context of sport organisations where their feelings were generated. In an interpretive socio-phenomenological view, the actions of mainstream organisations seem irrational, incoherent, unprecedented and unorderly to the realities of gay male athletes' lived experiences. Too often it is wrongly assumed that gay male athletes have continuous, logical or even interlocking selves, as if their sexuality was central to their identity.

In summary, the key findings in this study related to reconciliation are new to the literature and/or beyond what was anticipated in relation to the research questions and guiding framework. Notably, many of the findings are unique in the sense that most of the men could compare their experiences of playing gay rugby to that of playing mainstream rugby.

- Gay men can enjoy (love) playing contact team sports such as rugby.
- Gay men find greater validation within gay rugby compared to mainstream rugby.
- Playing rugby can be a healthy experience for gay men.

- Gay and heterosexual rugby players are very physically and socially compatible.
- Gay men want to play rugby and contribute visibly to New Zealand sport.
- Gay players find emancipation by playing rugby.
- Visible gay men feel more productive.
- Visible gay men reconcile their sporting, sexual, and social identities into one.

The overall data presented in this study are related both to oppression theory and identity management issues as presented within the Conspiracy of Silence model. It was found that, among the men in this research, rugby is a site where individual rights and freedoms can be expressed when oppressive policies and homophobia are eradicated. This was possible as a result of the formation of inclusive and safe spaces for gay men. Such examples include Wellington's Krazy Knights gay team and Val and Bernie's mainstream teams. The meanings gay men attributed to their participation in the sport of rugby became very positive as they participated in inclusive environments as visible gay players. Feelings of inclusiveness, compatibility, emancipation, and productivity as well as acts of reconciliation and altruism create opportunities for their survival in the context of a gay rugby union team. With the exception of Val and Bernie's examples, the same feelings did not apply for other participants in the context of most mainstream rugby union organisations where underlying exclusionary currents based on homophobia remain.

CONCLUSION

Finally, it is important to note that all participants in this study did traverse many hurdles in order to find personal emancipation. Many still have hurdles to cross before aspiring to feelings of wholeness and integrity, but for those who have, they overcame their oppressive sporting experiences by integrating their sexual identity with their sporting identity. In other words, it is only when they felt completely comfortable in the context of sport (mainstream or gay) that they felt they had reached personal contentment and the sense of reconciliation of all their identities (e.g., social, sexual, and sporting) into one. Their silence had finally ended.

As we move forward in the 21st century there seems to be a greater acceptance and understanding of human diversity within sexuality. There is a new generation of gay males who are less socialised by earlier gender-inversion and the separate socialisation of men and women, which led to misogyny, or even of the political struggles of recent decades. The next generation of gay men is in a better position to break down the barriers to their integration into mainstream society and to have their sexual orientation accepted as natural and non-problematic. However, as this study indicates, the domain of sport remains a very much-contested terrain for the rights and freedoms of gay men. It is worth stating a key fact that in the history of sport no professional rugby union player has come out in New Zealand or elsewhere during his career. Evidence from this study indicates clearly that organisational policies and attitudes within the sport of rugby need to change if gay male rugby players are to be seen, treated and celebrated as equals to their heterosexual counterparts within mainstream rugby.

The practical use of the phenomenological knowledge gained from this study may suggest ways administrators could or should adapt the provision of sport to ensure it is meeting the expectations of all involved. By achieving insight into the lived meaning of certain sporting experiences of gay male athletes, administrators and other officials in rugby may need to reassess the provisions of the rugby experience to recognise the experiential meaning of being a gay male and playing rugby.

Hence, the results of this phenomenological study indicate that gay male rugby players are specifically concerned about the need for social change. These concerns are fostered within a social context where people who are different lack the respect, understanding and affirmation they deserve under the human rights act. If social justice is to exist for gay men in sport, social changes are essential for the following purposes.

- Social change is needed for visible players to be accepted within mainstream society teams and organisations.
- Social change is needed for visible players to feel positive about themselves in rugby.
- Social change is needed for all New Zealanders to altruistically make a contribution to the sport of rugby and to the next generation of athletes; gay and heterosexual.

Although the possibilities for gay men in mainstream sport seem to be limited at this point in time, it appears the way to change people's opinions is to educate them about gay athletes and that alliances should be formed between gay men and all other stakeholders of sport in general and rugby in particular. Billy Bean, the only living openly gay former major league outfielder, states that coming out within sport organisations "needs to be a positive experience, or no one will ever come out" during their professional career (Menez, 2001). For many, sport is not the demon, administrators and the media are. They often represent the voices of the vocal few who instigate negative public opinion perceptions towards gay men. The following example presents a moment in time and place where a positive public opinion is recognised. Val explains a different kind of silence; a silence that for some may seem positive; a silence that cannot be clearly expressed in the media; a silence that cannot be loud enough for organisers and administrators to understand its significance.

#2 Val: You know how wonderful it was to see a gay team play a straight team and some of the little things that happened. Like I've never seen two guys come off a rugby field holding hands before. Nobody went: 'Ohhhh!' They all reacted really positively by saying nothing; just being silent like if there was nothing wrong. You know I mean I wish I was 20. Coming out now at that age I mean [life] would just be so much easier.

Finally, homophobia in sport (rugby) is a problem for everyone, players, administrators and spectators alike. Although this research dealt exclusively with gay rugby players, this subject is part of a larger problem of a society that tends to favour homogeneity over difference and consequently rejects all forms of sexuality that communicate any deviation from the dominant heterosexual orientation. As stated, what is unique about being gay is that it is the one subculture that transcends all other social categories such as: age, gender, race, social class, nationality, religion, ethnicity, and the able/disabled. It has no barriers to all other social groups nor does it have any over/under-representation in any of these groups and that includes sport. It is a subculture that operates within others and where different individuals from different backgrounds and cultures do show commonalities of understanding of what it is to be gay. Consequently, rugby in particular, and society in general has much to gain by eradicating homophobia. By publicly addressing the inclusion rather than exclusion of gay men, organisations in positions of privilege such as the sport of rugby could enable all young athletes to play rugby to the full extent of their capabilities in a safe and supportive environment. Athletes should be able to use each other for a source of strength instead of a source of fear. By doing so they will also ensure that rugby and other sports are inclusive for all. The measure in which gay men in sport suffer (or not) depends on the involvement of heterosexual allies, ready to act on their behalf for the good of all. In the words of the Hon Justice Michael Kirby AC CMG during his speech at the opening ceremonies of the 2002 Gay Games in Sydney: "the days of exclusion are numbered ... it is the truth that makes us free ... you who come together on this magical night to affirm the fundamental unity of all human beings ... let us be an example of respect for human rights. Not just for gays, *for everyone*" (Kirby, 2002).

As a final reflection on the existing silence of gay men in mainstream rugby union teams in Aotearoa/New Zealand, Ron describes in a few words what he thinks keeps *Player X*, our fictional All Black, from coming out publicly.

> #3 Ron: The only things stopping an All Black from coming out are the other 14 All Blacks because it is that exalted position in New Zealand society where rugby is still the domain of heterosexuality and macho New Zealand male behaviour and homosexuality is still misunderstood and unaccepted within mainstream rugby's public opinion.

The sporting experiences presented in this study show how we can account for the multiple ways in which the silence of gay men in rugby is constituted, thus enhancing our understanding of the complex and paradoxical world in which they live and play. Obtaining these perspectives may be the initial step needed in assisting rugby union officials in transforming its policies and political practices in order for it to be truly an inclusive sport for all New Zealanders.

In light of current inaction and the continued silence from both gay and heterosexual allies we can only speculate about what lies ahead for impressionable athletes who are young, gifted, and gay. Will they shy away from sport, fearful of not fitting in? Will they repress what comes naturally to them off the field to excel at what comes naturally to them on the field? What will it take for the sports world and indeed, the whole world, to overtly accept and include gay athletes?

The ongoing exclusionary silence of professional gay rugby players speaks volumes. Research that seeks to understand the gay athlete's perspective on the existence of silence and invisibility is made all the more pertinent as gay rights and equality are currently manifested within social institutions other than mainstream sport.

REFERENCES

Andrews, D. (2000). Excavating Michael Jordan's blackness. In: S. Birrell & M. G. McDonald (Eds), *Reading sport*. Boston: Northeastern University Press.

Bingham, M. (2001). In Mark's Own Words. Northern California Rugby Football Union, September. Available at http://www.sffog.org/about.

Birrell, S., & McDonald, M. G. (2000). *Sport readings*. Boston: Northeastern University Press.

Cahn, S. K. (1994). *Coming on strong*. New York: The Free Press.

Coakley, J. (1979). Sport as an opiate. In: D. S. Eitzen (Ed.), *Contemporary Society: An anthology.* New York: St Martin's Press.

Genasci, J., Genasci, J., & Griffin, P. (1994). Addressing Homophobia in Sports and Athletics. 11th Annual Conference on Counseling Athletes: Assisting Today's Athletes Toward Peak Performance. Springfield, Massachusetts.

Griffin, P. (1991). Identity management strategies among lesbian and gay educators. *Qualitative Studies in Education, 4,* 189–202.

Griffin, P. (1998). *Strong women, deep closets.* Champaign, IL: Human Kinetics.

Grossman, A. H. (1995). Until there is acceptance. *The Journal of Physical Education, Recreation & Dance, 66,* 47–48.

Johnson, R. B., & Christensen, L. B. (2004). *Education research: Quantitative, qualitative, and mixed approaches.* Boston, MA: Allyn and Bacon.

Kirby, H. M. (2002), Courage. Gay Games VI Sport and Cultural Festival Opening Speech. Available at http://www.sydney2002.org.au

Krane, V. (1997). Introduction to special theme issue: Sexualities, culture, and sport. *Women in Sport & Physical Activity Journal, 6,* 1–6.

LeBlanc, R. G., & Jackson, S. J. (2007). Sexuality as cultural diversity in sport organisations. *International Journal of Sport Management and Marketing, 2,* 119–133.

Lenskyj, H. J. (2003). *Out on the field: Gender, sport and sexuality.* Toronto: Women's Press.

McKay, J. (1991). *No pain no gain? Sport and Australian culture.* New York: Prentice Hall.

Menez, G. (2001). The toughest out: Homosexuality in baseball. *Sports Illustrated (Los Angeles), 94*(22), 26.

Pronger, B. (1990b). Gay jocks: A phenomenology of gay men in athletics. In: M. A. Messner & D. F. Sabo (Eds), *Sport, men and the gender order: Critical feminist perspectives.* Champaign, IL: Human Kinetics.

Rhoads, R. A. (1995). Learning from the coming-out experiences of college males. *Journal of College Student Development, 36,* 67–74.

Rodman, D., & Silver, M. (1997). *Walk on the wild side.* New York: Bantam.

Woods, S. E. (1992). Describing the experience of lesbian physical educators: A phenomenological study. In: A. C. Sparks (Ed.), *Explaining Alternative Visions.* London: Palmer Press.

JAPANESE EDUCATIONAL SPORT AND THE REPRODUCTION OF IDENTITY

Brent McDonald and Hiroshi Komuku

ABSTRACT

This chapter examines the role of educational sport in producing and reproducing a particular version of Japanese identity. Despite the influences of globalisation on Japanese professional sport and the resultant increases in diversity both in terms of participants and of practice, Japanese educational sport remains a bastion of traditional values and the production house of the homogenising notion of 'Japaneseness'. Based on research conducted within sports at both high school and university this chapter examines the apparent contradiction between the increasing diversity of the elite model of Japanese sport and subsequent resistance to this model at an educational level, which in turn reinforces the reproduction of a particular notion of Japanese identity.

INTRODUCTION

This chapter examines Ministry for Education, Culture, Sports, Science and Technology (MEXT) policy towards diversification of sporting practice in

Social and Cultural Diversity in a Sporting World
Research in the Sociology of Sport, Volume 5, 97–110
Copyright © 2008 by Emerald Group Publishing Limited
All rights of reproduction in any form reserved
ISSN: 1476-2854/doi:10.1016/S1476-2854(08)05007-3

Japan on one hand and policy towards moral education on the other. We consider the effects of globalisation on Japanese educational sport, concerns of lowering rates of physical and emotional health amongst youth and the resultant government response through policy. In examining sporting practice 'in the field' at both high school and university we seek to investigate whether increasing diversity is encouraged or if educational sport actually serves to homogenise practice and reinforce more traditional notions of hierarchy, discipline and hard work. Is sport as a 'disciplinary power gradually losing its socio-cultural base' in Japan due to the effects of globalisation (Yamashita, 2006, p. 164) or does it reinforce traditional values and remain a production house of the homogenising notion of 'Japaneseness'.

During the past 15 years the effects of globalisation and the increased professionalization of Japanese sport has resulted in an increase in diversity both in terms of participants and of practice. This can be seen in terms of the proliferation of sport fitness clubs and new sports (Yamashita, 2006; Spielvogel, 2002); the advent of the J-League (Watts, 1998; Ebishima & Yamashita, 2006); the naturalisation of elite foreign athletes in order to represent and bolster Japanese national teams (Chiba, Ebihara, & Morino, 2001); the migration of Japanese baseball players to the Major leagues in America (Hirai, 2001; Nakamura, 2005); hosting global sporting mega events such as the Nagano Winter Olympics and the 2002 World Cup (Horne & Manzenreiter, 2004); the influx of foreign wrestlers into the top ranks of sumo wrestling (Light & Kinnaird, 2002; Amano, 2004).

According to Horne and Manzenreiter (2004, p. 198), research into the rise of football in Japan points to 'new ideals of masculinity, attitudes to full time paid work, attitudes towards place of residence and expressions of national identity'. However, whilst the 'cyber cultural' practices of volunteer groups offer a greater degree of 'cultural pluralism', their organizational structure suggests that only 'slight alteration to dominant principles' occur. In fact, 'new kinds of social groups' actually 'revived traditional cultural values' as opposed to challenging them (Horne & Manzenreiter, 2004, p. 198). This apparent contradictory outcome, the diversification on one hand and a strengthening of particular national identities on the other, is in keeping with Yamashita's (2006) observation that Japan's competition in the world market requires a strong nation and hence there is a reconstruction of national order utilising 'cultural apparatuses' in the form of the reinvention of tradition and traditional identity.

Examples of the strengthening of national identity in the face of potential diversification can be seen in the Japanese indigenous sport of Sumo, where foreigners had to satisfy strict requirements, that is, 'only foreign wrestlers who are sufficiently "Japanese"', could compete (Light & Kinnaird, 2002, p. 153). Exclusory tactics had been employed even further as foreign wrestlers threatened to reach the top Sumo rank of Yokozuna (Light & Kinnaird, 2002; Thompson, 1998). However, since the rise of Akebono (Hawaiian born Chad Rowan) to the rank of Yokozuna in 1993 the number of foreign Sumo has increased with the emphasis shifting instead to the 'Japaneseness', in terms of spirit, of these wrestlers (Amano, 2004). Chiba et al. (2001) track the processes of naturalisation and assimilation on foreign players to many sports in Japan so that they are perceived as 'more Japanese than the Japanese'. They point to the reality that in strengthening national teams in international competition foreign athletes actually 'strengthen nationalism' and reinforce the 'imagined community' of Japanese identity (Chiba et al., 2001, p. 215). Whilst many of these examples point to the diversification of Japanese sporting practice and therefore Japanese sporting identity in most cases in Japan, the effect is a strengthening of notions of homogeneity and tradition. The above examples demonstrate how the global hegemony of sport can be challenged particularly via the connection created between national identity and practice identity. This is a challenge that actually reinforces that which is commonsense and hegemonic within Japan, especially ideas about 'Japaneseness'.

At the same time there have been increasing concerns about

> A diminished sense of connectedness and a decline in the educational functions of communities ... . (T)these have adversely affected the mental and physical health of children, changing the way children approach play and reducing the everyday opportunities children have to exercise their bodies and interface with nature and society, experiences considered essential to forming a well-rounded character. (MEXT, 2004)

Policy response has been to attempt to shake up the delivery of sport by focusing on 'lifelong sport involvement' in which people can enjoy sports anytime and anywhere, in a manner that suits their respective physical constitution, age, ability, interests and objectives. Comprehensive community-based sport clubs based on European models are designed so residents not only engage in sports, but the 'clubs also provide a social forum, forming a foundation for the local community in both social and collective terms' where residents can gain a greater sense of pride as a member of their local community (MEXT, 2005). The final aim of MEXT policy is to develop programmes to 'train and strengthen Japanese athletes for international competition at events such as the Olympics' (MEXT, 2000) and enhance physical education and extracurricular sports clubs at schools in order to provide people with the basic foundation they need to enjoy sports (MEXT, 2004).

This educational reform also addresses the belief that younger generations in Japan have little 'understanding or experience of traditional Japanese spirituality' and have become 'accustomed to a more international and materialistic lifestyle' (Yasumura, 1998, p. 81). Sport and physical activity in Japanese education fall under the banner of what MEXT define as social education.[1] Social education involves amongst other things such as the delivery of a 'cultural curriculum' designed to enhance moral education, develop 'rich humanity' and reinvigorate traditional Japanese culture.

METHODOLOGY

The research in this chapter involves detailed examination of various Japanese government policies from MEXT towards the role of sport in education in Japan. Specifically we examine the 'Basic Plan for the Promotion of Sports' (MEXT, 2000) and various MEXT white papers since then regarding concerns of lowered rates of physical activity, declines in youth morality, increases in obesity and efforts to revitalise youth sport as a site for lifelong physical, social and emotional education. With MEXT policy as a backdrop we then consider practice in the field from ethnographic research conducted both in university rowing clubs and high school rugby and baseball clubs. The ethnographic research from the first author occurred intermittently over a 15-year period from 1994 to 2008, whilst the second author has researched extensively into school baseball in Japan. The ethnographic research utilises the multiple methods suggested by Fetterman (1998), Lincoln and Guba (1985) and Erlandson, Harris, Skipper, and Allen (1993).

Where informants have been 'heard' we have fictionalised identities and amalgamated data to provide a method for reporting 'subjective' information, including data based upon their informants' words and actions (Grenfell & Rinehart, 2003). Therefore, not only are the subjects or informants identities 'fictionalised' in order to preserve anonymity, but their narrative accounts/reports were amalgamated/blended so as to minimise detection of identities and more acutely capture the knowledge.

GOVERNMENT POLICY

In 1999, MEXT moved forward with unequivocal educational reform from four perspectives. The first perspective involved the concept of emotional education where it is 'imperative to reform the trend in overemphasizing intellectual education, the cramming system of education and to cultivate in children a "Zest for living" ... with the room to learn, think and act for themselves'. It is therefore important that education,

cultivates humanness blessed with a sense of justice, sense of ethics and a compassionate mind. Further, amidst the rapid progression of internationalization, it is indispensable to raise Japanese people who appreciate Japan's history, tradition and culture and have an enriched international mindset. To this end, a great emphasis on emotional education is required. (MEXT, 1999)

The second perspective is the development of a school system that helps children 'develop their individuality and gives them diverse choices'. This reform is an attempt to 'rectify the overemphasized egalitarianism and uniformity' of the current education system and ensure the opportunity of a 'second chance at any stage of the education'. The third concern involves promoting individual school's autonomy and a de-centralizing of administrative systems. The final perspective is to promote university reform and research activities establishing Japan as a 'nation based on creativity'.

The intended reform to education emphasizes a movement away from uniformity and towards internationalization, autonomy and diversity. Simultaneously, however, there is a clear directive towards the fostering of Japanese history, tradition and culture especially through the format of emotional or social education. How does sport as an important arm of the education system help deliver these changes and how effectively can diversity and social education be achieved?

GOVERNMENT POLICY AND MORAL EDUCATION THROUGH SPORT

After 1945, Japan was rebuilt under American occupation. Sport in school curriculum was altered to meet the intentions of the interim government. For example, all martial arts (*judo*, *kendo*, *karate*, etc.) were banned from school curricula for about 10 years for fear that they would be breeding grounds for traditional Japanese values which encouraged nationalism and militarism. In their place, sports such as baseball and volleyball were actively encouraged with the intention of creating 'democratic individuals'. Rather than the 'docile' bodies of the pre-war era, Japanese education now took on physical education from the perspective of egalitarianism, its aim to reshape individuals through the democratisation of sport.

The Ministry of Education (MOE)[2] moved from the educational liberalism of the early post-war period began to retighten its power over the system with various controls including stricter authorisation of school texts, revision of the social studies curriculum and the re-introduction of moral education (Okano & Tsuchiya, 1999, p. 39). During the 1960s emphasis on moral education continued to grow including its delivery through sporting and cultural club activity as schools and universities. The MOE's Moral Education for Junior High school in 1969, for example, took on a "Meiji" Confucian theme emphasising amongst other things the need to 'establish good human relationships with friends, male or female, understanding, respecting and encouraging each other' and 'to understand the significance and aims of the groups to which you belong and try to enrich community life' (in Beauchamp & Vardaman, 1994, p. 169). Much of the education system became re-geared around the needs of industry and Japan's rapidly increasing economic growth. Tertiary education became geared around an ideology of educational credentialism and merit. The prestige and reputation of the school attended became a direct influence on chances of progressing to higher education with a similar reputation and there developed direct links in the relationships between companies, universities, schools and even kindergartens (Sugimoto, 1997). Curriculum became based around passing entrance exams and required wrote learning and memorisation skills. Sporting clubs were developed on a model whose aim was to ensure the moral and cultural education of students (Kelly, 1998; Inoue, 1998). Sports clubs are predominantly autonomous student organisations at high school and university and membership usually involves an enormous time commitment for most of the year. In the case of sports such as rowing, baseball and rugby this may involve training sessions up to 5 or 6 days per week meaning that students can only be a member of one club. This mono-club model enhances the sense of collective identity members have to it. It also legitimates the hierarchical relationships existing in the group. Training revolves around a cornerstone of hard work and discipline, where displays of suffering are public and symbolic of a broader understanding of the importance of self-cultivation. Clammer (1995, p. 88) indicates that activities such as educational sport offer the view of self development as cultivation of character, moral qualities, endurance (which in Japan is a moral quality) and spirit which leads to an expansion of responsibility and human heartedness which ultimately defines the ideal person.

In 2001 MEXT put forward the 'Education Reform Plan for the 21st Century' or as it was labelled 'The Rainbow Plan'. The 'Rainbow Plan' comprised seven priority strategies to achieve this reform. These strategies included the encouragement of cultural and sports club activities and the improvement of moral and social education. MEXT (2001) goes on to add that social education is 'a general term for organised educational activities not covered in the regular curricula of elementary schools, secondary schools and institutions of higher education'. This new approach to sport delivery recognizes that

in order to improve this situation and bring about a lifelong sports society in which every member of the public can enjoy and engage in sports activities throughout life, it will be important to create community sports clubs that allow people with differing interests or hobbies to participate in sports regardless of age and regardless of their level of skill and technique. (MEXT, 2000)

The concept of lifelong sports involves the application of sport away from its traditional location centred on schools and companies. For example, 70.8% of junior high school students and 38% of high school students are members of school sports clubs (MEXT, 2000). However the implementation of community clubs has been problematic based on inadequate infrastructure, lack of community support, lack of recognition (as important) from sport associations and physical education practitioners and difficulty recruiting human resources with the 'enthusiasm and ability to promote the establishment of such' programmes (MEXT, 2000). Despite these problems, sport is still perceived as having a major role in the delivery of moral and social education.

Sports meet the instinctive need of people to exercise their bodies, generate exhilaration, a sense of achievement, and the mental fulfilment and pleasure of a sense of connectedness with others, and cultivate self-responsibility, self-control, and a spirit of fair play... .Sports are also a meaningful mechanism for pursuing the limits of human potential, and the single-mindedness of competitors who devote themselves to competitive sports also contributes to the formation of a vigorous and sound society, raising public interest in sports and inspiring the public with dreams. (MEXT, 2004)

Thus, whilst MEXT policy attempts to encourage a more diverse approach to sport and sport delivery in the 21st century its overall goal for this is in part a reinforcing of traditional Japanese values and identity. Despite the intentions to 'meet the diverse needs' of students including efforts 'to upgrade the instructors of the school sports clubs activities' and 'ensure a greater measure of flexibility for the school sports club activities' (MEXT, 2000), the emphasis on moral and cultural education ensures educational sport remains fairly static.

HOMOGENIZATION AND THE CAPITAL OF 'JAPANESENESS'

Despite the potential influences of globalisation, sporting practice in Rugby and baseball at high school and rowing at university in Japan have changed little over the past 15 years. These sports are student-driven, relying heavily on hierarchical relationships within the group and a rotation of hierarchy that occurs annually. Learning and leadership is achieved via observation and collectivism. Actual practice has altered little. Repetition and hard work are core components of arduous training regimes that involve most days of the week and most months of the year. These sporting clubs are homogenous in terms of ethnicity, all members are Japanese. The purpose of self-cultivation and belonging to the group are understood and given importance only in the context of an ongoing educational process grounded in the curriculum of social education.

In the case of the university rowers the ongoing bodily project is the intense, highly hierarchical and cyclical program of leadership and decision making. The four years of membership is a closed circuit program on permanent loop. Due to the *kohai/sempai* (junior/senior) relationships knowledge regarding technique, training and periodisation is passed down from senior to junior. Add to this the absence of significant influence from outside the club, be it lecturers, alumni or others and rowing clubs operate in a way that the knowledge transfer is stable, consistent and repeatable from year to year. Further we see the perception and appreciation of values that are grounded in a particularly Japanese cultural identity as demonstrated by the following responses of members:

> When I am in a hardship I can overcome it because I have gone through painful hard times in rowing, I can overcome hardship. (Musashi)

> The ordinary university student goes to class and has a routine. However, I am learning something that university cannot teach me. I have a special experience here so after graduating or in the future it will make sense, maybe not now but later it will help. The skill to make the teamwork together cannot be acquired just from studying at university. (Hiro)

I am the type of person who can advise other people without making them uncomfortable. I am the type of person who has the right mentality and social skills to be effective. I'm the sort of person who has a strong will and determination to stick things out and finish the job. Rowing has taught me this. (Taka)

Compared to other people who don't do club activities I think I understand more about physical strength, *joge kankei*, (hierarchical relationships) and *ningenkankei* (human relationships). (Kobe)

I have developed *seishin* (spirit) through perseverance, harmony and co-operation. (Kobe)

For the programme I will consult with the coxes, other senior members and training diary from the previous year. I think we should change some routines. For example we can improve winter training to become more effective and improve everyone's skill level, but many things will stay the same. (Hiro)

These students verbalise an understanding of important characteristics tied in with the notion of 'Japaneseness'. These characteristics particularly revolved around the concepts of individual suffering, the development of spirit and group harmony and co-operation based collective decision making and collective identity grounded in hierarchical and human relationships. Further these concepts can be seen in action at any high school training ground or university practice. The self-regulated 'Japaneseness' of training, that of hierarchy, repetition, autonomy and collectiveness are homogenous across most sporting clubs. As a result of this homogeneity these characteristics become universally recognisable and therefore representative of symbolic capital. The power of this capital is very stable rendering changes to practice unlikely.

MECHANISM OF MUTUAL OBSERVATION

Another feature that ensures the continued homogenous production of sport in education is the critical gaze extending from what Kuwayama (1992) describes as the 'mechanism of mutual observation'. This mechanism becomes extremely cogent in the club sport and extends from the training venue and into the more mundane day-to-day self-disciplining activities of the group.

Whilst rowers at university train on a shared venue with their rivals, sports in high school invariably share space with each other (e.g., rugby, baseball and soccer clubs may all share the same field for training). Training time is either regulated by the end of the school day or in the case of the rowers via an unspoken collective agreement. In all cases the consensual regulation of training time ensures the maximum opportunity to view others and to be viewed. The mechanism of mutual observation serves to regulate training further in regard to the amount (i.e., more is better), the intensity and the organisation. Clubs are constantly on display to the gaze of other clubs and their own members. The regulation time and space ensures that homogenised experience produces the homogenised identity of rowers, rugby players, base ballers, etc. This action can be seen to work as a type of 'quality control' of the capital imbued in the production of the self-cultivated, socialised club member.

Importantly these environments become largely self-regulatory. They act as a neighbourhood watch programme (that actually works) that keeps an eye on cultural property and social capital. With rowing for example, any time that one is being observed, the observer is more likely than not also a rower or connected with rowing. As a result, this becomes surveillance backed by knowledge, which in turn implies that judgements made by the observer possess a certain power. Whilst training rowers make a very public display of their physical capital, that is, their strength and technique, and also their symbolic capital as demonstrated by the way they go about their training. The noticeably standardised drills and exercises of most rowing clubs in the area can be viewed as, not so much wanting to fit in, but more not wanting to stand out. The level of risk inherent in adopting other forms of training practice invites attention and scrutiny from other practitioners and therefore the potential of ridicule, exposure and ostracism. Thus all rowers are subject to the critical gaze. Further, the cultural practice of learning via observation ensures that the power of the gaze endures from year to year.

However, the real strength of the mechanism of mutual observation is not its external force but rather the way these mechanisms are internalised by members so as to become self-regulatory. Bodily discipline and bodily control become central to the identity of the various sports club members. Self-regulation extends from training, to diet, to effort given during a session, to the appropriate way of expressing that the effort has been given (postures and facial expressions that designate effort, strength and sacrifice as opposed to weakness or lack of commitment or hardness). Interestingly one needs to possess the faculties of appreciation to recognise these actions. For example, screaming out in pain could be construed as weakness. However, in the context of a very difficult session, it can be an expression that one has really committed oneself to the task, to really pushing through the pain barrier. Similarly at the end of the final of the regatta the outpouring of emotion, in the form of weeping, by the competitors would be seen as weakness in the training environment but completely appropriate in the competitive one as this expression indicates the importance of the event and the disappointment of having given every last ounce of energy and failed or indeed having given every last ounce of energy and succeeded. As Light (1999) suggests from his observations of high school rugby in Japan, 'it is the value attached to restraint and emotional control that makes the shedding of tears, whether of joy or despair, a meaningful sign of total physical, emotional and spiritual commitment'. In all cases the internal regulation aims at impression management, of maintaining one's identity within the group and reaffirming one's commitment to its' collective values.

CONCLUSION

This chapter has examined the intersection of MEXT policy towards increasing the diversity of sporting expression in education whilst also fostering traditional Japanese values and identity. MEXT has identified that the rampant uniformity of educational practice and lowering rates of a sense of social justice need to be addressed through a change in approach to the structure of the education system. Educational sport operates with increasingly globalised professional sport as a backdrop. Despite this backdrop and some of the intended outcomes of policy, educational sports such as rowing, rugby and baseball continue to function in a way that reinforces a strong sense of homogeneity. The characteristics connected with the notion of 'Japaneseness' are awareness and understanding of hierarchical relationships within groups, an appreciation for the importance of harmony, collective identity and decision making, and a necessity for hard work, suffering and sacrifice. In this way Japanese educational sport is exceptionally effective at achieving its goal of fostering traditional values and identity. It points to belief from practitioners in the moral importance of self-cultivation, of organised time and recognition of traditional Japanese identity. All of these outcomes can be seen as a demonstration of an incredibly effective project of lifelong education. The curriculum of moral and social education becomes embodied in members of these sports to such an extent that by the time these students reach high school and university they require little or no direct supervision. They have internalised the concepts of 'Japaneseness' and, becoming appreciative of the symbolic capital such characteristics entail, play the game of being a member of a sports club below the level of consciousness.

When the capital accrued from sport is symbolic there is little incentive to alter practice. Altering the field has the potential of changing the value of this symbolic capital. In the case of educational sport in Japan the opportunity to embrace a diversification of practice and organisational setup runs the risk of devaluing such symbolic capital the embodiment of hierarchy, hard work, collectivism and the notion of self-cultivation.

Further the homogenous nature of students in these clubs, entirely Japanese, reinforces the notion of some form of specifically 'Japanese cultural character'. Whilst the professional model may display a world of diversity and expression, it is incongruous with the educational sport model and as a result plays little role in changing how sport may be experienced at a grassroots level. Even the development of community sports club rely heavily on the acceptance of the values espoused by the concept of 'Japaneseness'. This homogenous model of sport is reinforced further through the traditional method of learning through observation and repetition. This pedagogic feature ensures a strong stability in the identity created. The highly repetitious forms of practice have the intent of creating action without consciousness, action that is automatic. As action becomes automatic, it also becomes more commonsensical and therefore hegemonic. Ways of learning based on repetition and observation would appear to be very effective forms of identity construction and cultural reproduction. It is especially at the level of the mundane, the day-to-day routines and rituals, that ways of being are embedded in individuals so that such 'ways' take on a sense of naturalness or commonsense. Finally, the mechanism of mutual observation in force in the world of educational sport helps explain how the stereotypes of Japanese group think and conformity (Sugimoto, 1997) are created and maintained.

MEXT (2004) posits that as

> the average lifespan approaches 80 years, enhancing quality of life is a matter of common interest for the entire nation. This will require developing new lifestyles and new ways of thinking that address the issue of cultivating minds and bodies from childhood.

As these 'new ways' come into existence will this challenge the current model for Japanese educational sport or will it endure as a key player in the construction of Japanese identity?

NOTES

1. Sport accounts for a massive 600 billion yen or 27% of the total budget allocated to social education (MEXT, 2007). Interestingly this is a decrease from peak expenditure of 900 billion yen in 1995.

2. The Ministry of Education (MOE) changed to the Ministry of Education, Culture, Sport, Science and Technology (MEXT) in 2001.

REFERENCES

Amano, K. (2004). *Sumo and the challenge of globalisation*. Unpublished paper presented at Asian Sports Studies Forum: Reading Asia and Oceania through Sport. September 20–22, Otsu campus, Shiga University, Japan.

Beauchamp, E., & Vardaman, J. (1994). *Japanese education since 1945: A documentary study*. London: East Gate Books.

Chiba, Ebihara, & Morino (2001). Globalisation, naturalisation and identity: The case of borderless elite athletes in Japan. *International Review of Sociology of Sport, 5*, 203–221.

Clammer, J. (1995). *Difference and modernity: Social theory and contemporary Japanese society*. London: Kegan Paul International.

Ebishima, H., & Yamashita, R. (2006). FIFA 2002 World Cup in Japan: The Japanese football phenomenon. In: *Japan, sport and society: Tradition and change in a globalising world* (pp. 157–176). London: Routledge.

Erlandson, D., Harris, E., Skipper, B., & Allen, S. (1993). *Doing naturalistic inquiry: A guide to methods*. Newbury Park: Sage Publications.

Fetterman, D. (1998). *Ethnography: Step by step*. London: Sage Publications.

Grenfell, C., & Rinehart, R. (2003). Skating on thin ice: Human rights in youth figure skating. *International Review for the Sociology of Sport, 38*(1), 79–97.

Hirai, H. (2001). Hideo nomo: Pioneer or defector? In: D. Andrews & S. Jackson (Eds), *Sports stars: The cultural politics of sporting celebrity* (pp. 187–200). London: Routledge.

Horne, J., & Manzenreiter, W. (2004). Accounting for mega-events: Forecast and actual impacts of the 2002 football world cup finals on the host countries Japan/Korea. *International Review for the Sociology of Sport, 39*(2), 187–203.

Inoue, S. (1998). Budo: Invented tradition in the martial arts. In: S. Linhart & S. Fruhstuck (Eds), *The culture of Japan as seen through its leisure* (pp. 83–94). Albany: State University of New York Press.

Kelly, W. (1998). Blood and guts in Japanese professional baseball. In: S. Linhart & S. Fruhstuck (Eds), *The culture of Japan as seen through its leisure* (pp. 95–112). Albany: State University of New York Press.

Kuwayama, T. (1992). The reference other orientation. In: N. Rosenberger (Ed.), *The Japanese sense of self* (pp. 121–151). London: Cambridge University Press.

Light, R. (1999a). Japanese school rugby and the reproduction of hegemonic masculinity. In: T. Chandler & J. Nauright (Eds), *The rugby world: Race, gender and commerce* (pp. 105–127). London: Frank Cass.

Light, R., & Kinnaird, L. (2002). Appeasing the gods: Shinto, sumo and 'true' Japanese spirit. In: T. Magdalinski & T. Chandler (Eds), *With God on their side: Sport in the service of religion* (pp. 39–59). London: Routledge.

Lincoln, Y., & Guba, E. (1985). *Naturalistic inquiry*. Newbury Park: Sage.

MEXT. (1999). White paper. Retrieved on January 8, 2008 from http://www.mext.go.jp/b_menu/hakusho/html/hpae199901/hpae199901_1_003.html

MEXT. (2000). Press release. Retrieved on September 23, 2003 from http://www.mext.go.jp/english/news/2000/09/000949c.htm

MEXT. (2004). White paper. Retrieved on January 15, 2008 from http://www.mext.go.jp/ english/news/2005/10/05122201/003.pdf

MEXT. (2005). White paper. Retrieved on January 15, 2008 from http://www.mext.go.jp/ b_menu/hakusho/html/06101913/008.htm

MEXT. (2007). Expenditure on education. Retrieved on May 10, 2008 from http:// www.mext.go.jp/english/statist/07070310/007.pdf

Nakamura, Y. (2005). The samurai sword cuts both ways: A transnational analysis of Japanese and US media representations of Ichiro. *International Review for the Sociology of Sport*, *40*(4), 467–480.

Okano, K., & Tsuchiya, M. (1999). *Education in contemporary Japan: Inequalities and diversity*. UK: Cambridge University Press.

Spielvogel, L. (2002). The discipline of space in a Japanese fitness club. *Sociology of Sport Journal*, *19*, 189–205.

Sugimoto, Y. (1997). *An introduction to Japanese society*. Hong Kong: Cambridge University Press.

Thompson, L. (1998). The invention of yokozuna and the championship system, or, Futahaguro's revenge. In: S. Vlastos (Ed.), *Mirror of modernity: Invented traditions of modern Japan* (pp. 174–190). Berkeley: University of California Press.

Watts, J. (1998). Soccer *shinhatsubai*: What are consumers making of the J. League? In: D. Martinez (Ed.), *The worlds of Japanese popular culture* (pp. 181–202). Cambridge: Cambridge University Press.

Yamashita, T. (2006). The changing field of Japanese sport. In: *Japan, sport and society: Tradition and change in a globalising world* (pp. 157–176). London: Routledge.

Yasumura, H. (1998). Looking towards the 21st Century: Are Japanese cultural practices changing? In: D. Myer & K. Ishido (Eds), *Japan at the crossroads*. Tokyo: Seibundo Publishing.

AN OPEN LETTER FROM RUGBY BOYS IN NO-VOICE-LAND: REFLECTIONS ON RUGBY AND RACE BY SOUTH AFRICA'S 2007 SCHOOLBOY PLAYERS

Cora Burnett

INTRODUCTION

South Africa's rugby fraternity has achieved the highest honours in its national sporting history by winning the Rugby World Cup on 20 October 2007 in France. They also received international awards for the best team, player and coach of the year, as well as having its very own Mr. Rugby, Danie Craven being honoured by receiving a place in the International Rugby Board's Hall of Fame (Borchard, 2007). Yet, it was the most controversial and trying period for all sport-loving South Africans who were torn apart by exclusionary ownership and identification (Harmse, 2007). Not only was the team discredited because of its racial composition, having only six players of colour in the squad and fielding two Coloured players in the final, but the coach, Jake White was publicly scrutinized for not achieving 'transformation targets' (Pilay, 2007). In his controversial autobiography entitled *In Black and White,* he reflects on the 'politicking' in South African rugby such as the

Social and Cultural Diversity in a Sporting World
Research in the Sociology of Sport, Volume 5, 111–124
Copyright © 2008 by Emerald Group Publishing Limited
All rights of reproduction in any form reserved
ISSN: 1476-2854/doi:10.1016/S1476-2854(08)05008-5

forced inclusion of Luke Watson (son of a political activist) who was proclaimed 'an honorary black' (Ball, 2007; Ray, 2007), while the chairperson of the Portfolio Committee in Parliament threatened to have the 'lily white' Springbok team members' passports confiscated (Wyngaard, 2007).

Frustration mounted as the composition of the national team did not represent the country in its ethnic diversity and merely reflected the old division of white superiority and entitlement (Anon, 2007a). Although a broad understanding of such sentiments was expressed in the media, the fast-tracking and mechanism of doing so (affirmative action or racial targets) were opposed by those who advocated for merit selections and a winning team as a united force (Keohane, 2007). Fleeting moments of celebrating the victory were soon silenced by threats and demands for increased transformation targets and talent development of 'black ethnic players' (Coetzee, 2007; Majola & Ikaneng, 2007). It seems that little has changed in the national team as the Deputy President of Saru (South African Rugby Union) expressed his frustration of not having a transformed team 13 years after the black majority rule. He was reported saying:

> We must be honest with ourselves and realise that there are many different communities out there who play rugby – black, white, coloured, Indian and so forth. If those communities are not represented, how can we then say that we have transformed rugby ... We see in the South Africa Under-19 and Under-21 sides year after year, that there are nine or 11 players of colour in those teams. Why can't that happen in the Springbok team? (Anon, 2007b, p. 2)

The same scenario was repeated at different levels of the game – each side accusing the other of political 'foul play' (Ray, 2007). The selection of a black captain (Chiliboy Ralepelle) for a match against a World XV was criticized by the current Minister of Sport for using the player as a 'political pawn' – a once-off opportunity for Jake White 'to play politics' (McCallum, 2006, p. 23). White acknowledged the unique racial scenario of South Africa by saying: 'South Africa is the only country where when a winger is injured, you are obliged to change the prop' (Anon, 2007c).

The role of rugby as nation-builder is thus compromised despite widespread support for redressing past inequalities by perceived compromising of merit and demands to field a 'better shade of rugby' (Honey, 2003). It is clear that 'unity through sport' is a complex, highly emotional and value-laden issue for South Africans. Old political scores are being settled, new wounds are inflicted and the country is as divided as ever.

The chapter attempts to provide some insights into rugby as 'nation builder and divider' by deconstructing identity formation in the lived realities of young elite rugby players entrenched in the power games of decision-makers. It draws on a recent study where 359 Craven and Academic Week players reflected on their experiences in open-ended questions during the respective tournaments in 2007.

A CONCEPTUAL FRAMEWORK

National identity implies a sense of belonging to a nation-state of which one holds citizenship. It also relates to an imagined nation as collective and sense of 'nationness' embedded in socio-cultural constructions that are continuously communicated through a shared history, stories, memories and images (Tuck, 2003). In this sense political nationalism and sporting nationalism are closely interwoven (Bairner, 2003). Governments use sport to help create and manage national identity which is a highly fluid process, as sport symbolism and dynamics often undermine its capacity to exert a lasting effect (Houlihan, 1997).

From a figurational approach, sport is viewed as an important arena for the construction, maintenance and challenging of consumed national identities (constructed in histories and media reports) and embodied national identities (constructed by players) to which deep-rooted feelings, shared values and experiences create a sense of belonging – a social home (Schwartz, 1992). Sporting competitions provide expressions of an imagined community where the 'nation' becomes 'real' such as in having a national team winning a significant competition where a powerful nationwide feel-good factor is generated (Tuck, 2003). As sporting heroes, players become embodied symbols of national pride and patriotism, creating a sense of temporary union, often between distinct politically 'nations' within a nation-state. This may happen around unifying symbols such as an anthem, flag or team that evoke intense emotional involvement and self-labelling (Condor, Gibson, & Abell, 2006).

According to the self-categorization theory (Turner, Hogg, Oakes, Reicher, & Wetherell, 1987), people classify themselves and others into groups based on demographics, attitudes, ethnicity or other affiliations which explains the phenomenon of 'ethnic nations' within a particular nation-state. People have a need to maintain high self-esteem which is partly accomplished by comparing themselves to others. The social-identity theory (Turner, 1982) explains how people classify themselves into groups that are characterized by 'us' and 'them' dynamics as a dividing force, which makes social integration or the perceived belonging to a single social unit unlikely

(Gaertner & Dovidio, 2000). According to the relational demography theory (Riordan, 2000), in-group members will be afforded greater trust and will be beneficiaries of a more positive effect and intra-group bonding.

In-group members perceive themselves to be quite different from out-group members, and seek to maximize inter-group differences through positive interpretations of in-group members and less positive evaluations of the 'other' (Tajfel & Turner, 1979). Perceptions of diversity are relatively intense, often leading to emotional conflict (Hobman, Bordian, & Gallois, 2003) and in-group bias that exacerbates sub-group formations and social chasms (Cunningham, 2007). Studies have demonstrated that members of ethnic minorities often encounter access discrimination in the field of sport (Cunningham & Fink, 2006). Enforced change has unique behavioural consequences on satisfaction levels, stress, commitment and drop-out (Cunningham, 2006). The double-bind of minority or out-group status and coping with change may result in different behavioural changes such as resistance, compliance, cooperation and championing (Herscovitch & Meyer, 2002).

In the sporting context players are socialized through various phases of developing a group (team) and sporting identity (e.g. being a rugby player or winger), a process in which significant others such as parents (during the early formative years), coach and peers, especially team mates, play significant roles (Côté, 1999; Burnett, 2005). The type of involvement from significant others may change from a leadership role (during the 'sampling years'), to a facilitative role (during the specialization years) and finally to a supportive role (during the 'investment years') (Baker, Horton, Robertson-Wilson, & Wall, 2003).

During the process of socialization and identity formation into the rugby fraternity, young boys' participation is deeply situated in the social and cultural contexts they find themselves. Diverse social identities and political influences that upturn the in-group identity formation, may cause psychological discontent and translate into a struggle for power, dignity, acceptance and recognition (Light & Kirk, 2001). Non-merit selections, often part and parcel of meeting racial quotas in sports teams, may cause shifting identities of insider or outsider affiliation and behaviour that may not of itself be discriminatory or racist, but may have racial consequences (Long, 2000).

THE LEGACY OF A POLITICAL GAME

Sport is interwoven with the fabric of South African society and has for more than a century (even before the inception of the Springbok in 1906), remained largely entrenched within the bastions of the political power of the day (Nauright & Black, 1998). It carried with it the ideological baggage of the apartheid regime and resistance against British imperialism (Nauright, 1997). The first version of the game on South African soil was reported in 1862 when the 'manly' game of football was played at Bishops College in Cape Town (Nauright, 1997). It became increasingly popular, and in the aftermath of the Anglo-Boer War (1899–1902), Afrikaans-speaking rural folk ('Boers') took to the game and united around common values and an ethos of ethnic superiority, a rural lifestyle of hard work, sacrifice, toughness, physical prowess and patriarchal values (Archer & Bouillon, 1982; Van der Merwe, 1998).

The election of the National Party in 1948 set the South African society on a pathway of 'apartheid' with the development of fragmented national identities and a public discourse of white empowerment. Unity was expressed through national symbols such as a flag, anthem (*Die Stem*) and particularly rugby of which the Afrikaner elite claimed ownership (Grundlingh, 1996). White Afrikaner nationalists utilized rugby as a socio-political institution whereby racial attitudes and a masculine nationalist discourse became common sense reality in all spheres of public life (Nauright & Black, 1998). In the 1960s and 1970s it became a form of *Volksgodsdiens* (Folk religion) (Du Preez, 2002, p. 18).

Local and global resistance from various apartheid movements and activists (Lapchick, 1975; Ramsamy, 1982) tore South Africans apart, and bitter battles were fought to 'not have normal sport in an abnormal society' (a slogan made famous by SACOS – South African Council of Sport). Rebel tours organized in the 1970s and 1980s contributed to the fact that rugby was isolated for only six years, which included not participating in the 1987 and 1991 World Cups (Kidd, 1988; Nauright, 1996).

The post-1995 years evidenced a reformed political landscape which also claimed rugby as instrument for achieving a 'new national unity'. With the winning of the 1995 World Cup, a virtual South African society was mediated as being united with the newly elected President Mandela emulating the sentiment of 'one team one nation' (Griffiths, 1996). The process of Africanization and a new national identity found expression in a new anthem (*Nkosi Sikelel 'iAfrika*), flag and song (*Shosholoza*, a song about the plight of migrant mine workers from Zimbabwe) sung at rugby matches where the *Amabokoboko* were supported by supporters across the racial spectrum (Nauright, 1997).

The fast-tracking and drive for demographic representation on racial lines, became a priority as only one player of colour was fielded in the 1995 World

Cup (Griffiths, 1996). Ideological changes seemed tough to dismantle, and the government embarked on affirmative action strategies such as prescribing racial quotas at all levels of competition, with the expectation that the national side would have a new and 'darker' face in the future (Morris, 2002). The first racial quotas were implemented in 1997 for the Under-18 Coca-Cola Craven Week sides (Anon, 2002) and in 1998 for the Currie Cup (Nel, 2000), followed by the Super 12 in 2001 (Kruger, 2000; Del Carme, 2002). The development perspective was to begin with the younger age category at school boy level with the vision that if development could take place at that level, it would inevitably have a spill-over effect onto the more senior sides.

Schoolboy rugby has experienced the ripple effect of political changes across time. Since the inception of the Craven Week as an exclusionary competition for white players in 1964, Craven lobbied for the inclusion of a Coloured team in 1980, which resulted in some Afrikaner schools boycotting the tournament and caused a split in the National Party as conservatives resigned in protest to the reformist policies (Nauright, 1997). Since the implementation of the affirmative action policy of increasingly including a 'quota' of players of colour in the Coca-Cola Craven Week squads, accusations of 'racism' or neo-racism have appeared in media reports as divisions were created along racial lines (Gilbert, 2001).

Much controversy and resistance on a collective scale resulted in establishing a *Bokkie-week* for boys excluded from participation, and an attempt to reclaim socio-cultural identity for the white Afrikaans-speaking minority, escalated during the last decade (Isaacs, 2004). A newly composed song *De la Ray* (about a Boer general in the Anglo-Boer War who, in the lyrics becomes that mythical figure to 'come and lead the Boers'), is becoming increasingly popular at school and university rugby matches.

The political turmoil is but one major force that turned the rugby fraternity on its head. Legitimized professionalism brought about a complete change of values and attitudes. South African rugby players became highly paid professionals in the aftermath of the 1995 Rugby World Cup. Commercialization has since increased and at school level young players are recruited by 'rugby schools', lured by bursaries and incentives (Van Rensburg, 2004).

It is against this background that elite schoolboy rugby players have to compete for access to resources and opportunities that may result in a future rugby career. When listening to the voices of South Africa's upcoming rugby players, an understanding of the complexity, volatility, racial polarisation and a distorted sense of identity formation based on resisting versus expecting entitlement, is constructed.

THE BOYS FROM NO-VOICE-LAND

During the 2007 Academic and Craven Weeks, stakeholders (managers, coaches, parents and players) were invited to take part in a research project focusing on collecting data on influences, experiences perceptions and issues that mainly influence the sporting lives of the players. Participation was voluntary and anonymity guaranteed. A total of 359 Coca-Cola Craven Week ($n = 221$, 62%) and Adacemic Week players ($n = 138$, 38%) completed questionnaires. The race profile of the respondents from all the rugby unions, represents a relatively even split between players of colour ($n = 184$, 51%) and white players ($n = 174$, 49%) of whom the majority was Afrikaans-speaking ($n = 232$, 65%).

In these tournaments, the cream of schoolboy rugby players from all the provincial unions in South Africa compete against each other. A national squad is also selected that often paves the way for youngsters to embark on a professional rugby career and/or gain access to sports bursaries and contracts from rugby unions or academies. With the focus on 'development' and 'transformation', a 'quota-system' is stringently implemented to ensure an equal race representation (50%, 11 out of 22) in the Academic Week and (41%, 9 out of 22) representation of 'players of colour' in the Coca-Cola Craven Week teams. The monitoring of fielding a minimum of four 'players of colour' at the Coca-Cola Craven Week tournament, and eight at the Academic Week at all times, caused much controversy and intense feelings.

Several players were scared to speak about their experiences as they feared personal retaliation and/or victimization from coaches, managers and/or decision makers who constitute the fraternity in which they strife to 'find a place'. Youngsters have no official opportunity to share and give meaning to their experiences in such a way that they may escape 'punishment'. The mystification of 'ground rules' are further intensified when key political figures and spokespersons of the South African Rugby Union declared in the aftermath of the 2007 World Cup, that the focus will be on 'development' and 'merit selection' at the national level (Majola & Ikaneng, 2007). What are they to expect at the developmental levels of the game if 'transformation' (Maputi, 2007) will be the key drive for development in the foreseeable future?

Through their narratives, a story takes shape and will be written as an open letter to a wider audience in search of an understanding of their social worlds that to a large extent, entails collective identity formation within the South African rugby fraternity. In the analysis of qualitative data, the main negative experience communicated concerns perceived class and racial discrimination of not being afforded a fair opportunity for participation, mainly due to the implementation of 'racial quotas' and bias selections.

A collective voice of discontent from white players is expressed in *non-merit selections* that keep them 'warming the seats' for 'lesser talented players', as they have players selected 'in their positions' that clearly 'do not make the grade'. Some of the experiences tell a story of marginalization and emotional reactions. They reflected as follows:

> It is like in the Primary School Craven Week where a black player was chosen in my place because of his colour and now he doesn't even play rugby (a player from Griffons)

> Die kwota-stelsel is absurd. Ons kinders het niks met apartheid te doen gehad nie. Die patetiese base van SARU diskrimineer teen ons wit mense.' (Trans. 'The quota system is absurd. We as children did not have anything to do with apartheid. The pathetic bosses of SARU discriminate against our white people. (a player from South Western Districts)

> The fact that I had to sit on the bench while lesser players that are not even close to as good as I am (players of colour) played to fill a quota. (a player from the Blue Bulls)

> Kwotas is volgens my 'n vorm van rassisme. In die verlede kon 'n swart ou nie op 'n bus ry nie, want hy is swart. Ek mag nie vir 'n sekere span gekies word nie, want ek is wit en dit gebeur elke dag met talentvolle spelers.' (Trans. 'Quotas is to me a form of racism. In the past a black bloke was not allowed to ride on a bus, because he was black. I cannot be chosen for a certain team because I am white and this happens to talented players every day. (a player from the Blue Bulls)

> 'n Wit speler is bo my gekies sodat die span se kwota van 11:11 reg kon wees.' (Transl. 'They have chosen a white player above me in order to get the team quota of 11:11).' (a player of colour from Boland)

Self-labelling in terms of ethnic affiliation created an 'us' and 'them' identification that is inevitably linked to perceptions of superiority, inferiority and fairness for the collective, as well as acceptance for the individual. Discreditation of the 'other' is reflected in a victim mentality and loss of entitlement (Condor et al., 2006; Turner, 1982).

For some, the quota system awarded them an opportunity to be selected and showcase their talent that they otherwise would not have been able to do. As one black player from South Western Districts indicated: 'I play second and third team at school but always get selected for the Craven Week and not the first team players.' It is the *negative emotions* such as self-doubt, frustration, sadness, distrust and disillusionment that are inevitably linked to the strategy of affirmative action as evidenced in some statements.

> The white guys like calling us 'kaffers' and that makes one feel bad. (a player from the Leopards)

Ons het op die 3de teen SWD gespeel toe 'n Kleurling vleuel na my gestamp en stoot het en vir my: "jou *** wit plaas boer" geskree het.' (Transl. We played against South Western Districts on the third when a Coloured winger pushed me around and shouted at me: "you *** white farmer." (a player from the Blue Bulls)

I get lots of discrimination, because all my team mates are black ... they only communicate in Xhosa and I don't understand it. So I feel left out. I have received plenty of comments because I'm white from plenty of players, management and coaching staff. (a player from Border).

Some players and provincial coaches think that black players aren't good enough to play in their teams and make it far in life. Some white players not trusting black players with the ball in the field. (a player from the Falcons)

Sometimes you start to believe some of the bad things said about you and you just want to quit the bloody sports and concentrate on your academics. (a player from the Leopards)

The racial divide is broadened as players are emotionally affected by perceived unfair treatment, humiliation and 'hate speech' (Long, 2000). Acceptance by the 'rest of the team' seems to be problematic as some players mentioned that 'skipped passes' are played, and they are marginalized as their performance is seen as 'sub-standard'. Experiences of overt discrimination and marginalization is very much in the face of players – some by being belittled in front of team members, and others by being degraded 'and made to watch the weak players play in their positions as side benchers'. The negative labelling, humiliation, distrust, hatred, feelings of inferiority and superiority are contributing to poor team cohesion, increased racial divides through racial stereotyping and stacking (selecting players of colours as wingers). Such experiences fostered in-group identity formation and caused psychological discontent among those who perceived themselves to be 'outsiders' (Light & Kirk, 2001).

Another stumbling block seems to be the *lack of money and resources* for continued participation, especially players from relatively poor socio-economic backgrounds may be excluded as they cannot afford high level participation (Cunningham & Fink, 2006). Some explain:

The problem is that some provinces don't get sponsored and that (the) quota system is just putting all the black players under a lot of pressure. (a player from the Pumas)

Many opportunities must be given to the younger players and underprivileged ones like us. We study on a bursary in high school and they say we can't get (further) bursaries because we were in privileged schools, we need to further our careers. Some can't pay money to play in the U/16 and U/18 teams because they want R3000 to go on tour and some can't afford that money – that causes players to quit. (a player from the Pumas)

These experiences are also translated into views expressed by players when they were asked to give their opinion on the *current state* of rugby in South Africa. The depth of talent and the success of the two South African teams that played in the final of the 2007 Super 14 League were inspirational and were to many a 'proof' of rugby being 'in their blood', and the potential for them to follow in the footsteps of 'great players' (role models) by one day playing for the Springboks. The success that was referred to by the players, excludes the winning of the 2007 Rugby World Cup as the data was collected three months prior to the competition. They expressed themselves as follows:

> We have it all we must just keep on working harder to be the best. Since the Super 14 Final was in SA it has given not only the players, but the whole South Africa supporters of rugby a massive boost. (a player from the Free State)

> Rugby in South Africa, it is growing to a state where youngsters get to be skilled (and) being strong. (There are) lots of opportunities like Coca-Cola Craven Week which brings up the school youngsters to live up their dreams and also getting lots of club rugby around their provincial regions. (a player from the Falcons)

The majority however felt very *negative* towards the 'current state' and management of rugby in the country, mainly because of the implementation of the *quota-system* and not being selected on merit, factors that weaken the teams. For them, 'politics' is the main factor that contributed to their decision to either drop out of the game or wanting to join an overseas club. The following narratives give voice to such sentiments.

> The rugby in South Africa is getting worse because of the quota structure in schools. Players who are talented and need to be in the teams are kicked out or didn't make it to make place for quotas who can't even play. They weaken the teams and poor positions are achieved. If the quotas are good then let them play but not if they mess up the team. The whites are mostly on the bench and the quotas playing. Never get time to show their talent and to be spotted by the universities to get bursaries for rugby, most of them need it. (a player from the Leopards)

> At the moment it is brilliant however if they do what they have said, and do (it) after the World Cup, South Africa's rugby is going to go to the gutters. (a player from KwaZulu-Natal)

> Ons land se rugby is besig om die groet ... Die kwota-stelsel beïnvloed baie van die spelers se besluite om oorsee te gaan. Die media kraak baie van die spelers af.' (Transl. Our country's rugby is busy saying good bye. The quota-system influences many of the players to go overseas. The media negatively portrays many players. (a player from the Leopards)

In offering solutions that will 'work for them', the majority suggested that quotas should be abolished ($n = 38$) and players with commitment be selected on merit ($n = 32$). Another issue that they felt strongly about, is a well-focused thrust toward grassroots player development, giving players a say in the game, and revoking the ethos of 'loving the game' and 'playing with passion, not for the money'. An urgent call is for player integration, feelings of inclusion and intra-team acceptance where rugby players may find a social home in the rugby fraternity (Schwartz, 1992). Such sentiments are worded as follows:

> Die talent is hier ons moet dit net begin gebruik, hoeveel wit en swart spelers word nie die kans van Craven Week gegun oor kwotas nie? Spelers moet op meriete gekies word soos in al die ander lande. (Transl. 'The talent is here and we have to start using it. How many white and black players do not get the opportunities of Craven Week because of quotas? Players should be selected on merit as is the case in all other countries. (a player from Griffons)

> They (SA) really started getting good ... but one thing is the quota in SA rugby, they must pick the best player for the position (it) doesn't matter what colour – we are all equal in South Africa. (a player from South Western Districts)

> More players should be selected on merit and general team dynamics should be maintained. (a player from Kwa-Zulu Natal)

> We would do a lot better if more academies were set in place to get the better players of colour, so the better white players could not have not (sic) reason to be angry. If they are better, there will be no reason for (the) quota system. (a player from the Blue Bulls)

> The black players get too easily into the teams. The white ones have to work hard. If this doesn't change, our rugby will fall. (a player from the Leopards)

As a player from the Blue Bulls said: 'Let us unite and be the rainbow nation', indicating the need for talent identification, development and merit selection as boys just want to play, following the inherent ethos of competitive sport – to play as a team, excel and get recognition and acceptance as a player.

CONCLUSION

It is clear that the legacy of apartheid and the implementation of racial quotas as strategy to redress the racial representation in the branding of 'nation-building', has devastating unintended consequences. In-outsider affiliations are strengthened, the racial divide deepened and 'no normal society created in the abnormal (world) of South African rugby'. True nation building at the grassroots level should focus on the development of racial tolerance, acceptance and inclusion that transcend the momentary euphoria of magic moments, but place an enduring responsibility on decision-makers to act wisely, with insight and compassion to optimally develop players as future custodians of rugby in South Africa.

Outside public and private agencies cannot be held solely responsible for building a truly representative and/or national team that will uphold the national prestige of excellence on a global competitive stage. Significant others such as parents and coaches should realise the vital role that they have to play in socializing young players into responsible and informed citizens, nation-builders and part of the rugby fraternity of a proudly South African legacy.

REFERENCES

Anon (2002). The quota system is bearing fruit. *Star*, July 8, p. 9.

Anon (2007a). South Africa: Critic of White heads coach selection panel. Available at http:// allafrica.com.stories/2007//051239.htm. Retrieved on November 3.

Anon (2007b). Seven black Boks far from enough, says Sasu's Stofile. *Pretoria News*, September 11, p. 2.

Anon (2007c). White had to buck odds. Available at www.citizen.co.za/index/ article.aspx?Desc = 50681,1,11. Retrieved on October 18.

Archer, R., & Bouillon, A. (1982). *The South African game: Sport and racism*. London: Zed Press.

Bairner, A. (2003). Political Unionism and sporting nationalism: An examination of the relationship between sport and national identity within the Ulster Unionist tradition. *Global Studies in Culture and Power* (10), 517–535.

Baker, J., Horton, S., Robertson-Wilson, J., & Wall, M. (2003). Nurturing sport expertise: Factors influencing the development of the elite athlete. *Journal of Sport Science and Medicine* (2), 1–9.

Ball, D. (2007). The merits of merit in sport. *Reporter*, July 2, p. 3.

Borchard, De J. (2007). Doc Craven vereer. 'Meneer Rugby' in Heldesaal opgeneem. [*Translation Doc Craven honoured. 'Mister Rugby' had been given a place in Hall of Fame.*] *Rapport* (News Section), November 18, p. v.

Burnett, C. (2005). Influences on the socialisation of South African Elite Athletes. *South African Journal for Research in Sport, Physical Education and Recreation*, 27(1), 37–50.

Coetzee, G. (2007). Politici kry Bok-koors. [*Translation Politicians gets Bok-fever.*] Available at www.dieburger.com/Stories/news/15.0.3203702397.aspx. Retrieved on October 16.

Condor, S., Gibson, S., & Abell, J. (2006). English identity and ethnic diversity in the context of UK constitutional change. *Ethnicities* (6), 123–158.

Côté, J. (1999). The influence of the family in the development of talent in sport. *The Sport Psychologist* (13), 359–417.

Cunningham, G. B. (2006). Examining the relationship among coping with change, demographic dissimilarity and championing behaviour. *Sport Management Review* (9), 253–270.

Cunningham, G. B. (2007). Opening the black box: The influence of perceived diversity and a common in-group identity in diverse groups. *Journal of Sport Management, 5*(21), 58–78.

Cunningham, G. B., & Fink, J. S. (2006). Diversity issues in sport and leisure. *Journal of Sport Management* (20), 455–465.

Del Carme, L. (2002). More black players must be given a chance to prove themselves – Rian. *Star*, April 10, p. 14

Du Preez, M. (2002). Keep yesterday's manne away from rugby. *Star*, September 5, p. 18.

Gaertner, S. L., & Dovidio, J. F. (2000). *Reducing intergroup bias: The common ingroup identity model.* Philadelphia: Psychology Press.

Gilbert, M. (2001). Pleidooi aan Sarvu oor Cravenweek. [*Translation Plead to Sarfu about Craven Week.*] *Beeld*, July 16, p. 3.

Griffiths, E. (1996). *One team, one country: The greatest year of springbok rugby.* London: Viking.

Grundlingh, A. (1996). Playing for power? Rugby, Afrikaner nationalism and masculinity in South Africa, c1900–c1970. In: J. Nauright & T. J. L. Chandler (Eds), *Making men. Rugby and Masculine Identity* (pp. 181–204). London: Frank Cass.

Harmse, J. J. (2007). Kwota-skok vir rugby. Bokspan moet tot 12 swartes hê. [*Translation Quota shock for rugby. Bok-team must have up to 12 blacks.*] *Rapport*, August 5, p. 1.

Herscovitch, L., & Meyer, J. P. (2002). Commitment to organizational change: Extension of a three-component model. *Journal of Applied Psychology, 5*(87), 474–487.

Hobman, E. V., Bordian, P., & Gallois, C. (2003). Consequences of feeling dissimilar from others in a work team. *Journal of Business and Psychology, 5*(17), 301–325.

Honey, P. (2003). Kick the political football. *Financial Mail*, November 28, p. 24.

Houlihan, B. (1997). *Sport, policy and politics: A comparative analysis.* London: Routledge.

Isaacs, A. (2004). Skolerugby 'wil ook na Rugga SA skuif. [*Translation School rugby also wants to move to Rugga SA.*] *Burger*, August 9, p. 4.

Keohane, M. (2007). SA rugby's 2001 black player plan. Bosses committed to seeing seven in World Cup starting XV. Available at http://www.sundayindependent.co.za/index.php?Articled = 3969061. Retrieved on October 12.

Kidd, B. (1988). The campaign against sport in South Africa. *International Journal, 63*(4), 643–664.

Kruger, P. (2000). Indaba aims to thrash out racism in rugby. *Business Day*, May 31, p. 36.

Lapchick, R. (1975). *The politics of race and international sport: The case of South Africa.* Westport, CT: Greenwood Press.

Light, R., & Kirk, D. (2001). Australian cultural capital – rugby's social meaning: Physical assets, social advantage and independent schools. *Culture, Sport, Society, 4*(3), 81–98.

Long, J. (2000). No racism here? A preliminary examination of sporting innocence. *Managing Leisure*, 5, pp. 121–133.

Majola, B., & Ikaneng, T. (2007). Let World Cup euphoria not blind us to rugby racist realities. Available at www.thetimes.co.za/PrintEditon/Insight/Article.aspx?id = 598104. Retrieved on October 29.

Maputi, S. (2007). Stofile prefers merits to quotas. *Citizen*, September 12, p. 3.

McCallum, K. (2006). It was an honour to captain Springboks – Chiliboy. *Star*, December 6, p. 23.

Morris, M. (2002). An empty numbers game in the name of transformation. *Cape Argus*, January 11, p. 6.

Nauright, J. (1996). Colonial manhood and imperial race virility: British responses to post-Boer War colonial rugby tours. In: J. Nauright & T. Chandler (Eds), *In Making Men: Rugby and Masculine Identity* (pp. 121–139). London: Frank Cass.

Nauright, J. (1997). *Sport, cultures and identities in South Africa*. Cape Town: David Philip.

Nauright, J., & Black, D. (1998). Sport at the center of power: Rugby in South Africa during apartheid. *Sport History Review*, 5(29), 192–211.

Nel, B. (2000). Bulls to be quizzed on the quota scandal. *Pretoria News*, September 9, p. 5.

Pilay, U. (2007). Rugby lessons for SA soccer. Available at www.businessday.co.za/specialist/aricles/AgonyRant.aspx?ID = BD4A621385. Retrieved on November 22.

Ramsamy, S. (1982). *Apartheid: The real hurdle*. London: International Defence and Aid Fund.

Ray, G. (2007). *In black and white. The jake white story*. Cape Town: Zebra Press.

Riordan, C. M. (2000). Relational demography within groups: Past developments, contradictions and new directions. In: G. R. Ferris (Ed.), *Research in personnel and human resources management* (pp. 131–173). Greenwich, CT: Jai Press.

Schwartz, B. (1992). England in Europe: Reflections on national identity and cultural theory. *Cultural Studies* (6), 198–206.

Tajfel, H., & Turner, J. C. (1979). An integrative theory of intergroup conflict. In: W. G. Austin & S. Worchel (Eds), *The social psychology of intergroup relations* (pp. 33–47). Monterey, CA: Brooks/Cole.

Tuck, J. (2003). Making sense of emerald commotion: Rugby union, national identity and Ireland. *Identities: Global Studies in Culture and Power*, 5(10), 495–515.

Turner, J. (1982). Toward a cognitive definition of the group. In: H. Tajfel (Ed.), *Social identity and intergroup relations* (pp. 17–40). Cambridge: Cambridge University Press.

Turner, J., Hogg, M. A., Oakes, P. J., Reicher, S. D., & Wetherell, J. S. (1987). *Rediscovering the social group: A self-categorization theory*. Oxford, UK: Blackwell.

Van der Merwe, F. (1998). Rugby in the prisoner-of-war camps of the Anglo-Boer war. *Occasional Papers in Football Studies*, 1(1), 76–83.

Van Rensburg, E. (2004). Skolerugby word vendusie. [*Translation School rugby becomes an auction.*] *Beeld*, July 30, p. 4.

Wyngaard H. (2007). Transformasie, nie getalle, moet getakel word. ANC se laaste woord: Vermoë, nié kwotas. [*Translation Transformation, not numbers must be taken on. ANC's last word: Ability, not quotas.*] *Rapport*, June 24, p. 12.

SHALOSH, SHTAYIM, ECHAD, MACCABI: JEWISH JUNIOR GIRLS BASKETBALL☆

Michael Burke and Chris Hallinan

ABSTRACT

An ethnographic approach was used to investigate the increasing significance of basketball participation for junior women to the development of an athletic Jewish female identity in Melbourne, Australia. Informants, especially parents of the players, suggested that participation in basketball, allowed them to remodel adolescent Jewish female identity in positive and community-enriching ways. However, this positive, identity-affirming participation by Jewish girls sometimes resulted in violent opposition from players and parents from other clubs, possibly a by-product of the 'wedge' politics that is now part of the broader Australian community.

☆Translated as "Three, Two, One, Maccabi", a pregame chant in Hebrew by an under 15 Maccabi girls' basketball team.

Social and Cultural Diversity in a Sporting World
Research in the Sociology of Sport, Volume 5, 125–139
Copyright © 2008 by Emerald Group Publishing Limited
All rights of reproduction in any form reserved
ISSN: 1476-2854/doi:10.1016/S1476-2854(08)05009-7

1. INTRODUCTION

Greenberg (1981 cited in Dufour, 2000, p. 92) explains:

> [Halakhah, Jewish Law, is the] religious institutionalization of sexual and social status ... what was a sociological truth about women in all previous generations- that they were the "second sex"- was codified in many minute ways into Halakhah as religioethical concepts, binding upon future generations as well.

The effects in the Jewish religion had been that God remained a masculine concept with masculine values, and the images of women as sexual temptresses and evil demons had been used to prevent them from becoming rabbis. At the same time, many of the values that patriarchal religions such as Judaism espouse, such as love, commitment and justice, appear to be 'consonant with some feminist values' (Dufour, 2000, p. 92). In addition, a commitment within Judaism to be flexible and change has allowed females in the religion to experience increasing levels of responsibility, opportunity and protection. Women in Judaism, with the exception of Orthodoxy, can now become rabbis, may experience *Bat Mitzvahs*, and participate actively in religious services (Beecher, 1999; Dufour, 2000; Zaidman, 1996).

According to Rubinstein, the position and status of women in the contemporary Jewish community appears also to be 'highly contradictory' (1991, p. 117). He explains:

> Judaism has always been a male-dominated religion and a male-dominated culture, with traditional Judaism narrowly prescribing the role of women to the expected one of mothers and homemakers ... Yet Jewish women have, *de facto*, probably been more independent and visible than in most other cultures ... Jewish women have formed, and comprise today around the world, a very disproportionate share of 'liberated' women activists and achievers, as well as radical feminists. (1991, p. 117)

Whilst Australian-Jewish women may be characterised as more traditional in their orientation than Jewish women in the United States, they still participate actively in the spheres of education, business, workplace participation, philanthropy, the media and culture (Rutland, 1987; Rubinstein, 1991).

Sport in Jewish Australian communities has also presented as a site of female activity. According to Hughes, Jewish sporting organisations have always accepted the participation of women both as athletes and administrators (1997, p. 113). Interstate sporting carnivals for Jewish communities in Australia began in 1926 (Rutland, 1988). A prime motivation in this development of Maccabiah sporting festivals in Australia was a concern that a distinctive Jewish identity would die out because of assimilation and intermarriage with non-Jewish people (Hughes, 1999, p. 382).[1] It was a Jewish woman, Hannah Hart, who wrote a letter to the editor of the *Hebrew Standard* in 1924, suggesting the idea of a combined Jewish sports carnival in Australia (Rutland, 1987, p. 118). Sporting carnivals were viewed as an important site for involving Jewish youth in organisations within the community (Rutland, 1987). It was felt that 'sporting and social activities for young people would provide a rallying point for the unaffiliated and so help reduce the rising intermarriage rates' (Rutland, 1988, p. 154 cited in Hughes, 1999, p. 382). This matrimonial function of Jewish sport ensured that women were always a part of Jewish sporting carnivals and clubs (Hughes, 1997). The Judean girls' gymnasium and the Jewish girls' sports club both came into existence in Melbourne in 1930 (www.macvic.com.au).

This chapter describes and analyses the site of Jewish junior female basketball in Melbourne, Australia using the Maccabi basketball club as a case study. The AJAX/Maccabi basketball club in Victoria was established in 1951. Initially it was located in East St. Kilda and serviced Jewish basketball communities in both the south and northeast. In more recent times, these communities have been serviced by two separate organising committees, and play in two separate local region competitions. Both organising committees remain under the control of the governing body, Maccabi basketball, and both send players to the various Jewish sports carnivals that occur nationally and internationally. This research is limited to participants in the larger southern basketball club that has a number of teams that play in the local competitions in the south central Melbourne metropolitan area. We shall commence by explaining the significance of basketball participation to identity issues for young females within this Jewish community. We will move on to explain some dangers that arise from the maintenance of a Jewish cultural/religious identity in contemporary Australia.

2. JEWISH DIASPORA IN MELBOURNE

The Jewish community in Melbourne makes up approximately 1% of the total population of the metropolitan region. There are approximately 120,000 Jews in Australia, with a population nearing 50,000 in Melbourne (Dacy, 2002). The Jewish population in Melbourne is now mostly concentrated in two regions. A large community exists in a band of Southern suburbs from South Yarra to Glen Iris with an impressive array of day schools, synagogues, shops and Jewish institutions in this area, and makes up approximately 75% of the Melbourne Jewish population. The most populated suburbs of this band are Caulfield and St. Kilda. A smaller community exists across the Northern and Eastern suburbs from Doncaster to Malvern. The historical community base that once existed in inner Melbourne suburbs such as Carlton and Fitzroy has now almost disappeared (Rubinstein, 1991; Cohen, 1988).

According to Rubinstein (1986, pp. 10–12; 1991, pp. 1–50), two distinct periods can be observed in the relationship between the Jewish community and Australian society from 1788 to the present time. The first period from 1788 to the 1930s was broadly assimilationist with the Jewish community asserting that there is little cultural or practical difference between it and the general community, or, as Hughes describes following Rutland, 'an ideology of nondistinctiveness' (Rutland, 1988, pp. 141–146; Hughes, 1999, p. 377). Gouttman (2005) argues that since settlement, anti-Jewish stereotypes have been present in Australia, and many Jews approached a wary Australian community by avoiding the word 'Jew' as a descriptor of themselves. Most Jewish immigration before the end of the nineteenth century came to Australia from Britain, which added to their acceptability and nondistinctiveness in a mostly White, Anglo-Saxon society. Rubinstein comments: 'Jews have thus never been considered to be aliens to quite the same extent as elsewhere' (Rubinstein, 1982, p. 163). The second wave of mass Jewish immigration occurred in the 1930s and 1940s as refugees from the Nazi juggernaut (Gouttman, 2005; Rubinstein, 1986). The Australian government, supported by mainstream Australia, inserted 'Jewish clauses' in application documents for immigration that singled out Jews. As Gouttman (2005) explains: 'If Jewish immigrants were to come [to Australia], those from the latter [Europe's west] were preferred because they were considered able to assimilate much more quickly.' This immigration wave was large enough and sufficiently different enough to provoke prejudice. Some members of existing Jewish communities were also apprehensive about this second wave of immigration fearing that it would bring an outbreak of anti-Semitism in Australia (Gouttman, 2005; Rubinstein, 1986, 1987; Rutland, 1988).

The period since 1940 has been marked by an increasing assertion of both Jewish difference and the necessity for tolerance towards this difference. The Jewish community has been one that has benefited from the acceptance of multiculturalism in Australia in the early 1970s. According to Rutland, this new philosophy of tolerance has 'encouraged the development of Jewish culture, of the Yiddish and Hebrew languages, and has allowed the community to be open about its unique cultural heritage' (1988, p. 370). This changing philosophy has resulted in an expanded participation by the

Jewish community in Jewish institutions, clubs, synagogues and especially day schools. The establishment and growth of Jewish day schools has been instrumental in asserting Jewishness in the face of assimilationist forces. According to Goldlust (1993), nearly 65% of Melbourne's Jewish children were enrolled in Jewish day schools in the early 1990s. Within Jewish communities, there are also a variety of institutions, clubs and organisations that contribute to the maintenance of some form of Jewish identity in the Diaspora. The response has also included the development and expansion of Jewish studies at university level including teacher training, Jewish community and political organisations, Jewish media and Jewish museums (Rutland, 1988, pp. 365–381).

The development of Jewish sporting clubs in Australia spanned the change from assimilation to assertion of Jewishness. Many of these sporting clubs grew out of a desire to assert and protect Jewish identities from total assimilation, whilst maintaining a 'harmonious relationship with the wider society' (Hughes, 1999, p. 381). The *Jewish rule* in these clubs explains that non-Jews are not permitted to play. The justification for this exclusion is that sport is seen as an important site to knit the Jewish community together and reassert a separate Jewish identity in the Diaspora (Kaufman, 2005). Further, as Kaufman (2005, p. 147) (also see Borish, 1999 regarding Jewish womanhood) explains the development and practice of a Jewish sports identity would be important in 'repudiating the biases surrounding the Jew's alleged physical inferiority' through the creation of the 'New Jew' and 'muscular Judaism' in the contemporary world.

3. METHODOLOGY

Interviews were conducted with a representative sample of Maccabi basketball players, parents, coaches and administrators. We employed a qualitative method so as to enable the elicitation of the interpretive frameworks used by the people we interviewed (Denzin, 1989; Lincoln & Guba, 1985). Other data was gathered by means of observations and field notes made over the extended period that one of the authors acted as a coach for the Maccabi basketball club. In addition, both authors have spent hundreds of hours observing matches and training sessions and have thus established credibility among the participants of the sport of basketball.

Our observations, led to a working hypothesis that participation in the sport of basketball was a means of expressing Jewish identity for young female basketball players. The interview data was gathered by interviews with a purposive sample of 20 coaches, parents and administrators. Subjects were asked a set of open-ended questions that probed their interpretations of the Jewish community, the importance of sporting participation in the Jewish community, and the specific importance of participation for young Jewish women. Interviews were transcribed in full and then analysed following the steps outlined by Lincoln and Guba (1985) and Miles and Huberman (1984). The research was constantly shaped and reshaped as the data was collected and analysed, and new aspects of the study emerged from interviews and observations (Erlandson, Harris, Skipper, & Allen, 1993 Erlandson et. al. 1993).

At the same time, it is important to note that neither of the authors are well versed in Jewish religion, culture or history. The research project grew out of the perception by the coach-author of the significance of basketball participation in developing an athletically female Jewish identity, and the common desire amongst the parents of the players that basketball/sporting participation could protect their daughters from some dangerous social and sexual practices that were engaged in by many adolescent females in the community. The naiveté of the authors regarding this community required constant methods of checking. Different methods were used in order to establish trustworthiness, such as the use of thick descriptions, triangulation and peer debriefing.

4. DISCUSSION

Because our sample was drawn from a very small community basketball club, we have used the concept of identity amalgams to protect the individual identities of our informants. This was thought to be particularly important when utilising comments from parents in the closely knit Jewish community in Southern Melbourne. These amalgams are made up of comments from a number of different interviews, but the comments selected reflect general ideas that emanated from a number of sources. We hope that no individual informant will be able to be identified through the selective quotes that have been used.

4.1. Female Identity Issues in Jewish Basketball

The elite junior basketball league in Victoria, Australia conducts its competition on Friday evenings. Thus, many talented Jewish junior basketball players find themselves excluded from this elite league without an option to compete at that level, unless they choose to abandon parts of their religion and custom. Regardless of how strictly an individual observes the Sabbath, many Jewish players and coaches expressed some conflict over being required to play a sport on the Sabbath:

> in terms of basketball ... all the junior kids play the top league games on Friday nights. So it does ... if they want to observe *Shabbat* then they can't play at that level, and it starts preventing them from going further.

One of the authors has a long-term coaching role with the Maccabi basketball club. The coach is not Jewish. He was brought into the club 10 years ago by the then club president to offer a level of expertise in coaching to the junior girls program. The Maccabi sports programs regularly employ coaches from outside of the Jewish community to instruct the players. According to a number of administrators, this is justified in the basketball program to compensate for the inability of the club to offer opportunities for its players in the elite-level Friday night junior competition.

On arrival at the club, a standing joke made by a number of the parents was that the author-coach would be making the world safe from the JAPs. The author had no idea what the parents were talking about until one parent kindly offered that the term JAP was short for Jewish Australian Princesses. With further questioning, the parents made the following observations:

> We love our daughters, as do all parents in the community ... But it is difficult to get them to commit to anything. They are concerned with shopping, parties, dressing up and hairstyles ... They are pampered and spoilt. We have given our children everything and we have sacrificed much to do so.[2] Many parents may compensate for their absences in their children's lives by providing them with luxuries. But in so giving, we have produced a generation of children that do not work hard, do not commit ... It will have a long-lasting effect on the survival of our community.

The final comment explained a concern that was widely voiced amongst parents at the basketball club 10 years ago – the children were not committed to the welfare of the Jewish community in the ways that the parents and grandparents had been. Whilst the parents and grandparents had built both wealth and status within the Melbourne region, the children did not appear to want to attach to much more than the social side of Jewish-Melbourne female identity. The parents, and the broader community, were concerned about the ongoing existence of the Jewish Diaspora in Melbourne. They saw their children's attitudes as being dangerously hedonistic, and hoped that sporting participation might turn their daughters away from the sex and drugs that was available to them as young, middle to upper class, adolescent members of society.

The term, 'Jewish Australian Princesses' continues to be frequently used by parents at basketball but is now used as a term of derision for those Jewish girls who are not involved in Jewish sports teams or cultural activities. The disdain associated with the term captures the anxiety that many Jewish parents feel about their daughters. It was expressed by one group of parents in the following way:

Q: Why is your daughter's basketball participation important to you?

A: If my daughter gives up her basketball, then she will spend her Saturdays at the shopping centre with the other JAPs ... Wasting her time and money buying clothes and accessories ... And she will get into trouble without sport- she will want to take drugs, drink alcohol and go to parties like some of her school friends ... At least at basketball, we know she is safe. She may not have a future as a basketballer, but at least she will survive her teenage years.

One of the parents who offered these insights also stated that this concern is probably shared by parents of young women from several non-Jewish private schools across Melbourne. She felt that young, middle to upper class, females in private schools had to withstand the same forces towards consumption and dangerous behaviour that the Jewish children do. However, she then went on to add that the concern regarding individual behaviour is amplified in the Jewish community by the concern regarding the ongoing survival of that Jewish community. She lamented that many of the girls who her daughter had grown up with in basketball, and who had now retired, spent most of their leisure time 'drinking vodka and chasing boys at Chadstone,' a major shopping mall near Caulfield, or 'doing Chaplaps,' a reference to parading up and down Chapel Street, another major fashion strip shopping area in Melbourne.

The community has been active in addressing the assertion of Jewish identity in a number of ways. The Jewish day schools always rate highly in terms of educational results and outcomes. This success leads to a strong presence of Jewish academic, political and business leaders in the broader community. Moreover, the Jewish day schools promote studies of Jewish achievement, language, community and history within their curricula.

Further, as Hartman and Hartman (2003, p. 38) explain:

Jewish identity is strengthened during adolescence and young adulthood by exposure to non-formal Jewish educational experiences, such as participation in Jewish youth groups (Cohen, 1988), Jewish camp (See, for example, Ettenberg & Rosenfield, 1989) or the college-level Jewish organizations, all of which foster cognitive knowledge, behavioural experience and affective attachments to Jews and Jewish heritage.

Whilst we are fairly certain that the basketball club has not fostered a great deal of cognitive knowledge about Jewish heritage, it has been active in the promotion of Jewish identity amongst the junior players. The author-coach, along with most of the non-Jewish crowd at some teams' games, is regularly amused and confused by communication amongst the players in Hebrew. This may involve calling plays or motivational cheers at the commencement and conclusion of play. The basketball club has also become a major Jewish community body with large crowds of Jewish children attending and cheering for the senior teams in the club, and with results and photos regularly appearing in the Jewish media.

The basketball club (and most other sporting clubs) has flourished with the increasing assertion of Jewish identity. The number of junior girl's teams and players playing for Maccabi basketball club has increased by 500% over the 10-year involvement with the club. One of the reasons for this increase has been the desire expressed by a number of parents to produce a strongly athletic identity amongst Jewish girls:

> I used to hate going to watch my daughter play and train. Players would turn up for training in jeans or dresses-gear that was inappropriate for sports. They couldn't bend to pick up the ball because their jeans were too tight. Or they couldn't jump because their skirts would fly up. Or they wouldn't run because sweating ruined their make-up. And their parents would dress them this way and convince themselves that their daughters were being active and healthy... Now, with the increased focus on health and sports at Jewish schools, parents expect their daughters to engage fully and expertly in sports. There is no longer the 'Jewish excuse'- our girls are uncompetitive because of their genes. Jewish parents now expect their daughters to be proud of their athletic skills.

4.2. Importance of the Jewish Sporting Community in Melbourne

Many of our older informants explained a changing position for sport in the Orthodox and Progressive Jewish day schools over the last few years, which reflected the increasing importance of sport to the assertion of Jewish identity. All of our informants had gone to Bialik or Mount Scopus, the two largest Jewish Day Schools in Melbourne. Whereas they thought that previous generations of students had not had sport promoted within the curriculum because of an emphasis on academic achievement, all of our informants argued that the day schools they attended had begun to promote sporting achievement as an important part of a holistic education. One of the largest Jewish day schools, Bialik College had recently built a $AU 14 M sports centre that is (Jewish) community sports oriented, and is used as the main stadium for the Maccabi basketball club. Many of the female basketball players engage in sporting carnivals against other private schools in metropolitan Melbourne.

The wider Jewish community had also taken up this tentative endorsement of sporting participation as worthwhile practice to promote a distinct Jewish identity that was not threatening to, and perhaps successful within, mainstream Australia, as well as being an exciting and achievable point of identity attachment for Jewish youth. An official of the basketball club expressed the wider purpose of Jewish basketball in the following way by conveying what an opposition coach had said about Maccabi teams:

> A lot of people fear our club a little bit because we are close-knit ... There are not a lot of community-based clubs in the league ... The aspect of the club that I like the most is that its community-based ... It brings our community closer together which is very important. As a community we need to stay together ... There are a lot of Jewish people in Victoria, 45,000 Jewish people ... and a number of them do not attend Jewish schools, sometimes because of the cost of private school fees and sometimes for other reasons. Maccabi basketball is a community club that allows all Jewish people to be part of the community through sport.

Another common theme that emerged from our informants was that they all displayed great pride in being in a Jewish sporting team. Some saw the Jewish team as a place to find companionship and comfort, utilising the symbolic imagery of the State of Israel. Again, several informants contributed to the following sentiment:

> *Q:* Do you think it's important to have a Jewish team?
>
> *A:* Definitely. Definitely. Somewhere that ... Even if you don't make the top team, you're welcome to play, you can get a game, in a team, because you're Jewish. I guess it's like, if I can draw a parallel, it's kind of like, Israel, you know. Somewhere to go where it doesn't matter who you are or where you're from. If you're Jewish you've got somewhere to go and just be amongst other Jewish people ... But in Australia, it is sometimes hard to maintain Jewish identity, especially with young people. Maccabi provides you with sport. It provides you with social ... And it's a pretty good mix. Especially with the younger age-groups. So sport is important.

With the success of the Maccabi sports clubs and their Jewish players and teams come some negative consequences. The Melbourne Jewish community has recently had to deal with three significant incidents involving racial attacks on members of the community. In 2006, a court case involved members of the Ocean Grove football team who, whilst on an end-of-season football trip, had vilified and physically struck an Orthodox Jewish father, Menachem Vorchheimer in front of his two children, and stolen his *yarmulke*. And recently, two Caucasian men struck two Jewish adolescents, one with a baseball bat, whilst shouting 'Aussie pride,' on Carlisle Street outside Glick's takeaway food shop, a popular meeting place for Jewish adolescents (Singer, 2007). According to Asquith (2004, p. 407), physical acts of hate violence against Jews occur in only one percent of crimes. It is much more common to experience anti-Semitic hate crimes as threats of violence and intimidation. It is also common to experience these hate crimes at Jewish community organizations and places of worship through the internet or as graffiti. In 2007, cricketers from two local suburban clubs had published anti-Semitic comments about the Maccabi cricket club on a *Facebook* social networking webpage. In Australian society and Australian sport, it is becoming more difficult for minority ethnic groups to express their identities in a secure way without evoking violent responses from the mainstream community. In the recent era of social nationalism, 'wedge' politics and neo-assimilationism (Bulbeck, 2004; Greenfield & Williams, 2003; Brett, 2004), the assertion of a strong minority identity carries with it the danger of being considered 'un-Australian,' and being confronted with a violent response by white nationalists. Asquith explains that Jews, and some other groups of people in Australia, live their lives constantly aware that their identity and practices allow them to be marked as separate from their wider mainstream communities, and that this separation may be violently reinforced in the form of 'hate' crimes. Hence the lives of members of these communities are lived with a sense of terror and fear (2004, p. 401; see also Rutland, 2006), such that many minor forms of harassment are ignored for fear of encouraging more violent responses.

The Maccabi basketball club is identified/identifiable as a Jewish community organisation. In conversations with a group of non-Jewish basketball coaches who coach the Maccabi junior girls' teams, there was a general experience of some anti-Semitic behaviours, comments and attitudes. Many of the coaches had experienced the euphoria of opposition teams' parents on beating a Maccabi/Jewish team. And for these coaches, all of who had widespread coaching experience with a number of non-Jewish teams, none had witnessed these overt displays in any other environment of coaching. It was summed up after one game for one coach when a parent from a rival team was overheard expressing great delight in 'whipping the Jews.' One administrator relayed the following:

> Two parents on the scorebench had heard a young female player from an opposition team say, 'fuckin' Jew,' during a game against Maccabi. The parents reported this to a Maccabi club administrator, who was also at the game. The administrator went over to the opposing coach and advised him that the Maccabi club would be putting in a formal

complaint about the comments. After the game the opposition player denied that she had used those words and said she said 'dirty little rat'.[3]

Eventually the matter went to a formal tribunal. In her response prior to tribunal the player again denied what she said. And then all of a sudden the player and her coach stated that her comment was 'if only it had been fucking true,' and that this was in response to a bad umpiring decision. The player's version of events was not accepted by the tribunal, and she was found guilty of vilification.

When she was questioned at tribunal she said this was her first season at this particular basketball competition and her brother, who was the coach of the team, was also in his first season. Both people claimed that they had never heard of Maccabi and didn't know they were a Jewish club. The Maccabi club then went to the competition administrator and asked for the player's registration information to confirm her claim that it was her first season in the competition. The competition administrator refused to give this information to the club, as he was concerned about issues of privacy. The Maccabi club had to go to the statewide organising body for junior basketball in Victoria to get the administrator to release this information. Apparently the player had been playing in this competition for several seasons. When the offending player was challenged at a second tribunal hearing she denied having said it was her first season.

The administrator of the Maccabi club said that she realised that such protestations would draw claims from other people that the Jewish groups are whinging again. Yet this incident was not the first time that a Maccabi player had been racially vilified by either opposing players or parents at this competition. At the same time, several of the Maccabi club administrators felt that local sports organisations, such as those that had run the competitions that Maccabi football and hockey teams had played in, went out of their way to accommodate the special demands of the Jewish athlete, and were to be commended for their tolerant attitudes.[4]

5. CONCLUSION

The aim of Maccabi Australia is 'to promote Jewish identity through sporting, culture, Zionist and social activities' (Hughes, 1997, p. 384). Sport plays an important role in identity promotion and maintenance in the Jewish community, and is especially important in reproducing community identification for Jewish youth. This aim, according to members of Maccabi, is achieved both by exclusivity, and by sporting achievement in mainstream sports. As one of our informants so eloquently explained:

I think it's important that the community has a team because, we want to unite and stay together and also to show that we can be competitive, we are not disadvantaged, because we are from a different religion or race so … yeah, that's very important.

Given the popular contemporary stereotypes that are attached to the Jewish community by some members of the dominant white Anglo-Celtic population, and especially to Jewish female identity, the twin hopes of protection of a Jewish cultural identity and development of an able and esteemed Australian-Jewish female sporting identity, which is not viewed as deficient, is 'very important.' As with Morgan's (1998) explanation of the importance of the victories of the Algerian Islamic female distance runner, Hassiba Boulmerka, at the Olympics and the World Championships, elite Jewish basketball participation may both breakdown stereotypes held about Jewish females by other subgroups in society, and allow Jewish females to see themselves as strongly athletic. However, more important than identity issues according to our respondents, is the belief that sporting participation for young adolescent females may keep them safe from some of the social and sexual practices that are available to their non-playing peers.

NOTES

1. Assimilation, intermarriage with non-Jewish people, and the loss of Jewish identity remain a major concern for the Jewish community, to the extent that the Victorian Anti-Discrimination Tribunal permitted an exemption from the Equal Opportunities Act 1995, to allow Miss Ann Ivamy-Phillips to refuse to provide the services of her introduction agency to people who refused to identify themselves as Jewish. The judgement was based on the acceptance of the argument that Jewish family life was critical to 'the preservation and transmission of Jewish religion and traditions, and for the preservation of Jewish identity' (AIP Consultancy No. 2, 1998).

2. After two years of coaching one player, the author-coach approached the adult who was regularly at games and training and said, 'your daughter is really improving.' The adult replied: 'I'm the nanny. Her parents work very long hours to pay the school and sporting fees.' Whilst such a situation is rare, although not isolated, in the Maccabi club, it is still the only experience of this situation that either author has had in 25 years of coaching.

3. This was interesting in itself, as the player had resorted to the type of maledictive hate speech that pathologizes 'the other' (Asquith, 2004). Perhaps a combination of the two quotes would have expressed the players feelings best— '"fuckin" dirty little Jewish rat.' This combines a 'loathing of a too visible other' with a pejorative naming of the otherness (Asquith, 2004, p. 410).

4. In contrast, the Maccabi club asked for the movement of a final match of one of its teams because a girl's *bat mitzvah* was going to clash with her final. The chief administrator of the competition suggested that the girl should change the time of her ceremony. A Maccabi official responded with the following e-mail correspondence:

> For your future information, Batmitzvahs are planned at least 2 years in advance and take place during the course of a regular Sabbath Service (Saturday in our religion). It is

a hugely important day for the immediate and extended family and a time for great celebration. They involve not only the 200 or so invited guests but the entire congregation of the synagogue. Therefore it is not possible to change the time.

The administrator was also reminded that this team agreed to a previous fixture change because of an opponent's Catholic first communion ceremony.

ACKNOWLEDGEMENT

This chapter emanated from part of a larger project that is being supported by VicHealth (Victorian Health Promotion Foundation, a statutory body established by the Victorian State Parliament). The larger project is investigating participation and leadership issues for girls and women in Victorian basketball programs. The author would like to thank VicHealth for funding this study.

REFERENCES

AIP Consultancy No.2. [1998] VADT 2 (28 August 1998). Viewed on March 13, 2006 at www.austlii.edu.au/cgi-bin/disp.pl/au/cases/vic/VADT/1998/2.html

Asquith, N. (2004). 'in terrorem; "with their tanks and their bombs, and their bombs and their guns, in your head. Journal of Sociology, 40(4), 400–416.

Beecher, S. (1999). The treasure chest of diversity: Contemporary Australian Jewish women respond to feminism. Australian Feminist Studies, 14(30), 267–280.

Borish, L. (1999). An interest in physical well-being among the feminine membership': Sporting activities for women at young men's and young women's Hebrew associations. American Jewish History, 87, 61–93.

Brett, J. (2004). The new liberalism. In: M. Robert (Ed.), The Howard Years (pp. 74–93). Agenda, Melbourne, Australia: Black Inc.

Bulbeck, C. (2004). The "White Worrier" in South Australia: Attitudes to multiculturalism, immigration and reconciliation. Journal of Sociology, 40(4), 341–361.

Cohen, M. (1988). Australian Jewry: An overview. Viewed on 17 May, 2007, from www.jewishaustralia.com/communityhistory.htm#communal

Dacy, M. (2002). Brief history of Australian Jewry. Viewed on 20 May, 2007, from judaica.library.usyd.edu.au/histories/History.html

Denzin, N. (1989). Interpretive interactionism. Newbury Park, CA: Sage.

Dufour, L. (2000). Sifting through tradition: The creation of Jewish feminist identities. Journal for the Scientific Study of Religion, 39(1), 90–106.

Erlandson, D., Harris, E., Skipper, B., & Allen, S. (1993). Doing naturalistic inquiry- A guide to methods. California: Sage.

Goldlust, J. (1993). The Melbourne Jewish community: A needs assessment study. Canberra: Australian Government Publishing Service.

Gouttman, R. (2005). Was it ever so? Anti-Semitism in Australia 1860–1950? In: B. Penny (Ed.), *Bigotry and religion in Australia, 1865–1950, Humanities Research* (Vol. XII, No. 1) Canberra, Australia: ANU E-Press.

Greenfield, C., & Williams, P. (2003). 'Limiting politics: Howardism, media rhetoric and national cultural commemorations. *Australian Journal of Political Science, 38*(2), 279–297.

Hartman, H., & Hartman, M. (2003). Gender and Jewish identity. *Journal of Contemporary Religion, 18*(1), 37–60.

Hughes, A. (1997). The Jewish community. In: P. A. Mosely, R. Cashman, J. O'Hara & H. Weatherburn (Eds), *Sporting immigrants* (pp. 103–115). Crows Nest, Sydney: Walla Press.

Hughes, A. (1999). Sport in the Australian Jewish community. *Journal of Sport History, 26*, 376–391.

Kaufman, H. (2005). Jewish sports in the Diaspora, Yishuv, and Israel: Between nationalism and politics. *Israel Studies, 10*, 147–167.

Lincoln, Y., & Guba, E. (1985). *Naturalistic inquiry.* Newbury Park, CA: Sage.

Miles, M., & Huberman, A. (1984). *Qualitative data analysis: A sourcebook of new methods.* Thousand Oaks, CA: Sage.

Morgan, W. (1998). Multinational sport and literary practices and their communities: The moral salience of cultural narratives. In: M. McNamee & S. Parry (Eds), *Ethics and sport* (pp. 184–204). London: E & FN Spon.

Rubinstein, W. (1982). *The left, the right and the Jews.* Canberra, Australia: Croom Helm.

Rubinstein, W. (1986). *The Jews in Australia.* Melbourne, Australia: A.E. Press.

Rubinstein, W. (1987). Introduction. In: W. Rubinstein (Ed.), *Jews in the sixth continent* (pp. 1–21). Sydney, Australia: Allen & Unwin.

Rubinstein, W. D. (1991). *The jews in Australia: A thematic history. Volume 2: 1945 to the present.* Port Melbourne, Australia: William Heinemann.

Rutland, S. (1987). The changing role of women in Australian Jewry's communal structure. In: W. Rubinstein (Ed.), *Jews in the sixth continent* (pp. 101–126). Sydney, Australia: Allen & Unwin.

Rutland, S. (1988). *Edge of the Diaspora: Two centuries of Jewish settlement in Australia.* Sydney, Australia: Collins Australia.

Rutland, S. (2006). Negotiating religious dialogue: A response to the recent increase of antisemitism in Australia. In: E. Coleman & K. White (Eds), *Negotiating the sacred: Blasphemy and sacrilege in a multicultural society.* Canberra, Australia: ANU E-Press.

Singer, M. (2007). Students assaulted in fascist attacks on Carlisle Street. *Australian Jewish News Online*, August 19. Viewed on 20 May, 2008 at www.ajn.com.au/news/news.asp?pgID = 3929

Zaidman, N. (1996). Variations of Jewish feminism: The traditional, modern, and postmodern approaches. *Modern Judaism, 16*(1), 47–65.

PACIFIC (WHITE) MULTICULTURALISM: RUGBY, PACIFIC PEOPLES, AND THE EGALITARIAN MYTH IN NEW ZEALAND

Andrew Grainger

ABSTRACT

In their very make-up the New Zealand national rugby team, the All Blacks, suggest that this erstwhile British-outpost has now arrived in what may be dubbed the 'postcolonial Pacific present.' In particular, the team could be read as denoting a (new) New Zealand in which its Pacific peoples are no longer marginalized in the national space, a symbol of the way in which Pacific peoples no longer occupy the position of the cultural 'other.' In this chapter, however, I propose that the discursive construction of the All Blacks is indicative of a phenomenon which I wish to call 'Pacific multiculturalism.' Adapted from Ghassan Hage's (Hage, 2000) notion of 'white multiculturalism,' Pacific multiculturalism not only softens the otherwise sharp edges of cultural difference, but serves to disguise persistent racial inequality and tension within the nation. Simultaneously the All Blacks engender a kind of cultural amnesia (Behdad, 2005) that

Social and Cultural Diversity in a Sporting World
Research in the Sociology of Sport, Volume 5, 141–165
Copyright © 2008 by Emerald Group Publishing Limited
All rights of reproduction in any form reserved
ISSN: 1476-2854/doi:10.1016/S1476-2854(08)05010-3

circumvents the question of history and thus perpetuates contemporary oppression. Notably, they do so not *by eradicating difference, by constructing a (false) sense of common national unity. Instead the All Blacks' version of Pacific multiculturalism functions through more liberal, inclusionary, pluralistic, and fragmentary cultural practices. Borrowing from Mackey (1999), it is my contention that the discourses of New Zealand identity, as embodied by the Al Blacks, make room for both erasures* and *inclusions. I conclude by suggesting, however, that difference is only ever incorporated in a way that preserves the (white) status quo. Pacific multiculturalism places the dominant (white) culture in a position of greater import because it suggests non-white cultures function only to 'enrich' the white, cultural core. In Ang's (2001) terms Pacific multiculturalism is built on the seemingly paradoxical process of racialization through "inclusion by virtue of othering" (p. 139).*

Writers on sport ... automatically put what was unpleasant out of sight even if they had to sweep it under the carpet. The impression they created was one of almost perpetual sweetness and light

– C. L. R. James, *Beyond a Boundary*

Culturally speaking, New Zealand has never been so self-aware, so unashamed, of itself as a 'Pacific nation' as it is today. Among statisticians and demographers 'browning' has become a popular reference to the fact that, as an 'ethnic group' (to use official parlance), the 'Pacific population' is growing at a rate far in excess of their 'European' counterparts. By 2021 the Pacific population is projected to grow by some 59 percent over 2001, while the proportion of Pacific peoples[1] is estimated to rise from 6 percent to 9 percent of all New Zealanders (Statistics New Zealand, 2006). Beyond the numbers and the statistics, that New Zealand is "becoming browner" (Macfie, 2005, p. 42) is also evident in how the country is both defining, as well as projecting, its cultural identity. The recent "'efflorescence' of things Pacific" (Teaiwa & Mallon, 2005, p. 210) has provided the grounds for what academic Misatauveve Melani Anae describes as the "infiltration of a Pacific identity at a national level" (Anae, 2004, p. 92). This is well-reflected in the arts, music, television, film, and literature – all areas where Pacific peoples are making major, and highly visible, contributions (for further discussion see Anae, 2006; Teaiwa & Mallon, 2005). The influence of Pacific culture has also "surfaced in institutional contexts" (Anae, 2004) including education, research and government departments and policy. Little wonder, then, that renowned photographer Glenn Jowitt should offer this vision of how New Zealand should promote itself to the world: "I think that representing 'us' as Polynesia is the way to go" (quoted in Smith, 2005, p. 22).

The list of New Zealand's Pacific people who have made their mark at regional, national and international level also provides a telling example. Though the machinery of state is slowly widening the gap between Pacific peoples and (so-called) 'mainstream' New Zealanders, at the ideological level 'Pacificness' is being allowed to flourish. We could point to, for instance, Scribe's seven Tui Awards, Ben Lummis' crowning as *New Zealand Idol*, the wildly successful animated series *bro'Town*, or the fact that a record 210,000 recently turned out for Auckland's Pasifika Festival. For some, Pacific peoples are "changing the face of New Zealand" (Smith, 2005, p. 22). And, for me there is no better example of the growing (cultural) prominence and significance of Pacific peoples than the appointment of Ionatana Falefasa 'Tana' Umaga as the captain of New Zealand's national rugby side, the All Blacks.

The first Pacific person to be named as such, Umaga was roundly hailed at the time as "a fitting reflection of New Zealand society" (Kayes, 2004a, p. 14). Certainly, he was an apt choice given the national game has been dominated in recent years by players of Pacific descent (his role in a team with "a predominantly brown look about it" wrote one columnist, "always seemed to be a logical choice" (Singh, 2006). Multiculturalism aside, at the same time Umaga neatly symbolized other tenets deeply ingrained in the New Zealand psyche. It is significant in the way it played out the myth of classless egalitarianism which remains one of the core elements of New Zealand's national identity (Consedine, 1989; Nolan, 2007). Alongside this egalitarian ideal, it has become commonplace to believe that racism has no place in New Zealand, that it applies to other societies, but *not here*. Umaga's becoming captain was this color-blind, egalitarian narrative writ large: born in the working-class suburb of Wainuiomata to parents who had immigrated from Samoa, he has become, despite the "odd stumble and fall from grace" (Kayes, 2004a, p. 14), one of New Zealand's most recognized and respected sportsmen, attracting "the same publicity usually afforded the prime minister and other high-powered celebrities" (Rees, 2005, p. 25).

On one level the beatification of Umaga could well be read as a sign that Pacific peoples are no longer marginalized in the New Zealand national space, that they no longer occupy the position of the 'other.' More likely, however, it reflects New Zealand's desire to see as an inclusive, multicultural nation. That is, it has less to do with celebrating Umaga, than celebrating ourselves. To borrow from Anagnostou (2003), Umaga is an example of how:

> To tell stories of ethnic success is to speak about the nation in all its benevolence and generosity. National ideologies such as ... mobility, openness, and inclusiveness come to life any time the nation's Others claim socioeconomic achievement (p. 279).

Umaga, I wish to argue, can be read as an apparent vindication of what Chock (1991) dubs the "myth of opportunity." And, as an "opportunity story" (Chock, 1991), he serves an important ideological function. First, as a tale of national redemption, a way of forgetting the racially-charged 'dawn raids' and expulsions of the past (see de Bres, 2005; Spoonley, 1981, 1990). And, second, his story represents what Ang (2001, p. 98) calls a "public fiction" that implies New Zealanders "live in a harmonious ... and peaceful country where everyone is included and gets along." That is, through Umaga the national subject can be interpellated as tolerant.

There is too a further ideological consequence of this myth. If New Zealand society in the popular imagination provides the unfettered opportunity for upward mobility, if the barriers once facing ethnic minorities have been removed, then equality of opportunity for all New Zealanders becomes a given. If individual talents, motivations, and morals account for social statuses, then the failings of minorities are purely their own (McNamee & Miller, 2004). This type of liberal individualist myth suggests difference is not an obstacle to achievement, abrogating the real structural constraints that affect minority socioeconomic mobility, and ignoring "current inequalities that fall primarily along racial lines" (Ebert, 2004, p. 174). In assuming an open, race-neutral context, the egalitarian narrative reinforces the current racial order, "suppressing a plain dealing and unsentimental consideration of the continuing constitutive role of processes of racialized and ethnicized othering" in contemporary New Zealand (Ang, 2001, p. 139).

And, this, I argue, is where rugby enters the scene. That New Zealanders still hold fast to the illusion of being an democratic, egalitarian society, without hierarchies entrenched in race or inherited privilege, has much to do with the continual invocation of a history of diversity and tolerance – something marred only by 'exceptional' events in a less-enlightened past. Such myths are structured and reproduced through variegated and temporally extended representational strategies, narrated, obscured and embodied in various elements of public culture. The narrative construction of the past can be found in a variety of materials; in texts, objects, monuments, landscapes, and images. And, of course, to this list we should add sport. As Nauright (2003) argues, "the nostalgic use of sport and the history of sport has been one of the most significant areas in the process of sustaining identities and solidarity through shared experiences of heroic deeds in specific societies" (p. 38). Sport is also imbued with a contemporary relevance, in that the sporting past is frequently drawn on to "legitimate a present social order" (Nauright, 2003, p. 35).

Against this symbolic power of the All Blacks, in this chapter I would like to offer a different reading. Rugby, I will argue, for all its cosmopolitanism, often serves to obfuscate deeper ethnic schisms. Beneath the united façade of Pākehā[2] men playing side-by-side with their Māori[3] and Pacific Island brethren, rugby is not nearly as inclusive as Kiwis would like to, or have been led to, believe. Though rugby may offer a context where New Zealanders can engage on mutual terms, it gives lie to the fact that the acceptance of Pacific peoples as fully fledged Kiwis is far from unanimous. Rugby is neither immune to the discourses of race and nation: they are always there, struggled over and occasionally erupting. In Gilroy's (1991) terms it could be argued that rugby is an "important site on which the limits of the nation as well as its character are routinely established" (p. 62). As such, the ideas of national belonging and ethnicity that it maps out are a window into the "ambivalent kinships" that have marked the Pacific migrant experience (Teaiwa & Mallon, 2005, p. 207). As much as rugby turns "the ethnic into the national" (Anagnostou, 2003, p. 279) it generates messages bearing significant ideological contradictions, creating feelings of both belonging and alienation, and revealing a fundamental unease with the growing cultural prominence of Pacific peoples. However much they may have succeeded in rugby, Pacific peoples remain an ambiguous presence in New Zealand.

RUGBY: THE GAME FOR ALL NEW ZEALANDERS?

To begin, it is important to first trace the rise of what could be called the 'rugby mystique.' By this I am referring to the way in which rugby has come to be seen, to borrow the title of Peter Bush's best-selling tribute to the sport, *The Game for All New Zealand* (Bush, 1989). In many ways it is remarkable that this is the case. Rugby began, after all, as the sport of an elite. As Dunning and Sheard (2005) have shown, in its distinguishing form, rugby emerged in the milieu of the English Public School System during the early 1800s. And, it would remain a sport played and administered by a relatively homogeneous upper-middle class well into the 1870s. Rugby arrived in New Zealand in the context of these class-bound origins. Here too it began among the elite. As Crawford (1986, p. 151) has argued, the "games cult" and the influence of muscular Christianity was transferred to the prestigious boys schools of New Zealand, in doing so creating a mystique that made the good "games player" a privileged person in society.

However, though clearly transported from English public schools by old boys to New Zealand, rugby in the new colony "spread quickly through other social classes" (Phillips, 1987, p. 90). As During (1998) observes, "What in England was mainly an upper-class game ... became in New Zealand a symbol of mateship, intrepidness, colonizer-colonized reconciliation. All this without the game losing its imperialist aura" (p. 35). Why the exclusive nature of the English game did not reproduce itself in New Zealand has been the subject of some debate (see Ryan, 2004). One oft-posited theory is that rugby provided an important basis for social integration in a nascent settler society (Crawford, 1985, 1986; Fougere, 1989; Perry, 2004, 2005). According to Erik Olssen the structure of rugby "allowed ethnic, religious and local loyalties to be expressed yet transcended them" (Olssen, 1992, p. 284). Geoff Fougere (1989) has similarly written of how "rugby tied together the collection of localities and provinces into a national body" even before New Zealand "had anything resembling a national market, or even a very effective national state" (p. 12). As he writes,

> what is achieved through rugby is the symbolic uniting of men over and against all of the differences of background, occupation, education, income, experience and belief that otherwise divide them. This vision of male comradeship is not imposed from above, but built painstakingly from the level of the local club through provincial and national levels ... At the peak of this structure, giving final definition to its meaning and purpose ... the national team—the All Blacks. (Fougere, 1989, p. 116)

Perry (2005) notes that in this way "distinctions between social classes, between town and country, between regions, between colonizers and colonized, were both dramatized and bridged" (p. 158).

Implicit here is the suggestion of rugby's (purported) classlessness; something that fit with New Zealand's image of itself as 'a working man's paradise' (to use the words of one erstwhile Prime Minister). As True (1996) notes, into the early-twentieth century "it was common for the people of New Zealand to be told by successive governments that they were a 'classless society'" (p. 112). If England was home to inequality, then in New Zealand it found its counter. Rugby moved to the center of this egalitarian myth. Echoing the pioneer community Crawford (1986) argues, "rugby was appropriate for, and complimentary to, a New Zealand community forged by a democratic press of 'mateship' and familiarity." The word 'mateship' here is worth noting. Mateship, which Mulgan (2004) defines as "the peculiarly colonial ideal of male solidarity and friendship" (p. 42), is a kind of fraternal egalitarianism deeply invested with connotations of communality. It came to be a signifier of the ideals shared by men living closely together in the harsh conditions of the frontier. Rugby, like colonial life, appeared hospitable to a rough-and-ready egalitarianism and the pioneer disdain for authority and commitment to pragmatism. As the novelist Lloyd Jones writes,

> In New Zealand, the sport [rugby] reinforced the vision of the classless and inclusive society. And in a society that had still to build its infrastructure, every pair of hands had its use. Much the same applies to the game of rugby. (Jones, 2003)

Rugby thus became a way through which (Pākehā) men came to understand themselves as a settler society within a domestic culture grounded in the rigors of the colonial life, rather than as an English satellite.

Today, rugby writers – 'rugby journalists' in particular – have been essential in facilitating and perpetuating this egalitarian myth. In the best-selling book *How to Watch a Game of Rugby* Spiro Zavos reflects on how

> Most New Zealand males, from erudite scholars to burly shearers, have experienced the dying fall of the light after a hard match and the linament-scented mateship of the dressing room. It is one of those tribal experiences that has helped to create that unique and underrated species, the New Zealand man. (Zavos, 1998, p. 118; see also Zavos, 2004)

Elsewhere, Zavos writes of his own experience:

> The sports arena was my path, perhaps my only way, to respectability and self-knowledge. Thinking about this, I realized that sporting achievement is—or should be—colour blind, because it is (or should be) focused on what a person does, not his or her background, culture, class, religion or looks. Kids who try to make it in society through sport, know this instinctively. (Zavos, 1997, pp. 77–78)

The former All Black Chris Laidlaw writes similarly of how "the secret of most of New Zealand's rugby success this century has been a simplicity of approach; a focus on essentials and an innate self belief by individuals who have had to make it on the basis of their own personal effort" (Laidlaw, 1999, p. 185).

Professionalism has subsequently, and in many ways, put paid to this myth of rugby as the game of the 'everyman' (Romanos, 2002; Ryan, 2005; Thomas, 2003), yet it has not affected the popular view that the game is nonetheless meritocratic. Perhaps this is unsurprising given that the perceived virtues of a meritocracy still hold firm sway in New Zealand. Liu (2005) has noted how New Zealand holds liberal-democratic values, anchored in ideals of freedom and equality, as central to nationhood. This has particular salience to race, where the predominant (Pākehā) view has long been that "all New Zealanders were 'one people' who enjoyed some of the best race relations in the world" (Macdonald, 2004, p. 218). McCreanor (1993) has referred to this normative account of New Zealand race relations as the "standard story":

> The standard story of Māori/Pākehā relations ... says that Māori/Pākehā relations are the best in the world ... Mutual respect for each other's strengths and tolerance for idiosyncrasies has integrated the Māori people into a harmonious, egalitarian relationship with the more recent arrivals, the whole thing working constructively for the common good. This narrative explains Māori failure as due to their inability to cope in the modern world because of inherent flaws in their character or culture (p. 61).

Rugby has played a critical part in sustaining this narrative. Like McCreanor notes more generally, central in this regard to rugby is the role of played by Māori. From the game's very inception in New Zealand the achievements of Māori rugby players have been "celebrated by Pākehā as solid evidence that the country was indeed a paradise of racial harmony" (Belich, 1998). Symbolically, Māori participation in rugby "became proof of assimilation, co-operation and racial harmony" (MacLean, 1999, p. 14), helping to "establish in Pākehā eyes a myth of racial integration" (Phillips, 1987, p. viii). Their participation, especially at the national level, "provided affirmation for the then dominant ... belief that race relations in New Zealand were among the best in the world" (Watson, 2007, p. 783).

To be sure, the race-rugby-nation homology has been frequently undermined – particularly by New Zealand rugby's problematic relationship with South Africa, and especially the divisive 1981 Springbok Tour to New Zealand (Chapple, 1984; Richards, 1999; MacLean, 1998, 2000). Academics, and occasionally even members of the mainstream media (see, e.g., *Sport a mirror of society*, 2006), have also exposed the rugby myth for what it is: precisely that, a *myth* (Ryan, 2005). Recent scholarship, in particular, has challenged the received understandings of rugby as an agent of national and racial integration. Ryan (2005) is particularly wary of the way rugby was perceived to be a 'level playing field.' He notes how the New Zealand Rugby Football Union (NZRFU) distanced itself from fixtures between Māori and touring sides by only according them 'unofficial status.' Watson (2007) makes a similar observation, suggesting "the NZRFU was, at best, ambivalent in its attitude towards Māori rugby between 1870 and 1914" (p. 785). Ryan also questions the belief that rugby was even widely played by Māori in the late-1800s. Finally, while MacLean (1998, 1999) suggests that a crucial element of the relations of symbolic power of a "singular New Zealand" was the inclusion of Māori as 'just like us,' he argues that incorporation has been decidedly ambivalent. For MacLean, the national hegemonic identity "suggests a number of areas of contention centerd primarily on the contradiction between hegemonic masculinity as incorporating Māori and colonial relations that exclude Māori" (MacLean, 1998, p. 24).

BROWN BOYS IN THE BACK-LINE: ON THE PROPER USES OF 'PACIFIC' ALL BLACKS

Often, however, myth is more important than reality. The accuracy of the 'rugby story' has obviously mattered less than the way the game functions as a symbolic display of bicultural partnership. As Francis (1997, p. 174) reminds us, when it comes to core national myths, "literal truth" has never been "a measure of their power or their usefulness." In a Barthesian sense, the myth is more palatable because it does not question the prevailing structures of power. Of course, to mention Barthes is to also recognize the *ideological* work of 'myth.' The myth is posited as the normal state-of-affairs, legitimating the status quo, suppressing difference. In rugby there is a familiarity proceeding from history, in that, for New Zealanders it affirms and promotes the supposed racial democracy in which they live. It should also be mentioned that race relations in New Zealand have, of late, taken something of a beating in New Zealand. Many were embarrassed by the 2006 report of UN special rapporteur Rodolfo Stavenhagen which concluded that "persistent disparities" continue between Māori and non-Māori, and that many of these were consistent with "a history of discrimination" (Stavenhagen, 2006; for further discussion see Mutu, 2007). Hence, the rugby myth today takes on an added ideological burden: as Francis (1997) notes, even if "the myths we have used to explain our history no longer make much sense," in an "age of anxiety" we revert to them like something of an "habitual tic," a "nostalgic hankering for the past rather than an accurate understanding of it" (p. 174). Because it is one of the country's 'central myths' – a story that seems to express a fundamental belief that New Zealanders hold about themselves – the deceptive idea of Māori and Pākehā being partners "in the scrum and wider society" (Brabazon, 2006, p. 182) has not died easily. As one reporter for the UK's *Guardian* rhetorically (and sardonically) asked: "Māori do very well, don't they, in all walks of life? And look at the All Blacks! New Zealand and the Māori, they're pretty much OK, aren't they? No big issues there" (Henley, 2007). What critical analysis there has been of the maintenance and perpetuation of this (false) image has largely concerned the deep contradiction between the wholesale (mal)appropriation of *tikanga* Māori and the fact that, in Stavenhagen's words, the "gap in social and economic conditions is actually growing larger and an increasing proportion of Māori are being left behind" (Stavenhagen, 2006): that is, critics continue to problematize rugby via its complicity in the depoliticization of culture, or what Fish (1997) may have called 'boutique [bi]culturalism.' Without wishing to dismiss nor diminish either the relevance or import of such work, the continued focus on the bicultural context of New Zealand identity politics would seem to deny the symbolic and representational rights of other minorities. Can those groups that are neither Pākehā nor Māori continue to be "frozen out of the debate on the identity and future of the country" (Thakur, 1995, p. 272) given the increasing cultural and ethnic diversity of New Zealand's population? This is a particularly salient question for rugby when Pacific people now account for more than 30 percent of New Zealand's professional rugby players. How can a New Zealand of "multicultural drift," the process, as Stuart Hall may have described it, whereby images of Pacific people are slowly pulled into the mainstream of representation (Hall, 2000, p. 29), be reconciled with a New Zealand still struggling with the "unfinished business" of Māori-Pākehā relations? (Kothari, Pearson, & Zuberi, 2004, p. 139). More pointedly, does the increasing visibility of Pacific people interrupt the flow of rugby's dominant narrative discourse as a compact between two 'founding cultures'?

On these lines, I wish to discuss what I herein call 'Pacific multi-culturalism.' Best exemplified in rugby, Pacific multiculturalism is first and foremost a form of multiculturalism that softens the otherwise sharp edges of cultural difference. Difference is incorporated into the national imaginary but only in a way which occludes or minimizes specific political activisms and their histories. More pointedly, in drawing on and reinforcing 'ethnic' difference it does so in a hierarchical way: while it provides an appa-rently more inclusionary construction of New Zealand national identity, it mobilizes difference as part of the crisis-management of monoculturalism. In the very celebration of their difference the All Blacks sideline bicultural anxieties and, ironically, perpetuate an unmarked and normative New Zealand (read Pākehā) ethnicity. For all the rhetoric, rugby is as much a conduit of division as an agent of integration and change. Beneath the united, multicultural façade, rugby is not nearly as inclusive as Kiwis would like to, or have been led to, believe. This is especially true with regard to Pacific peoples whose involvement in the national game continues to evoke feelings of ambivalence among both Māori and Pākehā alike (Teaiwa & Mallon, 2005).

Arguably, Pacific All Blacks have become every bit as powerful as Māori once were in projecting an image of acceptance. The successes of Pacific peoples in rugby are appealing in the way they offer faith in the New Zealand way of life, in the myth of egalitarian society. As journalist Gregor Paul describes the Pasifika contribution to New Zealand rugby: "as feelgood stories go, the happy marriage of cultures into the rugby fabric is hard to beat" (Paul, 2007). The parallels are striking here to the critical analyses of North American critics who have noted how the sporting successes of African Americans have been used to "reinforce an argument that the US is an open society, and that blacks are improving their economic and social positions" (Wonsek, 1992, p. 457). The high-profile successes are relatively few, but nonetheless they suggest African Americans can, and regularly do, achieve both economic success and upward social mobility. The implication is not only that sport is a space devoid of racial discrimination, but so is society more generally. Such thinking has long been echoed in New Zealand. Hokowhitu (2004b) elaborates on the New Zealand case, with particular regard to Māori:

> In a neoracist age, the overriding tenets of positivist discourse are egalitarianism, democracy, and social equality–the predetermined conclusions of an advanced and civilized western world. The successful Māori sportsman ... acts as an exemplar of a subject in an egalitarian state who has triumphed over adversity to succeed; combine this with the common notion that sport reflects society, and the essential suggestion is that Māori men are afforded equal opportunities in all walks of life (p. 271).

The situation is arguably little different for Pacific peoples, where those succeeding in the Pākehā world of rugby seem to prove that Pacific people at least have equality of opportunity.

In key socio-demographic indicators, however, and particularly education, occupation and income, there remain significant disparities between Pacific peoples and other New Zealanders. These social and structural factors are regularly effaced in favor of emphasizing the individual achievements of a small number of high-profile Pacific athletes. Recently, for example, Umaga was lauded by the popular media as living proof of the mythological Kiwi meritocracy. Much was made of his rise to prominence, despite hailing from the "unfashionable" (Kayes, 2004b, p. D6), "working class" (Harding, 2004, p. 18) suburb of Wainuiomata. "Tana Umaga" writes one biographer, "could have been just another statistic – the son of immigrant parents born on the wrong side of town with no hope of success, let alone greatness" (Matheson, 2006). "Through nothing but hard work," he continues, Umaga was able to "[turn] his career around to such an extent that his legacy now rests comfortable alongside the likes of Sir Wilson Whineray, Sir Brian Lochore, Graham Mourie and Sean Fitzpatrick – the All Blacks' greatest ever captains" (Matheson, 2006). The power of Umaga's image was in its suggestion that anyone in New Zealand could 'make it,' regardless of class or ethnicity. As Anthony Hubbard notes also of Umaga: "Conservatives can promote him as a sign of equal opportunity. The son of poor immigrants leaps to the top in our open society – from Wainuiomata to the White House" (Hubbard, 2006, p. C1).

The presence, as well as the success of Pacific peoples in rugby should not, though, be mistaken as evidence of the abatement of racist attitudes toward Pacific peoples in New Zealand. This is hardly surprising, for as Grant Jarvie reminds us, "such accounts of sport which make general inferences about the changing nature of racial relations in society based on a consideration of athletic participation rates" are misleading in their tendency to ignore "the broader issues of power and domination within society" (Jarvie, 1991, p. 3). While Pacific peoples may have been breaking into rugby in recent decades, they continue "to be depicted in all the wrong places: hospitals, courts, ghettos, welfare offices and prisons" (Loto et al., 2006, p. 103). They remain too at, or near, the bottom of all socio-economic measures, including education, housing, employment, income, and health (Ministry of Pacific Island Affairs, 1999, pp. 8–9; Statistics New Zealand, 2006). Moreover, the greater numerical involvement of Pacific peoples does not mean that rugby itself is non-racist. As Robyn Jones argues, "a situation that results in the presence of significant number of an ethnic minority people in the higher echelons of a sport is as indicative of racist social processes as if they were absent from it" (Jones, 2002, p. 47). Certainly, akin to the stereotyping of Māori (Hokowhitu, 2004a, 2004b), Pacific players continue to be stigmatized as "savage, emotionally impulsive, aggressive, and violent" (Hokowhitu, 2004b, p. 266).

A FORGETFUL NATION? WHITENESS AND PACIFIC MULTICULTURALISM

As in the past when the contributions of Māori to All Blacks successes "provided comforting evidence of New Zealand as a racially integrated society" (Phillips, 1987, p. 286), rugby today therefore works in such a fashion as to sustain its central place in the national imaginary precisely because of its continued efficacy as a symbol of social integration. Today, though, this is increasingly achieved through recourse to a partial history, via excising rugby's connections to a racist past (we forget, for instance, that Māori were barred from All Black tours to South Africa in 1928, 1949, and 1960). It holds a flattering mirror up to us that erases every distortion. Denuded of the complexities and complications of (real) history, rugby has become the model of a prospective future by way of a retrospective turn. Supposedly in rugby we can see how things have *always been* (a space of equal opportunity), how things *are* (proof of co-operation and racial harmony), and how things *could be* (a sign of our multicultural future). Demonstrating such political use of 'rugby nostalgia,' Laidlaw (1999) writes:

> differences between the races have always been set aside for rugby. It is a fascinating point of convergence for Māori, Pākehā and Pacific Islander; one of the few real bridges between each of the cultures. The romance, the legends, the folklore of the great matches and the great players are not a Pākehā monopoly. *They belong to all* (p. 22; emphasis added).

Such fantasies are typical of how rugby has provided a continuity and connection with past achievements, glories, and heroes in national culture – a culture that historically links it to war, mateship and, perhaps most importantly, racial tolerance. Within the national narrative rugby provides a symbolic reassurance that, as in the past, egalitarianism and opportunity are still alive in contemporary New Zealand.

Simultaneously the All Blacks also allow us to forget the past. They engender a kind of cultural amnesia that circumvents the question of history and thus perpetuates contemporary oppression. Behdad (2005, p. 23) argues of the United States that it is an "amnesiac nation;" a nation built on a "historical amnesia" that enables it to disavow a past and present built on the exclusion of others. This echoes Ernest Renan's famous description of how the political project of founding a nation often entails an act of forgetting, an erasure of those elements that might threaten the coherence of the national narrative (Renan, 1990). Those things which must be forgotten are not necessarily confined to the past but exist in the present: forgetting functions in both the diachronic and synchronic sense (Bhabha, 1994). What the All Blacks allow us to forget in the present is perhaps obvious: the real conditions that most Pacific peoples face – that Pacific peoples are, to use the words of the Ministry of Social Development "over-represented in all negative socio-economic statistics." What is forgotten in the past is the racial vilification of Pacific peoples during the 1970s and the way in which they were cast as outsiders, 'overstayers,' and a burden on 'real' New Zealanders. Even today something of the social stigma of once being 'undesirable' immigrants clearly persists in the discursive framing of Pacific peoples. Though they are clearly 'at home' in New Zealand, no longer 'out there' in the Pacific, one of the identifiable and recurring themes of dominant "Pākehā discourse" (McCreanor, 2005) is continued allusions to Pacific peoples as 'foreign,' as the 'Other.' References to Pacific people as 'overstayers,' 'coconuts,' 'bungas,' or 'FOBs' ('fresh off the boat') may now be a lesser feature of the New Zealand vernacular, yet as Loto et al. (2006, p. 100) have found, "the legacy of a domineering relationship between the Palagi [Pākehā] majority group and Pacific minorities that is captured by such derogatory terms is still evident in public forums such as the media." Put simply, citizenship has not been sufficient for Pacific peoples to transcend the prejudices of race.

There is an interesting parallel here to Wu's (2002) description of Asian Americans in the United as "perpetual foreigners" (p. 79). He notes that while discrimination on the basis of race is increasingly seen as immoral, the lines that distinguish 'citizens' from 'aliens' are largely considered acceptable. With Asian Americans, however, Wu contends that "it is clear that lines that appear to be based on citizenship can cover up lines that are based on race" (p. 91). By this Wu means to suggest that citizenship is always already defined by race, by whiteness, and that as a consequence

it becomes convenient to refer to the innocuous lines based on citizenship in lieu of the odious lines based on race. Non-Asian Americans can discriminate against Asian Americans by turning us into non-citizens, either officially ... or informally by casting doubt on our status. Our objection to such discrimination is obviated before it is even made, because the discrimination looks legitimate as having been founded on citizenship rather than race. (p. 91)

Regardless of their citizenship status, Pacific peoples are similarly dogged by such a "perpetual foreigner syndrome." And, even All Blacks – generally the preeminent national 'body' – are not immune. In one telling example after the All Black team for the 2003 World Cup was named a caller to a local talk back show aporetically asked, "Why in a country where we have so much rugby talent do we have to select four Samoans in the All Blacks?" (quoted in Teaiwa & Mallon, 2005, p. 213). There is unquestionably a certain contingency to a Pacific person achieving 'New Zealander' status. This is true also for Pacific All Blacks. Historically and materially, Pacific peoples have played crucial roles in the building and sustaining of

New Zealand identity. In particular, as 'immigrants' they have been "fundamental to the construction of the nation as a simulacrum of inclusiveness" (Lowe, 1996, p. 5). Yet this project of imagining the nation is haunted by the fact that Pacific peoples are still seen as 'the foreigner within,' even when born in New Zealand and the descendants of generations born here before (Lowe, 1996). They *enrich* New Zealand culture but are not *part* of it. They are only ever afforded a kind of "dependent integration" (Hage, 2000) which positions the Pākehā subject as the 'authentic' or 'normal' New Zealander.

Pacific multiculturalism, then, is akin to what Hage (2000) has labeled "White multiculturalism." For a long time New Zealand had a *de facto* 'White New Zealand' immigration policy whereas today the New Zealand government proudly touts itself as a multicultural Pacific nation. Yet White multiculturalism is a peculiar feature of dominant white groups (in this case Pākehā) that generously 'allow' others to co-exist with them. For Hage, multiculturalism is part of a "white nation fantasy" that works through "New Racist" practices that regulate and manage inclusion as a way of maintaining the white nation. As he writes,

> White multiculturalists ... share in a concept of themselves as nationalists and of the nation as a space structured around a White culture where Aboriginal people and non-White 'ethnics' are merely national objects to be moved or removed according to a White national will. (Hage, 2000, p. 18)

In New Zealand Pākehā ethnicity has similarly underpinned New Zealand culture, its institutions and the nation itself since the beginning of European settlement. Migration has undoubtedly changed New Zealand into a 'post-white' society (Hill, 2004). However, the new multicultural representations of nationhood emerging in recent years do not necessary signify a radical break with previous more exclusionary versions of nationhood. Instead Pacific multiculturalism merely reshapes and reinforces older identity discourses through recognizing limited and unthreatening forms of difference, through the containment of the "multicultural real" (Gilroy, 2005).

Politically, the popular elision of racism from rugby's past works to maintain this status quo, this Pākehā hegemony. It constitutes what Avril Bell (2004) calls "a refusal of discussion" (p. 92). As opposed to any critical reflection on colonial history, rugby draws on those mythological well-springs of New Zealand's egalitarian culture – no one is denied a place, success is open to all – as a means to "close off discussion before it can begin" (Bell, 2004, p. 92). The growing number of 'Pacific Islanders' representing New Zealand in recent years becomes proof-positive of an open, multiracial society – belying a past in which Pacific communities were subjected to dehumanizing dawn police raids and random street checks of their citizenship. In seeming to rise above the current contingencies of national race relations politics, the All Blacks offer New Zealanders what Bruce and Hallinan (2001, p. 266) may have dubbed "an easy way out." Without actually taking any action, without offering any practical approaches to dealing with *de facto* racial inequality, the continuing significance of race can be explained away and racism denied: *how can we be racist? just look at the All Blacks!* The issue of history as a site of moral wrong is sidelined in favor of a presentist fallacy of a multicultural unity in difference.

What must also be emphasized here is the way difference has long been appropriated as a defining characteristic of New Zealand. Nation-building it must be said is not simply a process of erasure. As a 'project' the nation is first and foremost a form of categorization premised on the imagining of solidarity. Numerous critics have suggested that this process is generally predicated on the construction of a common national culture, on national cultural homogeneity. That is, national identity must be seen to transcend individual and group differences. Homi Bhabha (1990), for instance, has argued that the "nationalist discourse" must suppress certain elements in its effort to construct the "impossible unity of the nation as a symbolic force" (p. 3). Linking nationalism to Western modernity and power, Bhabha continues, suggesting that "political supremacy ... seeks to obliterate ... difference." However, pace those critics who see nationalism as nearly always destructive of cultural difference, New Zealand is testament to Eva Mackey's claim that nationalism, and by implication power and dominance, may "function through more liberal, inclusionary, pluralistic, multiple and fragmented formulations and practices concerning culture and difference" (Mackey, 1999, pp. 4–5). Borrowing from Mackey, it is my contention that the discourses of New Zealand identity make room for both erasures *and* inclusions – they possess what Asad (1993) would call an "improvisational quality" that may (sometimes simultaneously) subsume, accommodate, or institutionalize difference.

Pace those who argue national identity as being "predicated on the elimination of ethnic distinctions" (Lesser, 1999, p. 3), in New Zealand difference has been pressed into the service of nation-building – and Pacific peoples are front and center in this national project. Yet this Pacific multiculturalism is a carefully managed form of difference. It appears as a negation of Pākehā ethnocentrism at the same time as it both needs and creates the 'Pacific other' That is, Pacific multiculturalism is "itself a vehicle for racialization": it establishes Pākehā culture as the "ethnic core culture while 'tolerating' and arranging others around its 'multiculture'" (Bannerji, 2000, p. 78). The "ethics and aesthetics" of Pākehāness, with its "colonial imperialist/racist ranking criteria," define and construct "the 'multi' culture" of New Zealand's Pacific others (p. 78). In other words, New Zealand's self-identity

> has been secured partly through the construction of internal Others, whose markedness assures the existence of a national identity that, remaining invisible or unmarked, is successfully inscribed as the norm ... the ethnic identity of the dominant group is privileged as the core of imagined community. (Alonso, 1994, p. 390)

Pacific people are perhaps first and foremost among the "necessary 'others'" who Mackey (1999, p. 16) suggests have become "central pillars" of an ideology of tolerance that expresses itself through the discursivities of 'difference' (multi/sub/minority/ethnic culture) and that must name 'others,' that must mark 'us' and 'them.'

CONCLUSION: THE CONTRADICTIONS OF INCLUSION

Spending any time in New Zealand one would be hard-pressed to not notice the sheer ubiquity of the 'one nation forged on a rugby field' rhetoric I allude to above. Yet in real terms there has been a growing disjuncture between rugby's social base and the characteristics of the society it purportedly represents: the expansion of the urban middle classes, the gains of feminism, the rising visibility of various Polynesian communities and the political resurgence of Māoridom all seem at odds with the traditional marriage of rugby to rural, Pākehā masculinity. But somehow rugby and the All Blacks persist as one of the more, if not the most, potent agents and symbols of national identity formation. What I have suggested above, however, is that rather than being 'a game for all New Zealanders,' contemporary rugby in New Zealand can be seen to "serve the functional needs of the dominant national group" (Triandafyllidou, 2001, p. 4). Rugby, and the All Blacks in particular, are part of the wider discourse of celebration, of claims that New Zealand, *as a nation*, has embraced the values of cultural pluralism and tolerance. As a narrative of progress, the game purportedly speaks to a "deeper truth about the new New Zealand and its people," the "exotic" nature of the All Blacks – "tattooed, dreadlocked, surnames festooned with apostrophes" (Macdonald, 2005,

p. C11) – patent recognition that Pacific peoples are officially "an increasingly large part of the New Zealand identity" (Laidlaw, cited in Hubbard, 2006, p. C2). In reality, however, to take the All Blacks as evidence of a new 'Pacific' identity for New Zealanders would be to ignore the liminal world of Pacific peoples: they live in New Zealand, are members of its civil society, yet as 'ethnics' they are never able to be fully-incorporated into the social body.

The discourse of Pacific multiculturalism ensures that they will always be different, wherein difference is measured in terms of distance from Pākehā culture. That is, diversity in fact works to sustain Pākehā power. As Wade (1998) argues,

> just as in colonial power relations the coloniser's sense of domination is fed by a narcissistic desire for the submission of the subordinate other, so the nation-builders define their own superiority in relation to the diversity they observe and construct–and desire. (p. 4)

My argument is that national belonging in New Zealand still functions according to an investment in an ethnonational 'core' (Brubaker, 1996; Mackey, 1999) around which a 'hierarchy' of New Zealandness is constructed – Pākehā of course being at the top. 'New Zealander' remains a racialized term with nation and race clearly intersecting in the bodies of Pacific peoples. This racialization operates via a model of 'normal' New Zealandness that is white and unmarked, and ultimately sustained by the exclusion-yet-retention of the foreigner, the other, within. New Zealand may no longer be a "white nation" (Hage, 2000) but the self/other divide – which, Ang (2001, p. 142) reminds us, "is the epistemological basis of the very possibility for racism" – is an inherent feature of the new Pacific multiculturalism. Forced into a place-taking politics within the dominant terms of belonging, the "structural hierarchy between majority (singular) and minorities (plural)" (Ang, 2001, p. 142) has not been nullified by the elevation of Pacific people onto the national cultural stage.

However pretty a picture the All Blacks paint, they do not stand outside the dominant hegemonic discourses of race that continue to infuse New Zealand culture. At the level of rhetoric and ideology, they project an image of New Zealand as open to diversity, the personification of the so-called liberal nation-state: rational, reflective, civic, egalitarian. They invite us, via a "discourse of enrichment" that works difference into an over-riding unity, to join in the chorus of "celebrating our national identity" (Hage, 2000). But we cannot ignore how this new Pacific multiculturalism functions as an *ideological* discourse designed to, in Ang's (2001) words, provide

New Zealanders "with a favorable, flattering, even triumphant representation of the national self" (p. 98). I emphasize ideological here in that Pacific multiculturalism is "forgetful of many things" (Behdad, 2000, p. 143), presenting the people of New Zealand "with a public fiction that they live in a harmonious, tolerant and peaceful country where everyone is included and gets along" (Ang, 2001, p. 98).

Openness to cultural difference should therefore be seen as intersecting rather than undermining New Zealand's (new) national identity. That New Zealand is, in the words of its Minister for Ethnic Affairs, a "multi-ethnic and multicultural society" has become a badge of national identity. As oxymoronic as it sounds, diversity is the means by which New Zealand constructs a unified national culture, differentiated and defined in difference to other settler colonies. The New Zealand twist in this regard is, *vis-à-vis* Australia or Canada, multiculturalism with a 'Polynesian' flavor. Rather than emulating its Pacific Rim counterparts, New Zealand has sought to emphasize what Minister of Pacific Island Affairs Phil Goff describes as "its Pacific character." "Migration from the Pacific has shaped and changed our identity as a Pacific nation," he has said in a recent speech. "The strong Pasifika community ... gives us a sense of identity" (Goff, 2007). Like Goff, other members of the Labour government are also increasingly playing up 'Pacificness' as part of what "makes us unique" (Laban, 2007). Yet this new form of Pacific multiculturalism and Pākehā dominance in New Zealand are not necessarily at odds. Pacific multiculturalism 'works' in New Zealand precisely because it contains the increasingly active role of Pacific Others in New Zealand's cultural and political life. The 'nation,' as Benedict Anderson (1983) famously reminds us, needs an ideology of unification and legitimation. Yet at the same time the cultural pluralist discourse of the All Blacks is evidence of how this ideology also needs and creates the Other: in this case, the once undesirable 'Pacific Islander' is "discursively inserted into the middle of a dialogue" of multiracial unity (Bannerji, 2000, p. 96). This introjection of belonging draws on and reinforces racial differences and hierarchies of difference (Triandafyllidou & Veikou, 2000). Pacific peoples, even as All Blacks, are never simply New Zealanders. They are, in Bannerji's (2000) terms, "pasted over with labels" that provide them with extraneous identities: Samoan, Tongan, Fijian, immigrants, Pacific peoples. For them New Zealand is always a hyphenated space, a space between two identities. The hyphen, as in Samoan-New Zealander, "links two identities together in an attempt to integrate the marginal into the dominant, while at the same time defining each as separate" (Russell, 2002, p. xviii). Only Pākehā have the privilege of being simply a 'New Zealander.' For Pacific peoples this is the paradox of belonging and not-belonging, of living in the national space while not being 'New Zealanders.' Even in rugby we see evidence of there being a cultural Pākehā core which generates a "coexistence of hostility and hospitality" (Behdad, 2005) that has been, and still is, fundamental to the construction of New Zealand's national identity.

NOTES

1. 'Pacific peoples' is the official term used by the Ministry of Pacific Island Affairs and the state sector to describe those people in New Zealand who identify as having Pacific Island origins. Pacific peoples generally includes both those born in the islands as well as those born in New Zealand.
2. Though a somewhat contentious term, 'Pākehā' is commonly-used in New Zealand to refer to a "New Zealander of European descent" (Moorfield, 2005, p. 108).
3. As Brendan Hokowhitu notes "'Māori' is a generic word that initially meant 'normal'", but it has now come – he notes, incorrectly – to represent "the tribal-based indigenous peoples of New Zealand" (Hokowhitu, 2008, p. 135).

REFERENCES

Alonso, A. M. (1994). The politics of space, time and substance: State formation, nationalism and ethnicity. Annual Review of Anthropology, 23, 379–405.
Anae, M. (2004). From kava to coffee: The 'browning' of Auckland. In: I. Carter, D. Craig & S. Matthewman (Eds), Almighty Auckland? (pp. 89–110). Palmerston North, New Zealand: Dunmore Press.
Anae, M. (2006). Samoans. Te Ara: The Encyclopedia of New Zealand, 21 December, [Online], Available at: http://www.TeAra.govt.nz/NewZealanders/NewZealandPeoples/Samoans/en
Anagnostou, Y. (2003). Model Americans, quintessential Greeks: Ethnic success and assimilation in diaspora. Diaspora, 12(3), 279–327.
Anderson, B. (1983). Imagined communities: Reflections on the origin and spread of nationalism. New York: Verso.
Ang, I. (2001). On not speaking Chinese: Living between Asia and the West. New York: Routledge.
Asad, T. (1993). Genealogies of religion: Discipline and reasons of power in Christianity and Islam. Baltimore, MD: Johns Hopkins University Press.
Bannerji, H. (2000). The dark side of the nation: Essays on multiculturalism, nationalism and gender. Toronto, Canada: Canadian Scholar Press.
Behdad, A. (2000). Founding myths of the nation, or what Jefferson and Hamilton forgot about immigration. Aztlan: A Journal of Chicano Studies, 25(2), 143–150.
Behdad, A. (2005). A forgetful nation: On immigration and cultural identity in the United States. Durham, NC: Duke University Press.

Belich, J. (1998). *The New Zealand wars and the victorian interpretation of racial conflict.* New York: Penguin.

Bell, A. (2004). Cultural vandalism and Pākehā politics of guilt and responsibility. In: P. Spoonley, C. Macpherson & D. Pearson (Eds), *Tangata Tangata: The Changing Ethnic Contours of New Zealand* (pp. 89–107). Southbank, Australia: Dunmore Press.

Bhabha, H. K. (1990). DissemiNation: Time, narrative and the margins of the modern nation. In: H. K. Bhabha (Ed.), *Nation and Narration* (pp. 291–322). New York: Routledge.

Bhabha, H. K. (1994). *The location of culture.* New York: Routledge.

Brabazon, T. (2006). *Playing on the periphery: Sport, identity and memory.* New York: Routledge.

Brubaker, R. (1996). *Nationalism reframed: Nationhood and the national question in the New Europe.* Cambridge, UK: Cambridge University Press.

Bruce, T., & Hallinan, C. (2001). Cathy Freeman: The quest for Australian identity. In: D. L. Andrews & S. J. Jackson (Eds), *Sport stars: The cultural politics of sporting celebrity* (pp. 257–270). New York: Routledge.

Bush, P. (1989). *The game for all New Zealand: Through the lens of peter bush.* Auckland, New Zealand: Moa Publications.

Chapple, G. (1984). *1981: The tour.* Wellington, New Zealand: Reed.

Chock, P. P. (1991). 'Illegal aliens' and 'opportunity': Myth-making in congressional testimony. *American Ethnologist, 18*(2), 279–294.

Consedine, B. (1989). Inequality and the egalitarian myth. In: D. Novitz & B. Willmott (Eds), *Culture and identity in New Zealand* (pp. 172–186). Wellington, New Zealand: GP Books.

Crawford, S. A. G. M (1985). The game of glory and hard knocks: A study of the inter-penetration of rugby and New Zealand society. *Journal of Popular Culture, 19*(2), 77–91.

Crawford, S. A. G. M. (1986). A secular religion: The historical iconography of New Zealand rugby. *Physical Education Review, 8*(2), 146–158.

de Bres, J. (2005). Dawn raids. *Spasifik* (7), 52–53.

Dunning, E., & Sheard, K. (2005). *Barbarians, gentlemen and players: A sociological study of the development of rugby football* (2nd edn). New York: Routledge.

During, S. (1998). Postcolonialism and globalisation: A dialectical relation after all? *Postcolonial Studies, 1*(1), 31–47.

Ebert, K. L. (2004). Demystifying color-blind ideology: Denying race, ignoring racial inequalities. In: C. Herring, V. M. Keith & H. D. Horton (Eds), *Skin deep: How race and complexion matter in the Color-Blind Era* (pp. 174–196). Urbana, IL: University of Illinois Press.

Fish, S. (1997). Boutique multiculturalism, or why liberals are incapable of thinking about hate speech. *Critical Inquiry, 23*(2), 378–386.

Fougere, G. (1989). Sport, culture and identity: The case of rugby football. In: D. Novitz & B. Willmott (Eds), *Culture and identity in New Zealand* (pp. 110–122). Wellington, New Zealand: GP Books.

Francis, D. (1997). *National dreams: Myth, memory and Canadian history.* Vancouver, Canada: Arsenal Pulp Press.

Gilroy, P. (1991). *There ain't no black in the union jack: The cultural politics of race and nation.* Chicago, IL: The University of Chicago Press.

Gilroy, P. (2005). *Postcolonial melancholia.* New York: Columbia University Press.

Goff, P. (2007). New Zealand in the Pacific, *Speech to the Young Pacific Leaders Conference,* Auckland, New Zealand, March 8.

Hage, G. (2000). *White nation: Fantasies of white supremacy in a multicultural society.* New York: Routledge.

Hall, S. (2000). Conclusion: The multi-cultural question. In: B. Hesse (Ed.), *Un/settled multiculturalisms: Diasporas, entanglements, 'Transruptions'* (pp. 209–241). New York: Zed Books.

Harding, G. (2004). Tana's the man. *New Zealand Rugby World, 72*(June), 16–22.

Henley, J. (2007). The Māori resistance. *The Guardian*, November 6, [Online], Available at http://www.guardian.co.uk/g2/story/0,,2205852,00.html

Hill, M. (2004). *After whiteness: Unmaking an American majority.* New York: New York University Press.

Hokowhitu, B. (2004a). Physical beings: Stereotypes, sport and the physical education of New Zealand Māori. In: J. A. Mangan & A. Ritchie (Eds), *Ethnicity, sport, identity: Struggles for status* (pp. 192–218). London, UK: Frank Cass.

Hokowhitu, B. (2004b). Tackling Māori masculinity: A colonial genealogy of savagery and sport. *The Contemporary Pacific, 16*(2), 259–284.

Hokowhitu, B. (2008). The death of Koro Paka: 'Traditional' Māori patriarchy. *The Contemporary Pacific, 20*(1), 115–141.

Hubbard, A. (2006). On the ball…always. *Sunday Star-Times*, January 15, pp. C1–C2.

Jarvie, G. (1991). Introduction: Sport, racism, and ethnicity. In: G. Jarvie (Ed.), *Sport, racism and ethnicity* (pp. 1–6). New York: RoutledgeFalmer.

Jones, L. (2003). Much is on the line as the All Blacks try to add to past glories. *International Herald Tribune*, 11 October, [Online], Available at http://www.iht.com/articles/2003/10/11/blacks_ed3_.php

Jones, R. L. (2002). The black experience within English semiprofessional soccer. *Journal of Sport and Social Issues, 26*(1), 47–65.

Kayes, J. (2004a). Selection of Umaga as captain another wise move by Henry. *The Dominion Post*, May 25, p. 14.

Kayes, J. (2004b). The boy from Wainuiomata the man to lead the All Blacks. *The Dominion Post*, May 28, p. D6.

Kothari, S., Pearson, S., & Zuberi, N. (2004). Television and multiculturalism in aotearoa New Zealand. In: R. Horrocks & N. Perry (Eds), *Television in New Zealand: Programming the Nation* (pp. 135–151). New York: Oxford University Press.

Laban, L. W. (2007). World Heritage Committee Meeting Pasifika Evening. 27 June, *Speech to World Heritage Committee Meeting*, Christchurch, New Zealand, 23 June–3 July.

Laidlaw, C. (1999). *Rights of passage: Beyond the New Zealand identity crisis.* Auckland, New Zealand: Hodder Moa Beckett.

Lesser, J. (1999). *Negotiating national identity: Immigrants, minorities, and the struggle for ethnicity in Brazil.* Durham, NC: Duke University Press.

Loto, R., Hodgetts, D., Chamberlain, K., Nikora, L., Karapu, R., & Barmett, A. (2006). Pasifika in the news: The portrayal of Pacific peoples in the New Zealand press. *Journal of Community and Applied Social Psychology, 16*(2), 100–118.

Liu, J. H. (2005). History and identity: A system of checks and balances for Aotearoa/New Zealand. In: J. H. Liu, T. McCreanor, T. McIntosh & T. Teaiwa (Eds), *New Zealand identities: Departures and destinations* (pp. 69–87). Wellington, New Zealand: Victoria University Press.

Lowe, L. (1996). *Immigrant acts.* Durham, NC: Duke University Press.

McCreanor, T. (1993). Settling grievances to deny sovereignty: Trade goods for the year 2000. *Sites, 27*, 45–73.

Macdonald, C. (2004). Putting bodies on the line: Marching spaces in cold war culture. In: P. Vertinsky & J. Bale (Eds), *Sites of sport: Space, place, experience* (pp. 85–100). New York: Routledge.

Macdonald, F. (2005). Tana's triumph signals payback time for the Pacific. *Sunday Star-Times*, November 27, p. C11.

Macfie, R. (2005). The future of us. *Unlimited*, April, pp. 40–52.

Mackey, E. (1999). *The house of difference: Cultural politics and national identity in Canada.* New York: Routledge.

MacLean, M. (1998). From old soldiers to old youth: Political leadership and Aotearoa/New Zealand's 1981 Springbok rugby tour. *Occasional Papers in Football Studies, 1*(1), 22–36.

MacLean, M. (1999). Of warriors and blokes: The problem of Māori rugby for Pākehā masculinity in New Zealand. In: T. J. L. Chandler & J. Nauright (Eds), *Making the rugby world: Race, gender, commerce* (pp. 1–26). London, UK: Frank Cass.

MacLean, M. (2000). Football as social critique: Protest movements, rugby and history in Aotearoa, New Zealand. *International Journal of the History of Sport, 17*(2), 255–277.

McNamee, S. J., & Miller, R. K. (2004). *The meritocracy myth.* Lanham, MD: Rowman and Littlefield.

Matheson, J. (2006). *Tana umaga: A tribute to a rugby legend.* Auckland, New Zealand: Celebrity Books.

Ministry of Pacific Island Affairs. (1999). *Social and economic status of pacific people report 1999: Navigating the currents of the new millennium.* Wellington, New Zealand: Ministry of Pacific Island Affairs.

Moorfield, J. (2005). *Te aka: Māori-english, english-māori dictionary and index.* Auckland, New Zealand: Pearson.

Mulgan, R. (2004). *Politics in New Zealand* (3rd edn). Auckland, New Zealand: Auckland University Press.

Mutu, M. (2007). Māori issues. *The Contemporary Pacific, 19*(1), 233–240.

Nauright, J. (2003). Nostalgia, culture and modern sport. In: V. Møller & J. Nauright (Eds), *The essence of sport* (pp. 35–50). Odense. Denmark: University Press of Southern Denmark.

Nolan, M. (2007). The reality and myth of New Zealand egalitarianism: Explaining the pattern of a labour historiography at the edge of Empires. *Labour History Review, 72*(2), 113–134.

Olssen, E. (1992). Towards a new society. In: G. W. Rice (Ed.), *The oxford history of New Zealand* (2nd edn, pp. 254–284). Auckland, New Zealand: Oxford University Press.

Paul, G. (2007). Pacifika players dominating ranks. *The New Zealand Herald*, March 4, [Online], Available at http://www.nzherald.co.nz/author/story.cfm?a_id = 196&objectid = 10426898

Perry, N. (2004). Boots, boats, and bytes: Novel technologies of representation, changing media organization, and the globalization of New Zealand sport. In: R. Horrocks & N. Perry (Eds), *Television in New Zealand: Programming the nation* (pp. 272–288). New York: Oxford University Press.

Perry, N. (2005). Close encounters of another kind: Nationalism, media representations and advertising in New Zealand rugby. In: S. J. Jackson & D. L. Andrews (Eds), *Sport, culture and advertising: Identities, commodities and the politics of representation* (pp. 154–171). New York: Routledge.

Phillips, J. (1987). *A man's country? The image of the Pākehā male-a history*. Auckland, New Zealand: Penguin Books.

Rees, P. (2005). Respect earned: All Black captain Tana Umaga hailed a rugby saviour in New Zealand. *PolyNation, 1*(December), 23–27.

Renan, E. (1990). What is a nation? In: H. K. Bhabha (Ed.), *Nation and narration* (pp. 17–25). New York: Routledge.

Richards, T. (1999). *Dancing on our bones: New Zealand, South Africa, rugby and racism*. Wellington, New Zealand: Bridget Williams Books.

Romanos, J. (2002). *The judas game: The betrayal of New Zealand rugby*. Wellington, New Zealand: Darius Press.

Russell, E. (2002). Introduction. In: E. Russell (Ed.), *Caught between cultures: Women writing and subjectivities* (pp. xi–xxi). New York: Rodopi.

Ryan, G. (2004). *The making of New Zealand cricket, 1832–1914*. London, UK: Routledge.

Ryan, G. (Ed.) (2005). *Tacking rugby myths: Rugby and New Zealand society, 1854–2004*. Dunedin, New Zealand: Otago University Press.

Singh, A. (2006). Farewell to the Bob Marley of rugby. *Hawke's Bay Today*, November 1, [Online]. Available at http://www.hbtoday.co.nz/storyprint.cfm?storyID = 3668045

Smith, N. (2005). The colony strikes back: Selling Kiwi culture to the mother country. *The New Zealand Listener, 201*(3421), 20–24, December 3–9.

Spoonley, P. (1981). The politics of the disadvantaged: Observations on work, race and the polynesian in New Zealand. *New Zealand Journal of Industrial Relations, 6*(2), 73–77.

Spoonley, P. (1990). Polynesian immigrant workers in New Zealand. In: C. Moore, J. Leckie & D. Munro (Eds), *Labour in the South Pacific* (pp. 155–160). Townsville, Australia: James Cook University of North Queensland.

Sport a mirror of society. (2006), *Sunday Star-Times*, June 25, p. C8.

Statistics New Zealand. (2006). *QuickStats National Highlights: 2006 Census*, 7 December, Statistics New Zealand, Wellington, New Zealand.

Stavenhagen, R. (2006). *Report of the Special Rapporteur on the Situation of Human Rights and Fundamental Freedoms of Indigenous People*, 13 March, Office of the United Nations High Commissioner for Human Rights, New York.

Teaiwa, T., & Mallon, S. (2005). Ambivalent kinships? Pacific people in New Zealand. In: J. H. Liu, T. McCreanor, T. McIntosh & T. Teaiwa (Eds), *New Zealand identities: Departures and destinations* (pp. 207–229). Wellington, New Zealand: Victoria University Press.

Thakur, R. (1995). In defence of multiculturalism. In: S. W. Greif (Ed.), *Immigration and national identity in New Zealand: One people, two peoples, many peoples?* (pp. 255–281). Palmerston North, New Zealand: Dunmore Press.

Thomas, P. (2003). *A whole new ball game: Confronting the myths and realities of New Zealand rugby*. Auckland, New Zealand: Hodder Moa Beckett.

Triandafyllidou, A. (2001). *Immigrants and national identity in Europe*. London, UK: Routledge.

Triandafyllidou, A., & Veikou, M. (2000). The hierarchy of Greekness: Ethnic and national identity considerations in Greek immigration policy. *Ethnicities, 2*(2), 189–208.

True, J. (1996). Fit citizens for the British Empire?: Class-ifying racial and gendered subjects in Godzone (New Zealand). In: B. F. Williams (Ed.), *Women out of place: The gender of agency and the race of nationality* (pp. 103–128). London, UK: Routledge.

Wade, P. (1998). Music, blackness and national identity: Three moments in Colombian history. *Popular Music, 17*(1), 1–19.

Watson, G. (2007). Sport and ethnicity in New Zealand. *History Compass, 5*(3), 780–801.

Wonsek, P. L. (1992). College basketball on television: A study of racism in the media. *Media, Culture and Society, 14*, 449–461.

Wu, F. H. (2002). *Yellow: Race in America beyond black and white*. New York: Basic Books.

Zavos, S. (1988). In praise of rugby. In: M. King (Ed.), *One of the boys? Changing views of masculinity in New Zealand*. Auckland, New Zealand: Heinemann.

Zavos, S. (1997). *Winters of revenge: The bitter rivalry between the All Blacks and the Springboks*. Auckland, New Zealand: Viking.

Zavos, S. (2004). *How to watch a game of rugby*. Wellington, New Zealand: Awa Press.

GAMES OF SELF-RESPECT:
A COLONY AT THE OLYMPICS

Boria Majumdar and Nalin Metha

> There are so many communities, so many different religions, so many languages and
> dialects, so many different customs and ideals, that it is almost impossible to select a
> national team.
> — Sir Dorabji Tata, President IOA, 1929

India was the first colonised Asian nation to take part in the Olympic
Games. Its embrace of the Olympic movement, while still a British colony,
was no mere coincidence. It was intricately linked to the forces of
nationalism, the politics of self-respect and indeed the inculcation of what
has been called the British 'Games Ethic' among Indian elites. Colonial
India's early Olympic encounter was born out a complex interplay of all
three factors and it forms a crucial missing link in the story of Indian
nationhood. Historians now widely recognise the important role played by
sport in the creation of identities and social imaginaries. Indeed it is now
widely recognised that Japan, the only Asian country, with a longer Olympic
history than India's, embraced Olympism partly because of a deep rooted
desire to showcase Japanese modernity after the Meiji Restoration and to
take on the 'West' on equal terms. Olympism became so important for
modern Japanese identity that when Tokyo bid for the 1940 Games it went
so far as to tie its candidature to the celebrations of the "2,600th anniversary
of the Japanese empire" pulling out all the stops in an aggressive diplomatic
campaign that split European nations down the middle. While campaigning
for Tokyo's bid for the 1940 Games, Count Soyeshima Michisima, Japan's

Social and Cultural Diversity in a Sporting World
Research in the Sociology of Sport, Volume 5, 167–191
Copyright © 2008 by Emerald Group Publishing Limited
All rights of reproduction in any form reserved
ISSN: 1476-2854/doi:10.1016/S1476-2854(08)05011-5

delegate to the IOC, convinced Mussolini to withdraw Rome's candidature largely on the back of the claim that 1940 coincided with the 2,600th anniversary of the *Kigen*. Baron Yoriyasu saw Tokyo's victory in the Olympic race as affirmation not just of Japan's athletic progress but as proof that "renascent Japan has advanced in worldly and grand terms" (Collins, 2006, pp. 1132–1133). Tokyo's emotional gambit, combined with some smart cultural hard-sell, succeeded when Mussolini withdrew Rome's bid. Though the 1940 Games never took place, the politics of Japan and the 1940 Games provide a fascinating study of just how central sport can become for nationalistic identity making (Collins, 2006). In this context, in India, a number of historians have finely documented how the imperial game of cricket became an arena for colonial Indians to fight for political recognition (Guha, 2002; Cashman, 1979; Bose, 1990). Yet, despite its great importance, cricket never gave 'India' – the nation – any significant international triumph until well after independence. It was in Indian hockey, and in the Olympic Games, that the nationalist aspirations of colonial India found full expression. This chapter draws out the pre-history of how this came to be so, of why colonial India embraced the Olympics and why the still nascent and obscure Games started by a Swiss aristocrat in 1896 became so important for the creation of a nascent Indian identity.

The history of Indian sport can only be understood in light of the fact that sport was always inculcated as a crucial binding factor in the British Empire. Forged in the nineteenth century by traders, military officers, missionaries and proponents of 'muscular Christianity', the bond of sports was not only maintained and extended by the governing circles, but carefully cultivated among a selective section of the population through informal forms of exchange rather than authoritative imposition. Sports became a source of considerable cultural power, conveying through its different forms a moral and behavioural code – the Games Ethic – to connect and unite the far-flung British territories in Asia, Africa, the Caribbean, North America, Oceania, and of course, the British Isles. The introduction of all organised Western sports in India, from hockey to cricket to soccer, can all be traced to this idea. It took until 1920 for India to participate in the Olympic Games and no formal institutional mechanism for supporting Olympic sport was established in the sub-continent till the early 1920s. But by the mid-1920s, driven by nationalist enterprise and princely patronage, India's Olympic structure was well in place.

The Indian Olympic Association (IOA) as we know it today was formed in 1927. It was the second oldest national Olympic Association in Asia after Japan, which was established in 1912. A strong Indian contingent participated in the Amsterdam Games of 1928 winning India her first gold medal in hockey in the very first year of official participation. A precursor to the IOA had been formed in 1923 with the same name and it had served the Olympic cause for three years till 1926 before being shut down. At a time when nationalist sentiment in India was gaining pace, the Olympics were the only international arena where Indian-ness could be projected in the sporting field. India's participation in the Olympics, from the 1920s, was an important watershed for the politics of colonialism. Indians went to participate in the Olympics, on equal terms with the British, at time when the colony was not even invited to the first British Empire Games (1930) (later Commonwealth Games) in Canada (Moore, 1989). Apart from Bermuda, British Guyana and Newfoundland, only the white settler dominions of Australia, South Africa and New Zealand were invited to the first Empire Games. The organisers even paid for the costs of athletes from the white settler dominions and the exclusion of non-white athletes from big colonies, despite India's success at the Olympic Games meant that the Empire Games were fraught with tension.[1] The decision to prohibit India from competing at the first British Empire Games ignited angry demonstrations from both the pro-British aristocracy and the nationalist middle classes.[2] India never participated in the Commonwealth Games until independence in 1947 and it is well documented that it was partly the chance to compete in the Games that persuaded Prime Minister Nehru to keep India in the Commonwealth. The Games helped provide an arena for nationalist ambition and anti-colonial sentiment and while they extended imperial cultural power, they also offered an opportunity for the once subordinate and colonised to 'beat the master at his own game.' This was now true for the African, Asian and Caribbean Commonwealth as it already was for the white settler dominions like Australia, Canada and New Zealand.

This chapter documents the origins of Olympism in India and what it meant for India, for the British Empire and for the global Olympic movement. As a movement led by nationalist elites and princes, the early story of Indian Olympism is also the story of a global league of upper-class elites, connected through patronage networks in Europe, who passionately pushed the Olympic ideal. Until the 1920s, the Olympics were largely a Euro-centric enterprise, but India's embrace of Olympism in the 1920s was also simultaneously accompanied by a powerful push for diffusing the Olympic ideal in Latin America and South-East Asia. As this chapter will show, in all three cases, the same strategy was followed: the use of the global network of the Young Men's Christian Association (YMCA) and the co-option of local elites with enough private resources and European contacts to liaise with the Olympic movement's center. In that sense, the origin of Olympic sport in India that this chapter documents is a missing piece in the global story of Olympism. In a Europe divided by war, the IOC pushed this expansion as a strategy for survival and in India the ideal was appropriated by elite nationalists as a new avenue for self-respect, modernity and identity politics in the sporting arena. Olympism came to India as part of the processes of globalisation, decades before the term itself became fashionable. But once it was initiated, it was appropriated by and became inseparable from the forces of nationalism to begin with, and the centrifugal regional tendencies thereafter.

"100 YARDS ROUND A BEND" TO ANTWERP: PEASANTS ON THE ATHLETIC TRACK

To Sir Dorab Tata goes the credit of starting systematic Olympic activity on Indian soil in 1920. The son of the pioneering nationalist steel baron Jamsetji Tata, Dorabji was intimately involved in fulfilling his father's idea of creating an indigenous and modern steel industry in India. He is widely credited with the establishment of the Tata Steel Company in Jamshedpur that became India's largest private enterprise of the time. Simultaneously, in the great tradition of Parsi philanthropists in colonial India, some of his most valuable contributions (greatest contributions) came as a benefactor for sport, culture and education. For instance, the Sir Dorabji Tata Trust funded the provided the seed money to fund the setting up one of India's premier scientific and engineering research institutions, the Indian Institute of Science, Bangalore. Before taking an interest in Olympism, Sir Dorabji had already played a key role in the establishment of school and college cricket in Mumbai in the 1880s. Till the 1890s the structure of cricket in Mumbai educational institutions was 'crude and indefinite'. It was under Sir Dorabji's initiative that the move to form the Bombay High School Athletic Association gathered momentum. Determined to eliminate differences of caste and creed on the sporting field, he wished to unite local clubs and inculcate notions of 'fair play' among young boys. At first, the success of the scheme seemed doubtful as there was a question mark over whether European schools would join in such a union. However, with the elite Cathedral School joining hands with Sir Dorabji, the Association came into existence in 1893 and initiated the famous Harris Shield tournament in 1896.

It is now the oldest surviving inter-school cricket tournament in India and it has been nursery for many Indian cricketers, most prominently Sachin Tendulkar and Vinod Kambli. It was in a Harris Shield game that Tendulkar first hit the headlines when he shared a world record partnership of 664 with Kambli. The Association also propelled the formation of cricket clubs in each school and ensured appointment of coaches, which served the dual purpose of providing employment to veteran cricketers, while also promoting the game. A principal obstacle that Sir Dorabji and his men faced was the paucity of playgrounds in late nineteenth and early twentieth century Mumbai. To redress this, a games fee was levied in most high schools, but in order to safeguard the interests of poorer students, students from modest backgrounds were exempt from this. With aristocratic and upper-class patronage coming their way, many schools revoked the levy in course of time (Majumdar, 2004; Polishwala, 1921).

Sir Dorabji was largely educated in England and his interest in sport was largely a product of his Western upbringing, which exposed him to the period ideology of athleticism and the 'Games Ethic'. The Games Ethic saw sports as a form of moral education and was central to the ideology of English education at the time, in public schools and in universities. It was the key to the socialisation in metropolitan Britain of the future administrators and conquerors of the Empire (Mangan, 2001; Stoddart, 2006).This concept of sport as an element of cultural power may also be set in the wider context of a strong theoretical literature emanating largely from the work of Antonio Gramsci whose analysis of hegemony shifted the Marxist analytical emphasis from the economic base to the cultural superstructure. Gramsci showed how even severe deprivation could not easily shake the belief of the masses in values shared with the ruling groups and conditioned by cultural attitudes formed in the superstructure. In that sense, sport was central to the British imperial setting as a powerful but largely informal social institution that could create shared beliefs and attitudes between the rulers and ruled while at the same time enhancing the social distance between them. It was seen as such a powerful cultural edifice that Cecil Headlam could write of cricket in 1902:

First the hunter, the missionary, and the merchant, next the soldier and the politician, and then the cricketer-that is the history of British colonisation...The hunter may exterminate deserving species, the missionary may cause quarrels, the soldier may hector, the politician blunder – but cricket unites, as in India, the rulers and the ruled. It also provides a moral training, an education in pluck, and nerve, and self restraint, far more valuable to the character of the ordinary native than the mere learning by heart of Shakespeare or an essay of Macaulay which is reckoned education in India.[3]

This was the underlying philosophy behind the colonial policy of most sports and of course, "it is wise to appreciate that there was no culturally monolithic response to attempts to utilise sport as an imperial bond ... the nature of interpretation, assimilation and adaptation and the extent of resistance and rejection" varied (Mangan, 1992). But there is no doubt that the appropriated virtues of athleticism, as taught in the British public school, were in turn reformulated by the educated colonial middle classes and subsequently imposed upon the masses. In Sir Dorabji's words:

> Having been educated in my youth in England I had shared in nearly every kind of English Athletics and acquired a great love for them. On my return to India I conceived the idea of introducing a love for such things there. I helped set up with the support of English friends, as General Secretary, a High School Athletic Association amongst numerous schools of Bombay, in the first place for cricket, and then for Athletic Sports Meetings which embraced nearly all the events which form part of the Inter-University contests every year in London.[4]

Adopting a game also meant adopting the entire paraphernalia of modernity that went with it. It didn't just mean playing a foreign game, it also meant adopting European clothes, European rules and European notions of order and 'fair play'.

Sport became the playing field where tradition and modernity met, clashed and fused. A good example here is that of the Deccan Gymkhana. After the successful start of the Harris Shield, the idea was modified in Pune with the creation of the Gymkhana. The committee, which ran the Gymkhana, was not conversant with the details of managing such Athletic meetings on European lines and wanted to develop their sports programme more in line with established Indian traditions. Sir Dorabji, who was nominated the President of the Gymkhana, played a central role in the meeting of foreign and indigenous cultures that ensued. At the first athletic meet the Gymkahana organised, Dorabji found that the competitors were "all boys of the peasant class working in the fields and living off poor fare ... ".[5] Naturally they had no idea of European rules or modern training of any kind. On attending a meeting of the Gymkhana, Sir Dorabji found that they were proposing to run their 100 yards heats round a bend without strings. This was because their sports ground was very small and the track was part of a rough unrolled grass field. To the peasants, running was running, but now it had to be undertaken under standardised and controlled conditions. In Sir Dorabji's letters on the subject, preserved at the International Olympic Museum, the one thing that strikes the reader most palpably is his sense of wonder at this clash of peasant and Western cultures in the races at the Deccan Gymkhana.[6]

Other popular events included the long distance race of about 25 miles, rightly designated the Marathon. The peasants who participated were used to running bare feet on hard macadamised or dirt roads. Despite their lack of training and the primitive conditions, the first three or four men ran the distance in fair time. As Sir Dorabji observed, their time "would compare well with the times done in Europe or elsewhere."[7] In 1919 some of their times were close to the times clocked in the Olympics. Suitably impressed, the Tata scion decided to send three of the runners, even at his own expense, to the Antwerp Games of 1920. This was the birth of India's Olympic encounter and nationalist sentiment was at its core. As Dorabji Tata described his motives in a personal letter to the IOC President Count Baillet Latour in 1929:

> I therefore offered to arrange for the sending of three of the best runners to Antwerp to run the Olympic Marathon at the next meeting, when I hoped that with proper training and food under English trainers and coaches they might do credit to India. This proposal fired the ambition of the *nationalist element* in that city to try and send a complete Olympic team.[8]

But the peasant athletes had little idea of what was required to participate in the Olympics nor of the standard of performance essential to qualify for any of the events. For instance, a key member of the Gymkhana when asked what time he thought was standard for a 100-yard race replied that it could be anything "from half a minute to a minute". He was "astounded" when told that it was not a matter of minutes but rather of tenths of seconds.

Despite their naivety on the rules of modern sport, Deccan Gymkhana members were all fired up by a strong nationalist imagination to send a team to the Olympics and started raising subscriptions to finance a team to Antwerp and set up an Indian Olympic Association. It seems that despite the enthusiasm of the organisers, public money at this early stage was not too forthcoming. This meant that India's first tryst with international sport came to be financed largely by a combination of money from Tata, sundry princes, public collections – these increased substantially in later years – and interestingly, the Government of India. Apart from Tata's own correspondence, a report published in *The Statesman* substantiates this point. The secretary of the Bombay branch of the proposed Indian Olympic Association sent the editor of the daily a letter appealing for support. The letter mentioned that a batch of six amateur athletes had been selected by a committee presided over by Mr. H.G. Weber and were soon to set sail for Antwerp by the Steamer 'Mantua' under the supervision of Dr. A.H. Fyzee, India's national tennis champion. The cost of the adventure was estimated at Rs. 35,000 rupees of which only Rs. 18,000 had been collected so far. Of this, the Government of India contributed Rs. 6,000, apart from helping to secure a passage for the touring party. The great cricketer, the Jamsaheb of Nawanagar, Ranji, was expected to represent the country at the Olympic Council in Belgium and he too had assured the team all possible assistance. *The Statesman* report ended with an appeal to the public to contribute to India's Olympic cause. Contributions were to be sent to the Secretary of the Indian Olympic Association located at Pragmahal in Bombay (The Statesman, 1920). The public response though was lukewarm. In the end Sir Dorab personally bore a great deal of the expenditure, apart from taking a keen personal interest in selecting the participants.[9] In return for his munificence he was asked to become president of the proposed Indian Olympic Association and head the Indian cause at the meeting of the International Olympic Committee in Europe.

India's hurriedly put together Olympic contingent hardly created an impression at Antwerp and, by extension, in India. A good barometer of this is the fact that the Olympic Games barely merited a mention in Indian newspapers. If it did, it was only in the nature of one-line news briefs. Sample this one-line update, probably inserted by a sub-editor at Calcutta's *Amrita Bazar Patrika*: "In catch-as-catch-can wrestling (featherweight) at the Olympic Games, Bernard (Britain) best Shimpe (British India) in 19 seconds."[10] Little else is known about the men who represented India at Antwerp but what one thing is certain: the Indian athletes did not do well and did not catch the nationalist imagination as their backers had hoped. As is clear in the preceding paragraphs, the six or seven athletes who traveled to Europe had little idea about modern sport. Moreover as Dorabji Tata recounts, there was plenty of discord among them, leading to a series of unpleasant incidents.[11] Tata, who was not in good health, only visited Antwerp briefly to meet his colleagues at the International Olympic Committee. On account of an ailing health he did not find time to witness the games or meet the Indian contingent. India's first appearance at the Olympics in Antwerp ended in sporting failure but the very fact that the athletes reached there was an achievement. At least, the journey had begun.

'INDIA' GOES TO PARIS

Not overtly concerned with the failure at Antwerp, India once again entered a team at the Paris Games of 1924 and this time the nine-man contingent was better organised. If the contingent for the Antwerp Games was more the result of a locally driven initiative, spearheaded by Tata and his experiences at the Deccan Gymkhana, by this time a truly national effort had developed. The team for Antwerp had been selected largely by Tata after seeing some local runners in Pune. Now, for Paris, the Indian team was selected after rigorous screening of athletes at what was called an "Olympic Games" in Delhi. These were the first "national" congregation of Indian athletes in any organised form. In the words of A.G. Noehren, leader of the Madras YMCA and Secretary of the newly established Indian Olympic Association, the Delhi "Olympic Games" were a

> unique contribution made to the country...and it is fair to state that these have been far more successful, have created a wider interest throughout the country and has produced more permanent results than any of us dared to hope for.[12]

In 1920, the money had largely come from Tata, the princes and the government. Back then it was largely an initiative driven from Pune and Bombay. But by 1924, the funding poured in from diverse regions across the country. The subscription drive undertaken to finance the Games and the trips of the selected members to Paris was a success. A detailed breakdown of public funding for the Games shows the marked progress of the Olympic idea in the public mind by 1924. The Punjab Olympic Committee took the lead, contributing Rs. 1,114, "which represented contributions made by Punjab school boys through 47 schools." Punjab, in total, contributed Rs. 2,500. UP, Bihar, Orissa and Madras contributed Rs. 2,000 each while Central Provinces contributed Rs. 1,500. Calcutta too contributed Rs. 4,000 towards the fund.[13] From the North to the West to the South, the Olympic ideal seemed to be catching the public imagination.

Besides, as before, the princes were also approached and the Maharaja of Patiala, the nation's leading sports patron, contributed enough to fund the participation of the Patiala long jumper Dalip Singh. The Army too was sounded out to contribute to the passage of its representative and the government was called upon to put in a sum of Rs. 5,000.[14]

That Olympic sports were gaining currency in India is evident from the manifold increase in press coverage between 1920 and 1924. Newspapers across the country carried news of multiple regional "Olympic Trials" and the "Olympic Games" at Delhi were reported thus:

> The All India Olympic meeting to be held at the Roshanara Club, Delhi on February 8–9 promises to be a unique event in the history of sports in India. Reservations have already been booked for the Indian team, which will proceed to France on the steamer 'Lancashire' ex-Colombo on 29 May. The team will be accompanied by a professional

coach who will continue to train the players on steamer deck and in France for a month
before the Olympic begins.[15]

The detailed programme of the meet and the timings of all the events
featured prominently in the dailies and provincial successes at the meet were
greeted with considerable aplomb in the regions. For instance, the fact that
Bengali athletes made the finals in nine events was reported at length in the
province and much was made of the fact that Bengal had beaten Madras,
which had six final qualifications and Punjab, which had made it to the final
of five events. The two stars from Bengal, T. J. Pitt and J.S. Hall, were both
eventually selected to travel to Paris. The overwhelming popularity of this
meet, and the regional pride it evoked, is borne out by the following report
in Calcutta's *Amrita Bazar Patrika*:

> The weather condition was excellent and spectators numbered several thousands.
> Viceroy and Lady Reading were present. In four events-hurdles, one mile, long jump and
> three miles, provincial and Indian records were beaten, although the world records have
> not been touched. Bengal was first in the composition of India's Olympic team having
> won three places ... At a meeting of the All India Olympic Committee held after the meet
> it was decided to send these men to Paris as the money is available-
>
> 1. Dalip Singh of Patiala for Long Jump
> 2. Lakshmanan of Madras (Hurdles)
> 3. M.R. Hinge of Bombay (Marathon)
> 4. T.K. Pitt of Bengal (100 and 440 Yards)
> 5. J.S. Hall of Bengal (220 Yards)
> 6. Sepoy Pala Singh of UP (Three Miles)
> 7. J.C Heathcote (Madras), High Jump
> 8. M.V. Venkatramaswamy (Madras), One Mile.[16]

Patiala in the West, Madras in the South, Bombay and Bengal: already the
regional composition of the Paris team was beginning to represent the wide
regional disparities of India. H C Buck of the YMCA College of Physical
Education in Madras, an American who had pioneered Athletics coaching
in India, escorted the athletes. Though the Indians did not win medals, they
acquitted themselves better than at Antwerp with two of them, T.K Pitt in
the 400 metres, and Dalip Singh, in the broad jump, performing well
(Sanyal, 1964).

The organised planning for the Indian participation at Paris Games was
driven by the formation of a permanent All India Olympic Association. Sir
Dorabji Tata was invited to assume the presidency of the new body[17] but it
did not survive for more than three years. In 1927, another body, the Indian
Olympic Association, was formed and it continues to administer Indian
sport till the present day. Once again Dorabji Tata was the president and

A.G. Noehren the secretary. It was the new IOA that led India's preparations for the 1928 Olympiad in Amsterdam where India had her first taste of Olympic success.

"A CONTINENT AS BIG AS EUROPE": THE YMCA, INDIA AND THE GLOBAL OLYMPIC MOVEMENT

To make sense of how the Olympic ideal progress in India through the 1920s, it is imperative to see it in the context of global trends about Olympism in the same period and the 'Olympic explosion' that took place in another under-developed region, Latin America. In both regions, the YMCA played a pivotal role in stimulating Olympism. The Olympic movement needed a vehicle of organisation in every new country it targeted. The YMCA, a global body, with finely organised national tentacles in many under-developing countries, provided a ready option. As we shall see, Dorabji Tata's association with both bodies proved a pivotal fulcrum.

The Latin American "Olympic explosion" in the 1920s, as Cesar Torres calls it, was largely possible because of a partnership between the IOC and the YMCA. According to Torres' masterful study, the "explosion" occurred de to a confluence of three factors: "Latin American sporting cultures at the end of the First World War; an appreciation of Coubertin's new strategies of globalisation developed during the war; and a recognition of the crucial role that an alliance between the IOC and the Young Men's Christian Association (YMCA) ... " (Torres, 2006).

During the First World War, Coubertin was gravely concerned that the Games might be exterminated by the tumultuous political conditions created by the continuing violence. This anxiety made it essential to seek newer pastures for his Olympic ideology and he began to see this expansion as the key to the survival of the Olympic Games. The emphasis was to spread the Olympic gospel to areas unaffected by the war. If he could globalise Olympic affairs, Coubertin thought, he would ensure that if not in Europe the Games would at least continue in other corners of the world. He was simultaneously growing more and more anxious about the potential of the Inter-Allied Games being organised in the United States. These Games, designated as the "Military Olympics", were being planned in collaboration with the YMCA. Nervous about its bearing on the Olympic endeavor, Coubertin, as Torres mentions, wrote to Elwood S, Brown, the International Director of the YMCA on 25 January 1919 objecting against the 'action of the YMCA in deciding to hold Olympics in France in 1919.' Brown immediately wrote back allaying Coubertin's fears, declaring that the Inter-Allied Games 'is not a rival of the Olympic Games in any sense.'[18] His assurance had a comforting effect on Coubertin and this started a long association between the two that lasted several years and transformed the fundamental nature of the Olympic movement.

It was at Brown's insistence that Coubertin agreed to utilise the wide reach of the YMCA to spread the message of Olympism across Latin America. Stressing the role of the YMCA, Brown declared:

> a most unusual opportunity now existed to give a great impulse to physical training throughout the world, to develop backward areas along the lines of Olympic ideas and ideals, and to contribute definitely to the extension of your Committee's influence.[19]

Assured of Coubertin's support, Brown officially presented his proposal to the IOC at Antwerp in August 1920. It is of great importance that Sir Dorabji Tata, representing British India, was present in this session and followed the entire deliberation with keen interest. The proposal stressed the issue that the YMCA and the IOC had similar goals and drew attention to the YMCA's global structure. All its branches played key roles in promoting physical education and "manly sporting activity" and its organisational strength, Brown noted, was expected to add manifold to the IOC's global potency.

The YMCA had already held regional games like the Far Eastern Games in 1913 that helped in stimulating popularity of Olympic sports across the world. IOC recognition, Brown insisted and Coubertin concurred, would impart legitimacy to these efforts and this was the primary reason why the IOC unanimously accepted the scheme proposed by Brown. "With the partnership fully endorsed and Brown named South American *charge-de mission*, the IOC and the YMCA embarked on the first project the YMCA had in store, the 1922 Latin American Games."[20]

Dorabji Tata had already learnt his lessons at Antwerp and soon after his return to India insisted on enlisting the support of Dr. A.G. Noehren of the Madras YMCA for India's Olympic cause. It was no accident that the selection trials in Delhi for 1924 team were conducted under the expert supervision of H.C. Buck, staff of the Madras YMCA College of Physical Education (De Mello, 1959).

On the IOC's part, it did everything possible to encourage British India to join the Olympic family. The YMCA presence did much to boost the IOC's confidence and even though there was no permanent Indian Olympic institution in 1920 or 1924, the IOC allowed the Indian delegation to participate in the Games as part of its vision to globalise the movement. While Tata acted as a bridge, the IOC was also independently in touch with the Indian YMCA. There is evidence for this in a letter from Dr. J. Henry Gray, National Physical Director for the YMCA for India, Burma and Ceylon to Count Latour on 28 December 1928. The letter was primarily meant to update the IOC President on the progress of Olympism in India. To start with, Dr. Gray thanked the IOC President for sending him back issues of the "International Olympic Bulletin" and also for including him in the IOC's mailing list. He then suggested that Olympic organisation in India had begun on a positive note in 1922 and the power behind this, as in Latin America, was the YMCA.[21]

Though the involvement of the YMCA had lost sheen with the resignation of Dr. Noehren in 1927, YMCA cadres were still carrying on the bulk of the work in the provinces to promote Olympic sports and were instrumental in maintaining the fabric of the provincial sports organisations. In a country the size of India, this was no small concern. As Tata noted:

> India is such a vast continent, as big as Europe without Russia. When I went to Calcutta to see the Olympic Games last month, for the eight days that I was away from Bombay five of those were spent in the train.[22]

The YMCA's early role in the Indian Olympic movement cannot be emphasised enough. Its national network provided a lifeline for those who wanted to set up a national sporting movement.

"IMPOSSIBLE TO SELECT A NATIONAL REPRESENTATIVE": THE 'NATION' IN THE GAMES

The YMCA provided a vital crutch in the early years and nobody knew better than Tata that the Olympic movement in India was still in its infancy. Central to the challenge was the problem of creating a national consciousness, in a land divided along the multiple axes of region, caste and language. Writing in 1929, a year after India had won its first hockey gold in Amsterdam, Tata acknowledged:

> India is not yet ripe for the International Olympic Games. The love of such things is not ingrained here. There are so many communities, so many religions, so many languages and dialects, so many different customs and ideals, that it is almost impossible to select a national representative that would meet all requirements.[23]

There were two other major problems: the lack of stadiums and the relatively small size of a leisured class that could patronise sport as a watching public. As Tata noted at the end of his tenure as the head of the Indian Olympic movement, the foremost necessity were permanent stadiums, which would allow the organisation of the Games in at least two of the provinces. He had already approached the provincial municipalities and the government for funds to implement his projects of stadium building but nothing had come out of such overtures. Local stadiums were an urgent necessity because of the vast nature of the country, which made it impossible for the poor to travel long distances. Distances made it difficult for athletes to spend the time and money required to travel to these meets. Dorabji also stressed the point that the leisured class in India was much smaller than in Europe and the majority of Indians had little leisure time to devote to sports, making the progress of Olympic sports increasingly difficult. Finally, each province had its own indigenous pastime and people did not take much interest in other events.[24]

It may be mentioned here that Dorab Tata was not alone in pressing for the building of stadiums in India. In Bengal too, the Raja of Santosh, Sir Manmatha Nath Roy Chowdhury, emphasised a similar need for a permanent venue for sport in the 1920s:

> Speaking for Bengal, I may say, without any fear of contradiction, that a sports stadium in Calcutta is the need of the moment. Sport in Bengal will receive a serious check if we fail to provide at the psychological moment a central home for sports. Besides, in a city like Calcutta where the huge sporting crowds always cause anxiety to the police and people alike, the problem of providing accommodation for spectators can no longer be ignored ... We must have a sports stadium, which could accommodate in its auditorium no less than 60,000 people.[25]

Be that as it may, the Tata–Noehren combination successfully created the Indian Olympic Association in 1927. However, within months of its establishment the organisation entered troubled waters with both leaders resigning on personal grounds. Noehren resigned because he was leaving India permanently for England while Tata gave up the presidency for reasons of ill health. In a letter to the IOC President Count Latour on 21 February 1927 he outlined his reasons in detail:

> I have sent in my resignation as President of the All India Olympic Committee and I also wish to resign from the international Olympic Committee. I feel that with my advancing age and infirmities I can no longer devote the time and energy necessary for the position. It is with very great regret that I feel compelled to resign ... It has not been decided who the new President or Secretary will be.[26]

In view of his vision for the promotion of Olympic sport in India it was not surprising that the IOC only accepted Sir Dorab Tata's resignation with considerable reluctance.[27]

PATIALA AND THE REST: THE PRINCES AND THE POLITICS OF COLONIAL SPORT

The issue of picking successors for Dorab Tata and A.G. Neohren had become politicised from the start. At the heart of it was the battle between the Indian princes for control over Indian sport which was seen as an avenue for social mobility. In this context, there is no more celebrated example of the importance of sport for many princes than that of Ranji. It is now well documented that Ranji, a disinherited prince, won back his crown of Nawanagar largely because of the social capital he had gained as cricketing icon in England.[28] By the time Tata resigned from the presidency of the IOA, the Olympic movement too had become a prized catch for the princes to fight over. In fact, in his very first letter, acknowledging Tata's resignation, the IOC President noted that the name of the Prince of Kapurthala had been suggested to him as a possible successor.[29] The debate over succession raged on at several levels: at one level it was about which Prince would now get to establish control as a patron; at another level it was about whether the issue was solely a domestic one with the IOA unilaterally empowered to nominate a successor and third it was about whether the IOC, which had helped India right through, could justifiably interfere in the succession dispute.

With the princely spheres of influence in cricket and football already well demarcated[30] and with Olympic sport gaining in prominence, it was not unnatural that the succession dispute became a battle royale between several Indian princes with an interest in sport. Key players were soon split along lines of allegiance and each player tried to make a case for his candidate being the most suitable replacement. Of all the qualities sighted as essential in the successor, the one common denominator was that the candidate had to have the personal means and influence to visit Europe frequently. This was considered crucial to keep a tab on international developments, liaise with the IOC, learn of its plans and programmes and having thus imbibed new ideas implement them back home. Sir Dorabji Tata repeatedly emphasised that a regular presence in Europe was a necessary precondition in all his correspondence with the IOC.[31] This pointed towards two things.

First, the global Olympic movement at this stage was still league of gentlemanly elites from various countries. Second, though the movement rode on nationalist emotions within India, it was still top-driven and controlled by moneyed and political elites. The days of democratisation of the movement were still in the future and many would argue that this is a process that, at least in India, is still far from completion as the subsequent chapters highlight.

Reacting to the IOC's suggestion that the Maharaja of Kapurthala, a frequent visitor to Europe, be nominated his successor, Tata in a hand written letter to the President from Geneva on 16 June 1927 stated that the Indian Olympic Association had already requested His Highness the Maharaja of Burdwan to assume the presidency. Burdwan had not yet said yes and Tata appeared apprehensive about his candidacy:

> The Maharaja I know has been the local President for the Presidency of Bengal, but I am not aware that he has taken any personal interest in the working of the All India Olympic Association. I do not know with whom the nomination of the President for All India rests, with your committee or the Indian committee. I imagine that they will be a little jealous of their privileges and claim the right to nominate their own President.[32]

In a clear indicator the battle for control among Indian princes, he admitted that his own presidency so far had created a lot of discord in India from a rival section, which wanted Ranji, the great princely icon of Indian sport, to lead the Olympic movement. That crisis had only been averted because Tata, himself good friends with Ranji, heartily acquiesced with the suggestion only to be told by the Jam Sahib of Nawanagar that he did not want anything to do with the IOA at that stage.[33]

Tata personally was in favour of the Maharaja of Kapurthala, who, he thought, was better qualified to represent India at the IOC, more appropriate than Burdwan. "Kapurthala is every year in Europe and unlike me or Burdwan can be present at all European functions." Because he traveled to India every winter after his European vacation was over, he was also in a position to closely monitor the day-to-day activities of the Indian Association.[34]

As the names of Kapurthala, the Jam of Nawanagar and Burdwan were doing the rounds, the powerful Maharaja of Patiala, already a key figure in Indian cricket, threw his hat into the ring. It can be surmised that Patiala's coming into the fray was the principal reason behind Ranji's backing off. This was because Patiala's had been Ranji's strongest source of financial support at times of crisis. In fact, the connection between Ranji and Patiala was very well known in Indian sporting circles. Ranji had played for

Patiala's team in 1898–1899 and had been his ADC in the years before he won the crown of Nawanagar. While touring Bengal in 1899, Ranji and Patiala had been accorded a royal reception, the Kolkata Town Hall spending the huge sum of Rs. 3,000 on the occasion.[35]

Patiala's interest in Olympic affairs fundamentally transformed equations in India. By September 1927, Tata was informing his friend Count Latour that the Maharaja of Kapurthala had already declined the presidency of the IOA. Burdwan too had decided to withdraw his candidature clearing the turf for Patiala.[36] The dispute lingered and by early 1928 Tata had developed serious doubts about the suitability of princes, who themselves were not sportsmen, heading sporting organisations. In a letter to the Count, he suggested that though the Maharajas were keen on shooting, hunting, polo and other sporting activities, they had little knowledge of track and field events and not all of them were frequent visitors to Europe. He emphasised that the only reason that he had backed Kapurthala so far was because Kapurthala visited Europe regularly. However, he had since then realised that the Maharaja had little knowledge of Olympic sports and would hardly be of any practical assistance to the IOC's cause. In Tata's words:

> The same applies to the Maharaja of Burdwan who has declined the Presidentship... It is going to be very difficult to find a prominent man in India who takes interest in running, jumping and this type of sport who can spare the time to come to Europe every year... I think that if the Maharaja Jam Saheb of Nawanagar could be persuaded to accept the appointment he would be the most suitable man as he is a good general all round sportsman."[37]

Worried about the leadership vacuum, in October 1927, the IOA once again requested Tata to reconsider his resignation. His refusal to do so meant that by the end of 1927, Patiala was the lone candidate left in the fray in the race for the presidency. As he had so often done in cricket with his affluence, he had successfully outmaneuvered the others and posited himself as saviour of the Olympic cause in India. Soon after assuming charge, he took the perfect diplomatic step in appointing Dorab Tata as honorary Life President of the IOA in recognition of his efforts to promote the Olympism in India.

The Patiala Era

Aside from Ranji, if there was one Indian prince who was genuinely interested in sport for its own sake, it was Maharaja Bhupinder Singh of Patiala. He first became interested in Olympic matters in 1923 when a

Patiala athlete, Dalip Singh, failed to make it to the Indian Olympic team to Paris. As Anthony De Mello writes:

> His failure was, apparently, because he had been unavoidably prevented from attending the trials, which had recently been held at Lahore. Dalip Singh appealed for help to the Ruler of Patiala, who not only helped the young man to get his rightful place in the team, but also ordered the formation of the Patiala State Olympic Association.[38]

It was this incident that aroused Bhupinder Singh's interest in Olympic matters and "already he was rehearsing for the role he was soon to play."[39]

Soon after taking charge as President of the Indian Olympic Association, Bhupinder faced the difficult task of sending a team to the Amsterdam Games of 1928. With virtually no official funds available for the purpose, the task was an onerous one. It was as a result of his labors that India managed to send seven athletes and fifteen hockey players to Amsterdam. As De Mello asserts, "Without the efforts of Bhupinder Singh it is more than likely that our hockey wizards would not then, nor for many years to come, have had the opportunity so completely to baffle the game's experts from the rest of the world."[40] He goes on to suggest that the "self imposed task of sending our Olympic team to Amsterdam was only one of many such undertaken by Bhupinder Singh. He was instrumental in sending teams to the Far Eastern Games in Tokyo (1929), the Olympic Games at Los Angeles (1932), the Western Asiatic Games at Delhi (1934), the Empire Games of 1936 and also the Olympiad at Berlin in the same year."[41]

But Patiala's rise as the preeminent patron of Indian Olympism created serious resentment, not only among other princes but also among the power players in the Indian Olympic structure. Efforts to discredit him and preempt him from appointing Punjab's GD Sondhi as India's delegate in the IOC continued. With the influence of Tata and the YMCA gradually decreasing, Sondhi, and educationist and the Secretary of the Punjab Olympic Association, emerged as Patiala's man at this early stage of India's Olympic encounter. As early as 30 March 1931, Patiala urged the IOC President to allow Sondhi to stand in for Sir Dorabji at the IOC session in Los Angeles in case he was unable to attend. As he argued, Indian representation in the IOC session was crucial because "India is becoming more and more conscious of the importance of its position in international sport and we wish for as full a representation as possible on the international sports bodies." India's success at hockey had strengthened its case for greater representation at the highest decision making body of the Olympics and Patiala pushed further, asking for a permanent place for Sondhi at the international Olympic table:

> By winning an international event like hockey in the first year of its entrance into international competition, India has a good claim to have two members in charge of her affairs at the IOC[42]

The IOC's subsequent acceptance of Sondhi as the official Indian representative gave the formal seal to Patiala's dominance in India's Olympic affairs.

The one body that was most miffed at the rise of Patiala was the YMCA which had played such an important role in the movement so far. Using his proximity with the IOC President Count Latour, Henry Gray, National Director of the YMCA for India, Burma and Ceylon, sent the IOC a scathing critique of India's Olympic affairs on 28 December 1928. He lamented that Olympic organisation was sagging nationwide and ascribed the loss of steam directly to Patiala's ascent. Gray argued that the new leadership was not "representative" and that control had passed to a very small group, chiefly three men in North India representing the Punjab and the Army. He minced no words in saying that, "This leadership does not have the confidence of the entire country, is not familiar with conditions nor acquainted with the leaders in the other parts of the empire." He felt that this was because that most local provincial committees had lost their voting rights after failing to pay their dues to the national body. Gray specifically criticised the management of the team to Amsterdam, where Patiala had played a central role. He argued that the "masses continued to remain uninvolved in Olympic activity across the country" and went on to suggest that unless immediately checked the "top control of the movement will be secured by a semi-interested small group of people who do not represent the country as a whole." Even the remedies he suggested were clearly directed at challenging the monopoly established by Patiala over India's Olympic affairs: that a "really worthy" successor be appointed to fill the vacancy left by Tata at the IOC and the restoration of the active leadership of the YMCA as the "best qualified body in India" to lead the Olympic cause.[43]

That nothing resulted from any of these complaints was because of the affluence and influence of the house of Patiala and the paucity of funds from other sources to promote Olympic sports in the country as a whole. Funding continued to be a crucial concern even for Sondhi, Patala's own envoy. As he wrote to the IOC President on 1 May 1935:

> It costs me a great deal of money to attend the Olympic Games, which I regard as a work of national importance and national credit. I am therefore asking if it would be at all possible for you to write to Lord Willingdon, the Viceroy and Governor General of India, who is also the Patron of the IOA, to request him to recognize the attendance of

the of the Indian representative on the IOC as a national service and to get me some
monetary help from the Government for attending the Games.[44]

While Patiala was thus consolidating his position at the helm of the Indian
Olympic Association, the IOC President repeatedly asked Dorabji Tata to
reconsider his resignation from the International Olympic Committee.
Tata's stature was such that the Maharaja of Patiala could not but support
this suggestion on being asked. As Latour mentioned:

> after a year of troubles and inquiries, he (Patiala) wires to me that you are the only
> possible man. What else can I do than to say to you: Please come back, we all welcome
> you. What else can you do than to answer: I am coming back. Please do so.[45]

But Tata, by now 70 years old, steadfastly refused, citing his old age and ill
health.[46] By stepping aside, he left the field open for Patiala's complete
dominance over the Indian Olympic firmament, a dominance that continued
over the next few decades even after independence, as the subsequent
chapters will show.

It can be suggested that Patiala, as he had done in cricket, had used his
trusted weapon – patronage, to gain control of Olympic matters in India. He
had not only funded Indian teams to various international meets but had
also built a grand stadium in Amritsar to promote track and field
competitions. Patronage worked well because at the time of his assumption
of the office of President, the IOA was in a sorry financial state. Most
provinces were in arrears in their contributions and some of them for over a
period of two years. Rs. 10,000 was all that was available to the IOA for
sending the team to Amsterdam. Immediately before submitting his
resignation, the YMCA's Neohren drew attention to the difficulties
confronting the IOA:

> It must be obvious that the whole success of India's participation rests on a financial
> basis and that the IOA will be powerless to send even a small team abroad, unless all
> Provinces pay up their outstanding obligations and that this revenue be further
> supplemented by private donations.[47]

The fact that Patiala could sideline the YMCA so effectively in taking over
Indian Olympism, despite the sterling role played by that organisation in
laying the early seeds of the Olympic idea in India and despite its influence
with the IOC, is a measure of his success. The opposition, however, refused
to give up the fight, borne out by the tumultuous story of India's Olympic
encounter all through the 1930s.

CONCLUSION

In his much acclaimed biography of Pierre De Coubertin, John J Macaloon writes:

> But in the final reckoning, his [Coubertin's] eyes remained too focused by the period in which he had forged an identity and the Olympics had been reborn, the 1880s and 1890s. He failed to see that the games had become not something different from, but something much more than, what he had intended. From a small public novelty of the belle époque, an athletic competition wrapped in a prepotent historical conceit and adorned with verdant social claims, the games had been transformed in four decades [by the 1920s] into a crucible of symbolic force into which the world poured its energies and a stage upon which, every four years, it played out its hopes and its terrors."[48]

A small part of this transformation was also enacted in India, which by the late 1920s, had entered the Olympic family in earnest and where, as in other parts of the world, control of Olympic matters resulted in fascinating battles of intrigue and power play that defined and transformed established contours of the domestic political landscape. However, it must be acknowledged that despite the recent splurge in Olympic writing across the world, there remain many Olympic encounters still to be documented. India's is one such. The uncovering of this story demonstrates beyond doubt that globalised sport was a potent reality in the early twentieth century and colonial India benefited significantly from its vibrations. Acceptance of this truth will ensure that historians of India bring our tryst with Olympism into their ambit of study to better understand the colonial past and dig deeper for the roots of popular culture at home and abroad.

This chapter has aimed to document the early history of Olympism in India and in doing so has attempted to demonstrate the already globalised nature of the colonial Indian elite. These men, educated in the West and inspired by the gospels of internationalism, helped to dramatically alter a narrow national outlook. Sir Dorabji J. Tata was one such. Following him, the Olympic torch passed into the hands of the Maharaja of Patiala and his trusted lieutenant G.D. Sondhi. Control of Olympic sport was, among other things, a time tested way of establishing "manly" credentials. As Rosalind O' Hanlon has argued, manly qualities:

> were displayed in very direct and physical ways: in the splendour of men's physiques, the dazzle of equipage, the grim efficiency of their weapons and the magnificence of their fighting animals. Here, allies, troops, patrons, and rivals continually weighed and judged, challenged and affirmed each other's possession of the manly qualities and competence deemed essential in the successful ruler, ally, military commander and warrior.[49]

Having already fashioned a stranglehold over cricket by the late 1920s, control over the nation's expanding Olympic horizon allowed Patiala to establish himself as the standalone patriarch in India's sporting landscape. His monopoly was challenged on occasions but such confrontations, more often than not, proved feeble retorts rather than strong rebuffs. Yet, such attempts continued in the 1930s and 1940s and are as much a part of India's Olympic encounter as the eight gold medals India won at hockey between 1928 and 1956.

NOTES

1. This was documented by Prof. Bruce Kidd at a course taught at the University of Toronto in May 2007 by Prof. Bruce Kidd and Boria Majumdar titled "The Politics of the Commonwealth Games".

2. *Ibid.*

3. *Ten Thousand Miles Through India and Burma.*

4. Personal letter from Dorabji J. Tata to the IOC President Count Baillet Latour, 21 May 1929. Housed at the International Olympic Museum, Laussane, ID Chemise 7334 CIO 3535 MBR-TATA-CORR, Correspondence de Dorabji Tata 1926–1930.

5. *Ibid.*

6. See the letters in ID Chemise 7334 CIO 3535 MBR-TATA-CORR, Correspondence de Dorabji Tata 1926–1930. International Olympic Museum, Laussane.

7. Personal letter from Dorabji J. Tata to the IOC President Count Baillet Latour, 21 May 1929. Housed at the International Olympic Museum, Laussane, ID Chemise 7334 CIO 3535 MBR-TATA-CORR, Correspondence de Dorabji Tata 1926–1930.

8. *Ibid.*

9. *Ibid.*

10. *Amrita Bazar Patrika*, 30 August 1920.

11. *Ibid.*

12. Letter from A.G. Noehren to Dorabji J. Tata on 1 April 1924 housed at the International Olympic Museum, Lausanne. File OU MO 01 14 36, CIO CNO IND CORR, Olympic Studies Center, IOC Museum, Lausanne. This file deals primarily with correspondence exchanged between the Indian Olympic Association and the International Olympic Committee. Also, all documents sent from India to the IOC – letters, pamphlets, constitutions, etc., have been retained in this file. Also see IDD Chemise 9404 CIO CNO INDE CORR, Correspondence India 1924–1963.

13. *Ibid.*

14. *Ibid.*

15. *Amrita Bazar Patrika*, 18 January 1924.

16. *Ibid.*, 13 February 1924.

17. *Ibid.*

18. Personal letter from Elswood S. Brown to Pierre de Coubertin, 3 February 1919, "Young Men's Christian Associations. 1909–1927" (hereafter YMCA, 1909–1927), IOC Archives, Lausanne.

19. Personal letter from Elswood S. Brown to Pierre de Coubertin, 23 January 1929, (YMCA, 1909–1927), IOC Archives, Lausanne.

20. (YMCA, 1909–1927), IOC Archives, Lausanne.

21. Personal letter from Henry Gray to Count Latour, 28 December 1928. IOC Archives, ID Chemise 7334 CIO 3535 MBR-TATA-CORR, Correspondence de Dorabji Tata 1926–1930.

22. IOC Archives, ID Chemise 7334 CIO 3535 MBR-TATA-CORR, Correspondence de Dorabji Tata 1926–1930.

23. Personal letter from Dorabji J. Tata to the IOC President Count Baillet Latour, 21 May 1929. Housed at the International Olympic Museum, Laussane, ID Chemise 7334 CIO 3535 MBR-TATA-CORR, Correspondence de Dorabji Tata 1926–1930.

24. Personal letter from Dorabji J. Tata to the IOC President Count Baillet Latour, 21 February 1927. Housed at the International Olympic Museum, Laussane, ID Chemise 7334 CIO 3535 MBR-TATA-CORR, Correspondence de Dorabji Tata 1926–1930.

25. For details on the stadium controversy see; Boria Majumdar, *Twenty two yards to freedom: A social history of Indian cricket* (New Delhi: Penguin-Viking, 2004), pp. 171–199.

26. IOC Archives, ID Chemise 7334 CIO 3535 MBR-TATA-CORR, Correspondence de Dorabji Tata 1926–1930.

27. Personal letter from IOC President to Sir Dorabji Tata, 22 April 1927. The IOC chief thanked Tata for his wonderful work in promoting the Olympic cause in India and indicated that the IOC was aware of the difficulties involved in replacing Sir Dorab with someone equally capable and equal to the task of assuming effective control of the Olympic movement in India. IOC Archives, ID Chemise 7334 CIO 3535 MBR-TATA-CORR, Correspondence de Dorabji Tata 1926–1930.

28. For details see; Boria Majumdar, *Twenty two yards to freedom: A social history of Indian Cricket* (New Delhi: Penguin-Viking, 2004), Chapter 1.

29. Personal letter from IOC President to Sir Dorabji Tata, 22 April 1927. IOC Archives, ID Chemise 7334 CIO 3535 MBR-TATA-CORR, Correspondence de Dorabji Tata 1926–1930.

30. For details see Boria Majumdar and Kausik Bandyopadhyay, *Goalless: The story of a unique footballing nation* (New Delhi: Penguin-Viking, 2006), Chapter 4.

31. For most of his letters see; IOC Archives, ID Chemise 7334 CIO 3535 MBR-TATA-CORR, Correspondence de Dorabji Tata 1926–1930.

32. Personal letter from Sir Dorabji Tata to Count Baillet Latour, Geneva, 16 June 1927. IOC Archives, ID Chemise 7334 CIO 3535 MBR-TATA-CORR, Correspondence de Dorabji Tata 1926–1930. Also see; File OU MO 01 14 36, CIO CNO IND CORR, Olympic Studies Center, IOC Museum, Lausanne.

33. *Ibid.*

34. IOC Archives, ID Chemise 7334 CIO 3535 MBR-TATA-CORR, Correspondence de Dorabji Tata 1926–1930. Also see; File OU MO 01 14 36, CIO CNO IND CORR, Olympic Studies Center, IOC Museum, Lausanne.

35. For details of the Ranji–Patiala proximity see; Boria Majumdar, *Twenty two yards to freedom: A social history of Indian cricket* (New Delhi: Penguin-Viking, 2004), p. 62.

36. Personal letter from Sir Dorabji Tata to to Count Latour on 13 September 1927. File OU MO 01 14 36, CIO CNO IND CORR, Olympic Studies Center, IOC Museum, Lausanne.

37. Personal letter from Sir Dorabji Tata to to Count Latour on 17 January 1928. File OU MO 01 14 36, CIO CNO IND CORR, Olympic Studies Center, IOC Museum, Lausanne.

38. Anthony S De Mello, A wardrobe of coloured blazers, in *Portrait of Indian sport* (New Delhi: Mcmillan, 1959), pp. 48–49.

39. *Ibid.*

40. *Ibid.*

41. *Ibid.*

42. File OU MO 01 14 36, CIO CNO IND CORR, Olympic Studies Center, IOC Museum, Lausanne.

43. All quotes in this paragraph are from a personal letter from Henry Gray to Count Latour, 28 December 1928. IOC Archives, ID Chemise 7334 CIO 3535 MBR-TATA-CORR, Correspondence de Dorabji Tata 1926–1930.

44. IOC Archives, IDD Chemise 9404 CIO CNO INDE CORR, Correspondence India 1924–1963.

45. Personal letter from IOC President to Dorabji Tata on 11 May 1929. IOC Archives, ID Chemise 7334 CIO 3535 MBR-TATA-CORR, Correspondence de Dorabji Tata 1926–1930.

46. Personal letter from Sir Dorabji Tata to Count Latoure, 21 May 1929 and letter from Sir Dorabji Tata to the Maharaja of Patiala on 6 May 1931. IOC Archives, ID Chemise 7334 CIO 3535 MBR-TATA-CORR, Correspondence de Dorabji Tata 1926–1930 and File OU MO 01 14 36, CIO CNO IND CORR, Olympic Studies Center, IOC Museum, Lausanne.

47. IOC Archives, IDD Chemise 9404 CIO CNO INDE CORR, Correspondence India 1924–1963.

48. John J Macaloon, Introduction, Revised and Updated edition of *This great symbol: Pierre de Coubertin and the origins of the modern Olympic Games*, Special Issue, *The International Journal of the History of Sport*, *23*(3–4), 2006, p. 344.

49. Rosalind O'Hanlon, Issues of masculinity in North Indian history: The Bangash Nawabs of Farrukhabad, in *Indian Journal of Gender Studies*, *4*(1) (New Delhi: Sage, 1997).

REFERENCES

Bose, M. (1990). *History of Indian cricket.* London: Andre Deutsch.

Cashman, R. (1979). *Patrons, players and the crowd.* New Delhi: Orient Longman.

Collins, S. (2006). Conflicts of 1930s Japanese Olympic diplomacy in universalising the Olympic movement. *The International Journal of the History of Sport*, *23*(7), 1128–1151.

De Mello, A. S. (1959). *In the Ramayana and Mahabharata: Nehru's favourite"*, Portrait of Indian Sport. New Delhi: Macmillan.

Guha, R. (2002). *Corner of a foreign field: The Indian history of a British sport.* New Delhi: Pan Macmillan.

Majumdar, B. (2004). *Twenty two yards to freedom: A social history of Indian cricket.* New Delhi: Penguin-Viking.

Mangan, J. A. (1992). *The cultural bond: Sport, empire, society.* London and Portland, OR: Frank Cass.

Mangan, J. A. (2001). *The games ethic and imperialism.* London: Frank Cass.

Moore, K. (1989). The warmth of comradeship': The first British Empire Games and imperial solidarity. *The International Journal of the History of Sport, 6*(2), 243–251.

Polishwala, P.N. (1921). School and College Cricket in India. Mumbai.

Stoddart, B. (2006). Sport, colonialism and struggle: CLR James and cricket. *Sport in Society, 9*(5), 914–930.

Sanyal, S. (1964). India and the Olympics. In: XVIII Olympiad Tokyo 1964: Official souvenir of the Indian Olympic association. Mumbai: Sportswriters Publishers, pp. 25–26.

The Statesman. (1920). Indian athletes at the Olympic Games: Team of six from Bombay. June 3.

Torres, C. (2006). The Latin American Olympic explosion in the 1920s: Causes and consequences. In: B. Majumdar & S. Collins (Eds), *Olympism: The global vision: From nationalism to internationalism,* Special Issue, *The International Journal of the History of Sport,* Vol. 23, No. 7, pp. 1088–1094.

EXERCISE PRESCRIPTION AND THE CLINICAL GOVERNANCE OF SOCIAL AND ETHNIC BODIES

Lone Friis Thing

1. EXERCISE PRESCRIPTION: FROM A NORDIC PERSPECTIVE

We are all ethnic. When the XVI ISA World Congress of Sociology was held in Durban, South Africa, I took that opportunity to travel around the country. In Soweto, for the first time in my life, I was seriously confronted by my own ethnic background ... that pale whiteness that radiated shamefully from the surface of my skin ... and if I had the choice of turning it inside out, I would have done it at that moment. Concepts of racialised social relations took on new meaning as I trekked across the dusty African soil. Later, during the World Congress, while working out at the hotel's fitness center on the 11th floor that was only accessible by means of magnetic access cards and was heavily monitored electronically, I understood from a physical perspective the concept of "gated communities". Hermeneutic tradition's focus on "contextual understanding" (Gadamer, 1989) suddenly became very clear. There is an opportunity in Scandinavia to exercise at night in any major city, whether female or male, without any life threats. Social democratic welfare programmes, to a certain extent, have secured equality amongst societal groups, and this has had a positive impact

Social and Cultural Diversity in a Sporting World
Research in the Sociology of Sport, Volume 5, 193–210
Copyright © 2008 by Emerald Group Publishing Limited
All rights of reproduction in any form reserved
ISSN: 1476-2854/doi:10.1016/S1476-2854(08)05012-7

on freedom of movement, to the point where violence and assault do not jeopardise movement.

A total of 8.7% of the population in Denmark is of foreign origin.[1] However, although immigration is not a quantitative problem in itself, integration issues monopolise the political agenda. Social inequality in general and social inequality in health care in specific affect the Danish welfare state's marginalised groups. This is seen by the relationship between hospital usage in Denmark and social circumstances. Adults with post-graduate educations have a hospital usage of ~35% lower than the average for the entire population, while individuals with no vocational education use hospital services at 20% above the average.[2] Denmark is amongst those countries with the lowest life expectancy in Western Europe despite the fact that only 13% of the Danish population is physically inactive. Furthermore, social inequality in obesity as well as in physical activity is noted. There is a clear association between the length of education and the incidence of individuals that undertake moderate to strenuous physical activity during recreational time; i.e. the more years of education, the larger the incidence of individuals who do moderate to hard physical activity.[3] Even the pattern of diseases amongst ethnic groups in Denmark does not deviate much. We can all be considered ethnic, but are afforded different opportunities for education and vocation within this Scandinavian welfare state. Migration status worsens socio-cultural conditions, and as such has an indirect impact on health and illness.

Over more recent years, I have discussed "prescribed exercise" from a critical sociological perspective (Thing, 2005a, 2007). "Prescribed exercise" is a welfare state treatment intervention that seeks to prevent and heal disease. "Prescribed exercise" is an interesting topic of discussion in relation to the "migrant body" because, as an entry point, exercise can be characterised as not being culture-specific. Physical activity seen from a health professional's perspective is linked to the scientific evidence base and treats the body as universal sizes. By discussing "prescribed exercise" in relation to the migrant body, further penetrating questions emerge. "Prescribed exercise" can be analysed as a transformation of the Nordic exercise culture. Exercise is transformed from its understanding of being gymnastics, dance or sport[4] to that of being treatment given at a clinic, under the supervision of physicians. This chapter provides an in-depth discussion of this very point. There is a need for sociological knowledge that highlights the interpersonal dimensions of treatment types. There is a need for further reflection about "prescribed exercise" as there is danger in hasty action that could place substantial cost on society. "Prescribed exercise" creates work for many lifestyle experts, however, the development *away from* exercise as a daily activity (Timm, 1997) *towards* becoming a health professional treatment regimen can result in unforeseen consequences and can create a client and expert group dependence. A description of how and why building clients and expert dependence is established will be the aim of the chapter.

The chapter begins by defining "prescribed exercise", and thereafter provides a method and theory introduction. The impact of medicalisation of physical activity from the perspective of the "migrant body" will then be discussed. The chapter will conclude with a discussion on the consequences and future perspectives.

2. WHAT IS "PRESCRIBED EXERCISE"?

More recent research shows that physical activity prevents and treats a series of lifestyle-related diseases such as obesity, high blood pressure, type-2 diabetes and ischemic heart disease (Danish National Board of Health, Sundhedsstyrelsen, 2003; Pedersen, 2004a; Pedersen & Saltin, 2006). On the backcloth of earlier evidence of the positive effects of physical exercise as treatment in a series of diseases, several counties in Denmark initiated research projects based on "prescribed exercise" (Rosell, Raahauge Madsen, Mortensen, & Iversen, 2005).

"Prescribed exercise" is use of physical exercise as a physician's agent that is prescribed in measured dosages, and is conducted under the supervision of exercise experts. In the Copenhagen County, for example, this type of treatment is carried out in four physiotherapy clinics. The patients train over a two-month period twice weekly, followed by one weekly session for a further two months (Roessler, Ibsen, Saltin, & Sørensen, 2007). In a literature review conducted by the Danish National Board of Health on the effects and organisation of this treatment, the concept is defined as interventions ordered by a general practitioner, when he/she refers physically inactive patients to undertake concrete training or counsels inactive patients to promote physical activity (Willemann, 2004). "Prescribed exercise" is conducted in Denmark often by a multidisciplinary and multisectoral health professional team comprising physiotherapists, dieticians, physicians or public health nurses who collaborate to aim to promote lifestyle changes and sustained physical activity in the population. "Prescribed exercise" is limited in some interventions to training of the body, but in several treatment centers also includes counseling on diet and self-therapeutic aspects. In Denmark, the concept is offered nation-wide. It is noteworthy that those citizens that are offered the treatment are not sick but are considered at risk to become ill. "Prescribed exercise" is launched as a preventive and treatment initiative, despite the fact that there are few existing studies that have researched its effects and international research shows that one cannot expect important changes in physical activity level in the majority of patients due to drop-out rates and lack of sustainability of an increased physical activity level (Willemann, 2004).

It should be noted that there is an intention to begin a debate on "prescribed exercise" that will hopefully result in innovative research initiatives and strategies. There is no intention of futile criticism of exercise as treatment and as a preventive initiative. There is a need to rethink prevention and treatment and it is necessary for the population to develop and sustain active lives, where body movement is incorporated. However, there is also a need to launch a chain of reflection about the concept and a need for societal contextualising of "prescribed exercise" as it triggers compliance problems. It is my strong belief that the drop-out and sustainability issues are due to the theoretic perspective of the concept. The definition is developed with the understanding that motivation for physical activity or choice to drop out of it is based on *rationale*-based behaviour. Cognitive behaviour theories, with the concept imbedded, is used to explain and understand the individual's physical activity behaviour (Rosell et al., 2005), whereby motives and attitude to carry out physical activity are measured and evaluated. This is a narrow persuasion method for handling people. This medical paradigm reduces what could be a physical and sensual life promoting and healing activity to being a rationale deliberate behaviour.

3. ANALYTICAL STRATEGY

The analytical strategy, as mentioned, draws in a sociological and public health theory perspective, inspired[5] by Foucault's perspective on the "conduct of conduct" in the neoliberal society (Rose, 1999; Dean, 1999; Vallgaarda, 2003). Discussing the truths and givens of the new evidence-based content opens a general discussion on technology's possible consequences and makes room for critical reflection about societal changes that unfolds specifically in the health care system. The chapter is associated to that of Dean (1999, p. 23) that sketches rotating axes for analysis of practice regimes generally. Applied to the field of exercise, the rotating axes for analysis are as follows:

1. Characteristic forms of visibility: A visualisation of the inactivation problem.
2. Practice regimen: The hospitalised exercise program.
3. Scientific technology: Making exercise evidence-based in relation to knowledge.
4. Characteristic ways of forming subjects: Entrepreneurial efforts.

Dean argues that the four areas in the governmentality perspective should be seen as distinct analysis areas but goes on to state that they overlap and coincide. The four dividing points are seen as analytical reduction points in the attempt to roll out the governmentality in all its complexity. For mitigating and limiting purposes, I have selected to focus on only three of these analytical points. Making the field of inactivity more apparent is discussed in Section 5.1 of the chapter. The issue will be tackled at the discursive level, as I believe that the problem of inactivity is made more visible through language that renews interest in exercise. The clinical practice regimen and scientific technology level are discussed (together) in Section 5.2. Looking at the organisational level will shine light on which control mechanisms, scientific forms and rationales are used in the "prescribed exercise" regimen. The third area of analysis includes: the regimen's entrepreneurial work, which highlights the forms of established subjective positions in the regimen. This point describes how the development of identities unfolds in the concept.

4. THEORY: THE GOVERNMENTALITY PERSPECTIVE

The government's perspective on the "conduct of conduct" in the Neoliberal society (Hindess, 1996; Barry, Osborne, & Rose, 1996; Dean, 1999) is used as a sociological analytical framework to form a perspective of evidence-based exercise seen within a broader societal context. Governmentality literature investigates forms of practice in which different social, pubic and political bodies and authorities attempt to control the actions of individuals and society at large from perspectives of ethical ideals, political/policy results, economic necessities and social goals (Dean, 1999). Foucault's concept of governmentality (Foucault, 1991) refers to all program types that, through thought and action try to guide control of the people. Technologies guide individuals in desired directions and are defined mainly by social practices that aim to manipulate the social and physical surroundings in relation to identified routines. Dean writes (1999, p. 23) that the analytical thinking from the governmentality perspective focuses on how to control and how people are controlled in different regimens; and finally under what circumstances these regimens are developed, continue to operate and to transform. The governmentality perspective underscores the *How question* that makes evident different control mechanisms and their consequences. The question regarding what knowledge forms the basis for "prescribed exercise" is analysed, and in which way and how the government's version/form constitutes action. More specifically, focus is placed on types of techniques and procedures that are favored as sustainable authorities in the field.

5. ANALYSIS: "PRESCRIBED EXERCISE" AS A MEDICALISATION OF BODY MOVEMENT

"Prescribed exercise" draws physical activity into the medical paradigm's area of knowledge. This incorporation can also be seen as a societal medicalisation trend that draws in social and general conditions, structures and life situations as having clinical relevance and relevant for action control (Gannik & Schmidt, 1990; Conrad & Schneider, 1980). With respect to "prescribed exercise", medicalisation can mean that physical activity is a very real concept and daily life activity is drawn into the biomedical way of thinking and acting. It can also be seen differently by highlighting that physical exercise is a sport or a dance (and as such are a goal in itself) that is then changed into a welfare state instrument for advancing a major health goal. More specifically, a sport that can play out on a football field or a dance floor is now transformed into an instrument to improve blood circulation by using a stationary training cycle in a clinical setting. Medicalisation in this case happens on three different and important levels, i.e. (1) on the discursive level; (2) on the organisational level and (3) on the level of the individual.

5.1. The Discursive Level: Making it Evident by Means of Language

The discursive level refers to concepts equating physical activity with medicine. The clinical terminology and language used in relation to exercise impacts how we think and understand movement activities. When physical activity is described as medical treatment given by prescription, one thinks of exercise as a means of enhancing an overall aim and exercise becomes an object (and not a state of being or an activity) that can be taken in rationed dosages over short or longer periods of time. For "prescribed exercise" to be meaningful in the individual's life, treatment should not end at the hospital or physiotherapist's office. As such, exercise cannot be directly compared to a medication nor to regularly taken tablets. Tablets are taken at home with little or no consequence to daily life. It is not as simple with "doing exercise".

Another and critical aspect of the concept of "prescribed exercise" in medical terminology is its implication of illness. When exercise becomes something that the doctor prescribes over-the-counter, there is a shift away from exercise as a voluntary and individual initiative instigated by desire, to being a "must do" treatment triggered by society's public health theoretical interest. This conceptual movement places exercise in a different perspective; a perspective even if established out of interest for the population's health, sees exercise as an illness combating phenomenon. This new language about exercise has consequences for the population's way of thinking about and doing exercise. In the Nordic sports culture, gymnastics and sports, has considerable impact on the development of democracy and for social movements and thinking (Bale & Philo, 1998; Korsgaard, 1982). These consequences and associated function of movement activity become invisible and are lost in hospitalised clinical language. Physical inactivity becomes a 'risk factor' to be eliminated. Governmentality studies indicate that focusing on risk is a way to regulate the reality and as such make it calculated and controllable. Physically inactive citizens are seen in the medicalisation paradigm as risk objects that require care. Language alone can establish practice by highlighting the risk to trigger an individual's understanding of her own physically inactive life as something that need managing.

If exercise is thought of as a treatment, how are we to perceive the "old boys" football match played on Sunday mornings? Perhaps it should be seen as an unsightly and treatment requiring activity that is unworthy of pursuit since "old boys" football can hardly been characterised as "healthy"?

5.2. The Organisational Level: The Practice and Knowledge Regimens

In the concept of "prescribed exercise", physical activity shifts into or is incorporated into the treatment regimen. Purely from an institutional perspective one sees a shift from an exercise culture that was localised in the clubhouse, community center or in the wood to being in the physiotherapist's clinic. When physical training is seen in a clinical context, whether in a private physiotherapy or at the hospital, a certain amount of hospitalisation of exercise occurs. This shift leads to expert orientation that implies "knowledge about physical activity" being found only by trained experts such as physiotherapists, health science graduates and physicians. Transformation of the exercise culture as such creates a clientele and expert dependence. In the treatment regimen, expert knowledge takes precedence, as evidenced or scientific knowledge leads to establishing guidelines for how "prescribed exercise" should be ordered and coordinated. Pedersen (2004a, p. 78), in relation to prevention, write that campaigns and advice to the population should be based on evidence-based knowledge (Pedersen & Saltin, 2006) as high technological clinical treatment. The evidence should be published and convincing and be implemented in daily life. Pedersen informs: "When evidence for change in clinical practice is established, it is the health sector's task to ensure implementation" (2004a, p. 79). This view of evidence-based practice in the health sector does not consider the patient perspective. A more recent article entitled "The patient's encounter with the health sector" that is included in the National Strategy on Quality Development in the Health Sector in Demark, highlights that effective communication between the patient and health care personnel assumes that health care personnel understand and accept the patients' views, feelings, values and opinions (2002).[6] The article furthermore highlights that there is a need for new supplementary methods to evaluate treatment results and health status that, apart from basing evaluation of the treatment's effectiveness against an objective biomedical goal, draws in the patients' own opinion of their general wellbeing. Opinions regarding quality development in the health sector are in accordance with that of the individual in a postmodern society (Beck, 1992; Giddens, 1991), where the individual is seen as reflective and self-oriented, and compliant to thoughts of empowerment (Cruikshank, 1999, 2003).

An evidence-based health sector is a more recent trend that primarily stems from North America. As far back as the 1980s, Sakett et al. developed the concept that to a large extent, medical practice should be based on scientific evidence rather than on by chance practice, tradition and habit. The word "evidence" comes from Latin, and means clarity, certainty (Bydam, 2003). An evidence-based health sector includes evidence-based medicine, evidence-based practice and evidence-based nursing care.

Evidence-based medicine is defined as (Sackett, Rosenberg, Muir Gray, Haynes, & Richardson, 1996):

> Conscientious, explicit, well-considered use of the best available evidence in decision-making regarding treatment of the individual patient. To practice evidence-based medicine requires integrating individual clinical expertise with the best accessible external evidence from systematic research.

Sackett, Straus, Richardson, Rosenberg, and Haynes (2000) which can be considered one of the leading sources of evidence-based medicine, includes the patient's perspective and, amongst other critical perspectives, points to the fact that the patient's perspective loses foothold when guidelines and reference systems in the treatment system integrates research-based knowledge. The critique about the evidence-based health sector points to the tendency towards knowledge simplification leading the practitioner towards being expert oriented, and the critique maintains that the development discards treatment and the consumer influence because the focus towards the clinical treatment shifts from dialogue and care for the patient and family towards the knowledge area and international technology development (Mitchell, 1999; Gregson, Meal, & Avis, 2002; Walker, 2003).

The governmentality literature research forms of practice in which different social, public and political organs and authorities attempt to control the actions of individuals and the public at large with ethical ideals, political results, economic necessities and social goals (Dean, 1999). The movement towards evidence-based sports medicine, can by means of this sketchy analytical viewpoint be seen as "managerialism". A national strategic maneuver or a regulating regimen that is based on epidemiological knowledge and has a perspective that focuses on the population and statistics. As Castel (1991) says, control of the individual (in this case the patient) shifts towards the group and the standard. The epidemiological clinic wins methodologically over the "face-to-face" -based clinical practice. Although randomised clinical research has the command and is seen as the methodological "golden standard" (Sackett et al., 1996), it is the epidemiological knowledge that focuses on generalisation, quantity, objectivity and complexity of cases, that forms the basis for developing and using evidence in evidence-based research. The rationale of epidemiological risk is based on the estimation of disease and fatality in population groups (Dean, 1999) and epidemiological knowledge weights heavily on the evaluation criteria's hierarchical evidence system. The epidemiological paradigm becomes the backcloth for the recognition that takes place.

As such, the epidemiological paradigm is the backdrop against which a finding becomes recognised but its research tools can weaken guidance in a clinical practice. Evidence-based practice implicitly claims the use of population-based knowledge to establish guidance at the individual level as unreliable and problematic beyond discussion.

It is therefore important to maintain that also evidence-based sports medicine such as "prescribed exercise" must integrate three aspects:

1. research-based knowledge;
2. clinical expertise;
3. patient values.

Moreover, the economic aspect is often integrated as a fourth element in evidence-based medicine. With respect to the "prescribed exercise" initiative, it can therefore be argued that people should be physically active as it would be beneficial from a pure socioeconomic perspective and because the obesity epidemic will otherwise ruin the welfare state. However, the question remains whether funding for "prescribed exercise" is being properly distributed if the drop-out problem and sustainability issues show that the concept does not pay off in the long term. Both short- and long-term perspectives must be considered when advising the public. Drawing in patients' perspectives in the form of feelings, thoughts and values about exercise and in relation to lifestyle changes could show themselves as being economically advantageous, as the patient's own manner of integrating physical activity into her daily life would probably be sustainable. Some illustrative examples are provided below.

The target groups for "prescribed exercise" are very different. Some interventions refer themselves to overweight people, others may target children and youth and some will focus on, for example, overweight expectant mothers. These specific target groups have differentiated needs and are not a homogenous group. A less illustrative example is drawn from the Danish context regarding the body and nudity. In the Nordic culture there is a tradition for bathing nude and taking saunas. This historical tradition means that the population at large does not find it problematic to bathe naked with others, both men and women. This culture of nudity is respected at clinics, swimming pools and in the clubhouse showers, changing rooms and bathrooms and bathing naked in public is expected as early as school-age. For indigenous Danes it is a given. The example shows that this relationship with the body is not universal but socio-culturally structured. The culture of bathing and dressing in training institutions in Denmark is very problematic for immigrants; so problematic, in fact, as to prevent some people from participating in physical activity. We live in a multicultural society but establish institutional structures such as, for example, the bathing culture that is anchored in tradition. If we analyse movement activities we must admit that the body is not a universal and homogenous size. Not all population groups like to cycle indoors on a training bicycle and not all are pleased to use weight lifting machines in fitness centers. Some target groups prefer the camaraderie of a sports club while others enjoy moving around in the quiet of the woods, and others like to swim in the sea with their family. Organised exercise in a treatment regimen can lead to creating a client group because the desire for physical activity is played down and replaced by the focus on clinical health and illness. When the patient's own motivation is not the driving force and when treatment with physical activity is oriented towards medical parameters such as maximal oxygen intake, blood sugar level, cholesterol count and insulin sensitivity, a dependence on experts is created, a dependence that presupposes that the participant is distanced from his own body. Lack of compliance in exercise as treatment can be blamed on an underestimation of the individual as an emotions-driven person and a lack of compliance can be blamed on the lack of dialogue with people of other cultures.

5.3. The Individual Level: The Entrepreneurial Self Work

With respect to the individual level, one thinks of the paradox of methodical tools in the treatment regimen (Vallgaarda, 2003), the question of motivating people to assume responsibility for their own health as well as responsibility-giving processes in the concept. The "prescribed exercise" initiative is comparable with other more recent public health theoretic efforts by the health authorities that shift the focus away from disease towards health promotion (Iversen, Søndergård Kristensen, Holstein, & Due, 2002; Petersen & Lupton, 1996). The imperative morale in public health initiatives is that the individual should be encouraged to better look after his own health, including help to optimise knowledge and ability and assisted with tools to train the citizens to self-realise these health goals. There is a considerable interest in empowering individuals with respect to health and wellbeing. These types of interventions call for the analysis of public health from a policy perspective (Vallgaarda, 2003). Public health is seen as a movement that stewards the citizens' self-conditioning (Aakerstroem Andersen, 2003). The good aim and the supportive health perspective is the offer of changing lifestyles, and the helping hand is knowledge as a means to healthy and unhealthy nutrition and tools that help to train citizens to reflect on their own health-related behaviour. "The New Public Health" esteems self-management rather than providing a control framework. More precisely, control of the citizens' health welfare occurs through responsibility giving processes where the citizens should illustrate their personal relationship to, for example, exercise and eating habits. This takes place in some interventions by holding open therapeutic sessions during which the individual together with others in a group are encouraged to express their feelings about eating and exercise (Thing, 2005b). "Prescribed exercise" as a preventive initiative spreads to the knowledge relay level as work with the citizen's self-conditioning is not limited to only education about food and exercise. This type of initiative draws in the citizen's self-confidence and self-respect. Vallgaarda (2003) writes that preventive efforts can be counterproductive and can give a double message as dialogs and intervention actions attempt to motivate patients to act as the authorities think they should and the way that is best for them. Treatment technicians say that focus is on "non-control" because the citizens become aware of undesirable lifestyle and because the goal for the interventions is an improvement of the citizen's health. "Prescribed exercise" can be described as a form of control that focuses on the participants' autonomy in order to force them to choose the "right thing for them". The prevention initiative contains a double meaning therefore: the technique is "self-control" and "laying responsibility on the individual for his own health", but the goal is established by authorities in advance. If one cannot work very actively with a few involved patients and if one does not actively do something to influence these patients then a dependence on experts occurs. Substantial research in the United States has already shown that expert dependence is often the result. American researchers are working seriously with computers that audibly inform inactive citizens when and how they should be activated as it has been seen that "inactive" citizens do not sustain their physical activity level shortly after finishing treatment with "prescribed exercise". These futuristic scenes are not sustainable in the Nordic context where voluntary sports have a 100-year tradition for body culture.

It is important for preventive initiative not to take away responsibility from the citizens. It is vital that lifestyle change be seen broadly and in relation to the socio-cultural context (Rycroft-Malone et al., 2004). Changes regarding physical inactivity cannot be understood within a clinical frame of thinking. This medical regimen is only a mixture of many perspectives about exercise and possesses a danger of medicalisation. In most western countries, social inequality in health and illness exist. Activating "risk groups" demands a view and understanding of cultural backgrounds. The body is not a machine and daily life is not a laboratory experiment. We need to tailor and make flexible the offer of exercise, in a way that creates a dialog with the people. Changing lifestyles is not like an insect's metamorphosis and it is not a question of leaving behind an ugly cocoon.

Eichberg (1988) developed in the 1980s, a triangular model to analyse body culture in society. He was inspired by the German Heineman's sports model. Eichbergs' triangular model (Bale & Philo, 1998) on body culture incorporates achievement sports; health pedagogic body movement and body culture of experience. These three forms of body culture tell us something about motivation for movement. Many other sports sociological models and theories conceptualise the relationship between the body, culture and society. The English sociologists Elias and Dunning (1986) say that tension and feelings are the driving force behind free-time sports. I believe that existing knowledge that is found in sports sociological and sports historical area is useful if we need to conceptualise motivation to physical activity. Knowledge gained about voluntary and organised sports pave the way to a deeper understanding about physical and sensual movement. The phenomenological entry point that weighs the physical meaning of identity and self-understanding could very well be a third offer to resolve resistance problems and lack of "compliance" in treatment with exercise.

6. EMPIRICAL EXAMPLES FROM THE EVALUATION PROJECT "THE BEST WAS TO DRIVE HEAD FIRST – MULTICULTURAL HEALTH CARE"

One of the results in evaluating the project "The best is to jump in head first – multicultural health care" is that the target group of women with another ethnic background than Danish stimulated an interest in swimming. The project with the immigrant women and their daughters took place in the local swimming pool but at a time when men were forbidden entry to the swimming pool and where there were cabins to change in. This structure which focused on "the women's room", opened up the possibility of meeting with immigrant women because a frame was established that considered specific cultural values. The recognised and developmental learning pedagogy (Andersen & Vittrup, 2007, p. 24) produced results. An unplanned teaching episode (that did not stem from a manual nor was associated with evidenced concepts but rather involved playful and creative elements) opened dialog and was able to integrate perspectives while considering the local society. The body related sociological point here is that we don't just *have* bodies that need to learn to swim. We *are* bodies that will learn to swim on our own conditions (Timm, 1997; Turner, 1992).

Other evaluations of lifestyle changes (Thing, 2005b, 2006) show that changes towards healthy nutrition and exercise are aspects that require time and resources (economic, psychological and social). To develop competency to take action which is defined here as the possibility to make a health-related choice both in relation to oneself and to others, is a slow process as lifestyle stems from childhood (Bourdieu, 1986, 1997). Evaluation of obese Danish women show that action competency to a large extent, was developed in relation to nutrition rather than in relation to exercise, amongst other reasons because exercise is not integrated well enough in daily life. Exercise is experienced within Danish projects with women whose BMI is over 30 as well as in families with small children who experience that time for exercise takes away from being together and from time with the children. The women highlight that time for exercising daily is an egotistical initiative that happens at the expense of the children. This aspect is important to note in the lifestyle-changing situation. It is therefore important to listen to the women's experiences with "prescribed exercise". If the participants' experiences are not taken seriously, and if one does not become involved with the participants' desires, the intervention becomes superfluous in the long term. All of these aspects that create ambivalence in participants towards exercise must be drawn in when redefining and restructuring lifestyles is required. Influence by and dialogue with the target groups is beneficial.

Exercise is for some citizens associated with deep disgust, discomfort and bad experiences. Increasing the pulse rate and sweating is not a positive experience for everyone, and especially not for all ethnical groups. Even if an exercise regimen is necessary for a body's healing process, the individual's considerations should be taken into account. Efforts can be made to retrieve the joy in movement with which we are born. As important to note is the fact that lifestyle – the manner in which an individual lives her life – should be balanced with her life conditions. Lifestyle and living conditions cannot be considered separately from each other and policy for preventive initiatives must consider maintaining a balance of the dynamics of the socioeconomic dimension as well as the psychological dimension. This important aspect raises the consideration that exercising may not be just the individuals' problem but perhaps a societal issue as well.

7. FUTURE SCENARIO

The issue of a lack of physical activity by a population, broadly seen, is also a matter of social structure, the institutional context and the organisation of daily life. This is often forgotten today when taking preventive measures focuses on the individual and means that she must assume responsibility for her own health. Substantial social change has taken place over the past 20–30 years. Several sociologists claim that we have moved away from a tyranny of minimalism to becoming an indulgent society where not placing limitations on what we consume (also in relation to the body) is of paramount importance (Featherstone, Hepworth, & Turner, 1990; Giddens, 1991). The obesity epidemic and the population's inactive tendencies, in this respect, can therefore be seen as a societal issue. This is a policy problem that we can do something about both institutionally and structurally, for example, through education, the labour market, transportation and not least when developing residential areas. Changing people's exercise habits can be achieved at the societal level by explicitly remaining alert to social change that occurs over time rather than focusing on the individual as is currently done. Considering the use of responsibility-giving technologies at the macro-political level could be a creative approach and would avoid blaming or shaming individuals. To what extent could we stimulate physical activity in schools, in the workplace, within the transportation system, in residential areas and during recreational time? How can we organise sports in a way that they do not marginalise specific population groups and so that the competitive aspect does not determine the extent of a child's involvement in sports?

"Prescribed exercise" used as therapy will not lead to lifestyle change, and this therapy will be over on completion of an exercise program undertaken at a hospital or physiotherapist's clinic. Drawing in exercise as a sustainable part of an individual's daily life calls for substantial change (nothing as easy as swallowing a pill). That is why it is important to reflect on existing conditions at the societal level and necessary to maintain that exercise is not a medical matter.

NOTES

1. At January 1, 2007, 8.7% of the population comprised immigrants and their descendents. Fifty percent of this group originates from another European country (Statistisk Aarbog, 2007).
2. Statistisk Aarbog, (2007, p. 147).
3. SUSY, 2005 (Ekholm et al., 2007).
4. The terms gymnastics, dance and sport will not be further defined, as the purpose in this instance is only to underscore that the Danish body culture has a tradition of over 100 years in differentiating between these terms (Pedersen, 2004b).
5. The analysis should not be read as an unfolding genealogy or archeological assignment that interprets forms of discourse (Foucault, 2005; Aakerstroem Anderson, 1999), but rather as constructive critique to destabilize the subjectivity forms and power strategies (Villadsen, 2003, p. 23) which are seen as necessary and natural in the "prescribed exercise" concept.
6. Sundhedsstyrelsen (2002). National strategi for kvalitetsudvikling i sundheds-væsenet: fælles mål og handleplan 2002–2006. Copenhagen: Sundhedsstyrelsen.

REFERENCES

Aakerstroem Andersen, N. (1999). *Diskursive analysestrategier: Foucault, Koselleck, Laclau, Luhmann.* Copenhagen: Nyt fra Samfundsvidenskaberne.

Aakerstroem Andersen, N. (2003). *Borgerens kontraktliggørelse.* Copenhagen: Hans Reitzel.

Andersen, L. S., & Vittrup, R. (2007). *Det bedste var at springe på hovedet i – multikulturel sundhedspleje. Evaluering af sundhedsvejledning og svømning for mødre med anden etnisk baggrund end dansk og deres døtre.* Copenhagen: CVU Øresund.

Bale, J., & Philo, C. (1998). *Body cultures: Essays on sport, space and identity.* London: Routledge.

Barry, A., Osborne, T., & Rose, N. (1996). *Foucault and political reason: liberalism, neo-liberalism and rationalities of government.* London: UCL Press.

Beck, U. (1992). *Risk society. Towards a new modernity.* London: Sage Publications.

Bourdieu, P. (1986). *Distinction. A social critique of the judgement of taste.* London: Routledge.

Bourdieu, P. (1997). *Men hvem skabte skaberne?* Copenhagen: Akademisk Forlag.

Bydam, J. (2003). *Evidensbaseret praksis – en grundbog for sundhedspersonale.* Copenhagen: Nyt Nordisk Forlag Arnold Busck.

Castel, R. (1991). From dangerrousness to risk. In: G. Burchell, C. Gordon & P. Miller (Eds), *The Foucault effect. Studies in governmentality. With two lectures by and an interview with Michel Foucault* (pp. 281–298). Chicago: The University of Chicago Press.

Conrad, P., & Schneider, J. W. (1980). Looking at levels of medicalisation: A comment on strong's critique of the thesis of medical imperialism. *Social Science and Medicine, 14A,* 75–79.

Cruikshank, B. (1999). *The will to empower. Democratic citizens and other subjects.* London: Cornell University Press.

Cruikshank, B. (2003). Viljen til at mægtiggøre: Medborgerskabsteknologier og 'krigen mod fattigdom'. *Grus* (70), 30–48.

Dean, M. (1999). *Governmentality. Power and rule in modern society.* London: Sage Publications.

Eichberg, H. (1988). *Det løbende samfund.* Slagelse: Forlaget Bavnebanke.

Ekholm, O., Kjøller, M., Davidsen, M., Hesse, U., Eriksen, L., Illemann, A., & Grønbæk, M. (2007). *Sundhed og sygelighed i Danmark 2005 & udviklingen siden 1987.* Copenhagen: Statens Institut for Folkesundhed.

Elias, N., & Dunning, E. (1986). *Quest for excitement. Sport and leisure in the civilizing process.* Oxford: Basil Blackwell.

Featherstone, M., Hepworth, M., & Turner, B. S. (1990). *The body. Social process and cultural theory.* London: Sage Publications.

Foucault, M. (1991). Governmentality. In: G. Burchell, C. Gordon & P. Miller (Eds), *The Foucault effect: Studies in governmentality: with two lectures by and an interview with Michel Foucault* (pp. 87–104). Chicago: The University of Chicago Press.

Foucault, M. (2005). *Vidensarkæologien.* Århus: Philosophia.

Gadamer, H.-G. (1989). *Truth and Method.* London: Sheed & Ward.

Gannik, D., & Schmidt, D. (1990). Sygdom – fra et lægevidenskabeligt til et samfundsmæssigt anliggende. In: P. Gundelach, N. Mortensen & J. Chr. Tonboe (Eds), *Sociologi under forandring* (pp. 415–447). Copenhagen: Gyldendal.

Giddens, A. (1991). *Modernity and self-identity. Self and society in Late Modern Age.* Cambridge: Polity Press.

Gregson, P. R. W., Meal, A. G., & Avis, M. (2002). Meta-analysis: The glass eye of evidence-based practice? *Nursing Inquiry, 9*(1), 24–30.

Hindess, B. (1996). *Discourses of power: From Hobbes to Foucault.* Oxford: Blackwell Publishers.

Iversen, L., Søndergård Kristensen, T., Holstein, B. E., & Due, P. (2002). *Medicinsk sociologi: Samfund, sundhed og sygdom.* Copenhagen: Munksgaard.

Korsgaard, O. (1982). *Kampen om kroppen. Dansk Idræts historie gennem 200 år.* Copenhagen: Gyldendal.

Mitchell, G. J. (1999). Evidence-based practice: Critique and alternative view. *Nursing Science Quarterly, 12*(1), 30–35.

Pedersen, B. K. (2004a). Klinisk medicinsk viden i forebyggelsesarbejdet. In: J. J. Bruun, M. L. Hanak & B. G. Koefoed (Eds), *Viden og evidens i forebyggelsen* (pp. 70–80). Copenhagen: Sundhedsstyrelsen.

Pedersen, B. K., & Saltin, B. (2006). Evidence for prescribing exercise as therapy in chronic disease. *Scandinavian Journal of Medicine and Science of Sports, 16*, 3–63.

Pedersen, I. K. (2004b). sport – et sociologisk laboratorium. In: H. Andersen (Ed.), *Sociologi – en grundbog til et fag* (pp. 328–345). Copenhagen: Hans Reitzels.

Petersen, A., & Lupton, D. (1996). *The new public health: Health and the self in the age of risk.* London: Sage Publications.

Roessler, K. K., Ibsen, B., Saltin, B., & Sørensen, J. (2007). *Fysisk aktivitet som behandling. Motion og kost på Recept i Københavns Kommune.* Odense: Syddansk Universitetsforlag.

Rose, N. (1999). *Powers of freedom. Reframing political thought.* Cambridge: Cambridge University Press.

Rosell, AC., Raahauge Madsen, L., Mortensen, EL., & Iversen, L. (2005). Motion på recept. *Et kvalitativt studie af ændringer i patientens adfærd og forestillinger om fysisk aktivitet. Månedsskrift for Praktisk Lægegerning,, 83*, 5–14.

Rycroft-Malone, J., Seers, K., Titchen, A., Harvey, G., Kitson, A., & McCormack, B. (2004). What counts as evidence in evidence-based practice? *Journal of Advanced Nursing, 47*(1), 81–90.

Sackett, D., Rosenberg, WMC., Muir Gray, JA., Haynes, RB., & Richardson, WS. (1996). Evidence based medicine: What it is and what it isn't. *British Medical Journal, 312,* 71–72.

Sackett, D. L., Straus, S. E., Richardson, W. S., Rosenberg, W., & Haynes, R. B. (2000). *Evidence-based medicine. How to practice and teach EBM.* London: Churchill Livingstone.

Statistisk Aarbog. (2007). *Statistisk Aarbog.* Danmarks Statistik: Copenhagen.

Sundhedsstyrelsen. (2002). *National strategi for kvalitetsudvikling i sundhedsvæsenet: fælles mål og handleplan 2002–2006.* Copenhagen: Sundhedsstyrelsen.

Sundhedsstyrelsen. (2003). *Oplæg til national handlingsplan mod svær overvægt: Forslag til løsninger og perspektiver.* Copenhagen: Sundhedsstyrelsen.

Thing, L.F. (2005a). *Motion på recept – er en svær pille at sluge. En sociologisk diskussion af motion som behandling i velfærdsstaten.* Available at www.idrottsforum.org

Thing, L. F. (2005b). *Evaluering af projekt "Sunde Familier".* Copenhagen: Universitetshospitalernes Center for sygepleje- og omsorgsforskning.

Thing, L. F. (2006). *Evaluering af 'Sundhed og aktivitet i skoler (2003–2006)' Et EU Interreg III A samarbejdsprojekt mellem Lübeck og Storstrøms Amt om at støtte unge mennesker i at føre en sundere livsstil.* Copenhagen: Universitetshospitalernes Center for sygepleje- og omsorgsforskning.

Thing, L. F. (2007). Motion på recept – er en svær pille at sluge. *Månedsskrift for Praktisk Lægegerning., 85,* 219–224.

Timm, H. (1997). At have en krop og at være en krop. *Grus, 18*(52), 24–36.

Turner, B. (1992). *Kroppen i samfundet. Teorier om krop og kultur.* Copenhagen: Hans Reitzels forlag.

Vallgaarda, S. (2003). *Folkesundhed som politik: Danmark og Sverige fra 1930 til i dag.* Aarhus: Aarhus Universitetsforlag.

Villadsen, K. (2003). *Det sociale arbejdes genealogi: om kampen for at gøre fattige og udstødte til frie mennesker.* Copenhagen: Sociologisk Institut.

Walker, K. (2003). Why evidence-based practice now?: A polemic. *Nursing Inquiry, 10*(3), 145–155.

Willemann, M. (2004). *Motion på recept: en litteraturgennemgang med fokus på effekter og organisering.* Copenhagen: Sundhedsstyrelsen.

CROSS-CULTURAL DIMENSIONS OF SPORTING GOODS CONSUMPTION

Fabien Ohl and Marijke Taks

After Zidane gave his shirt to Beckham, someone asked him what he was going to do with it and Beckham answered "I will hang it at home like a painting. It is a great souvenir from a great player and it is good to have souvenirs". (July 7, 2007, Lisbone, Reuters)

Studying sporting culture is a complex task because there are numerous dimensions and aspects of this culture. One way to observe sporting culture is through the lens of consumption theories, and in our case, through the consumption of sporting goods. A wide variety of sporting goods can be acquired by many types of consumers and for various, and sometimes contradictory reasons. This explains the complex phenomenon and the challenge of studying the consumption of sporting goods, but makes it also an interesting path to explore. Material culture can be seen as a reflection of culture. Gender, age and cultural differences are reflected through consumption. Nevertheless, sporting goods are part of the sporting culture, and strongly influence social experiences in sport.

Social and Cultural Diversity in a Sporting World
Research in the Sociology of Sport, Volume 5, 211–228
Copyright © 2008 by Emerald Group Publishing Ltd
All rights of reproduction in any form reserved
ISSN: 1476-2854/doi:10.1016/S1476-2854(08)05013-9

1. GOODS AND CULTURE: A SOCIOLOGICAL PERSPECTIVE

In an economical perspective, goods have a utility value and an exchange value. They are an important part of an exchange system based on money. Goods, and more broadly consumption, are defined by their utility. Sociologists focused on consumption to compare social class behaviour and to react against a narrow economical view of consumption (Halbwachs, 1933). However, sociologists were more interested in core topics such as work, beliefs, social classes, institutions or organisations than they were in consumption. Consumption started to receive more attention during the sixties, a period of social criticism on morality, religion and more generally, capitalist order. These critiques followed the analyses on popular culture consumption, which were initiated by the Institute for Social Research at the University of Frankfurt. Popular culture consumption, including sport, was defined as mass consumption, controlled by the industry, supposed to indoctrinate and to manipulate people. The consumption of popular culture legitimates and reifies social classes "by hiding social relations behind the relationships of things, commodities in the marketplace" (Gartman, 2004, p. 182). Thus, the consumption of sports events, services or goods was also considered as a way to oppress the working class. Consequently, pleasure or emotion while consuming sporting goods, or objects in a more sociological language, could be considered as the result of an alienation and oppression of the working class by capitalism. Consumption produces social conformity, passivity, manipulation and depoliticises these attitudes. This way of thinking considers consumers as being very passive and driven by marketing and advertising.

Active, but disconnected from reality, was the view developed by Baudrillard on the consumption of objects. One of his first contributions was rooted in a critical neo-Marxist perspective on consumer society, and focused on objects as a system of signs. Consumption and advertising produce a system of signs in which objects play a key role. Consumption of objects is endless because it is based on signs, it has no real significance, and needs can never be satisfied because consumption is a "systematic act of the manipulation of signs" (Baudrillard, 1968, p. 233). This perspective projects objects as a system of communication disconnected from uses and needs. It is not the object in itself that is consumed but the signs associated with it. Objects such as cars, paintings, clothes and jewelleries are often related to social status. Consequently, all other social divisions such as class, gender or race can be recalled by consumption and collected by the market when brands exploit, for example, black athletes or masculinity. Subcultures also enter this "sign culture". For example, black basketball players are used to recall urban black subculture for its "authenticity" to target a multi-racial global audience (Goldman & Papson, 1998, p. 56).

Baudrillard's analysis was a seminal work in the sociology of consumption. However, the goal of his analyses of the consumption of goods was mainly to critique the consumer society. He did not pay so much attention to what people actually do with their objects. This became a focus of the anthropological perspective in which researchers analysed the meaning of goods and the "social life of things" (Appadurai, 1986). In this perspective, consumption is observed as a social experience in which people can be active, in which forms of resistance are developed, and provides emotions, pleasure or pain. Using goods can be a resource to create, emphasise, strengthen or change identity. Goods play a central role in the exchanges between people while using, buying, giving or borrowing them. Thus, purchasing or acquiring goods is not only a material exchange; objects are an important part of the communication process. Goods provide visual information about people. They also bring about verbal exchanges in the purchasing or exchanging processes (Ohl & Tribou, 2004). Goods are commodities, but as soon as they are touched or used they become objects with their specific bonds with people. Goods are part of our environment and there is no chance to escape them. Material objects are part of the sport culture, and they changed it considerably through innovations, new technologies and the creation of new objects. They validate the existence of specific sports; i.e., no windsurfers without fibreglass, no paragliding without nylon, etc., but they also change our body experience while participating in sports. Running used to be a simple and basic activity which only required a pair of shoes. Nowadays, new technology completely changes the bodily experience; think about the wide variety of sports shoes (e.g., light and soft versions and basketball and running), gloves, heart rate monitors, injury prevention and recovery products, insoles, training suits, speed and distance monitors, just to name a few. Sporting culture has an important material dimension, which falls under the denominator of material culture. The aim of this chapter is not only to reveal how the usage of goods expresses social differences. We also want to understand sporting subcultures through the diversity of social uses and meanings of sporting objects. Material culture influences our social experience of sport and it cannot be treated as something marginal compared with what is considered as more crucial, such as values. Following a more anthropological perspective, we could say that through goods consumption, social bonds, identities and communication is at stake (Douglas & Isherwood, 1979). Goods are part of the experience of sport, they are a core element of our activities, and are closely connected to human networks.

2. UNIQUE CHARACTERISTICS OF THE SPORTING CULTURE

Appearances, components and qualities of sporting goods are not unique to sport, since technologies are shared with many other industries. Compared to other goods, however, consumption of sporting goods has a particularly strong symbolic efficiency and plays an important role in social biography and experiences. Four phases of consumption can be distinguished over time:

1. The absence of specific goods to play sport; practitioners use ordinary goods and adapt them to play sports (e.g., dresses for women, pants for men and leather shoes). Sporting styles refer to class styles; the consumption of sporting goods is mainly an expression of a supposed conspicuous consumption (Veblen, 1899/1970).
2. Sporting goods are specifically developed for participants, and marketed through athletes by focusing on the relationship between the technical qualities of the goods and the high performance levels of the athletes. This is a quest for goods that help to improve performance. The variety of goods is (still) very limited; differences in consumption are related to social classes but also to specific sport choices.
3. Sporting goods are spreading outside the sporting field. A sports-lifestyle refers to "being cool". Sporting goods consumption becomes mass consumption.
4. Sporting goods are related to the style of sportspeople. The usage of sporting goods not only recalls the excellence of sport heroes but also the lifestyles of participants. Sporting goods become fashionable within a culture of celebrities. Consumer choices are not necessarily based on the excellent performances of athletes, but are mainly driven by the celebrities' lifestyles. For example, Kournikova (tennis), Chabal (rugby) or Beckham (football) are not necessarily the best players, but their lifestyle and celebrity influence consumer choices. These celebrities are used in branding strategies of major sporting goods companies.

Although the first consumption period has phased out, consumption attitude of the three other periods coexist. For particular market segments, such as high-performance athletes, the technical component of sporting goods remains extremely important. However, the majority of consumers, influenced by the lifestyles of sport heroes, are only using sporting goods for leisurely purposes. Thus, the mass market reflects a shift from technical efficiency to symbolic and aesthetical efficiency. During the 20th century, the role of the esthetical aspects of goods increased. It is argued that the consumer has difficulties to make choices because of the technological complexity of sporting goods. The esthetical dimensions, on the other hand, alleviate some of these difficulties, and facilitate consumer choices. Aesthetic judgement allows the consumer to decide on his/her own, and to affirm his/her place in the market (Hetzel, 2002, p. 44). Nevertheless, it is difficult to oppose technical and aesthetical aspects of goods, since both include symbolic dimensions. For experts, the quest for technical efficiency is related to their subculture. Experts' choices depend on the symbolic organisation of their sub-field. The symbolic meaning of goods is to be understood in relation with the specific history of each sport. In addition, when sporting goods are used for recreational purposes, there is no real need for technological efficiency. However, the casual or recreational consumer likes to show off highly innovative sports equipment as a means of symbolic efficacy.

The usage of celebrities to influence consumers exploits both, the aesthetical dimension as well as the sport-specific attributes. Using sport celebrities' styles also helps to solve the dilemma of the complexity of choice. The question of technology is solved thanks to champion's advice; the doubts concerning one's style are lowered thanks to the legitimacy of the styles of the sports celebrity, which serve as a reference. Sport celebrities, and pop or movie stars show some similarities but also major differences. They both have fans, endorse products and receive media attention from paparazzi. However, the significance of sporting events and their heroes is different. Sport is considered to be a model of fair competition and is used as the paradigm of equity (Boltanski & Chiapello, 1999, pp. 403–405). This is not the case for music or movie stars, and very few of these heroes reflect local or national identities as is the case in sport. In sport, human beings reveal what they really are and what they can do. But champions do not only reveal their personal character, they also represent social groups and particularly cities, regions and nations reinforcing local and national identity (Birrell, 2001; Goffman, 1967).

3. SPORTING GOODS, YOUTH
AND GENDERED CULTURES

Sporting goods choices are an expression of social relations between people. Choices are influenced by youth, and they also reflect gender relations. The sporting culture is considered a sphere that expresses values and education. The increasing importance of the economics of sport with its numerous businesses (media, events, goods, fashion, etc.) and the huge amounts of money involved, has changed the image of many sports actors. It has been argued that the sporting goods industry is exploiting people, particularly the more fragile ones such as youth and minorities. Within capitalist modernity, "children" and "culture" are ideologically positioned as "sacred" in opposition to the "profane" sphere of commerce and industry (Langer, 2002). This can explain the sensitivity towards children's consumption, but in different and contradictory ways. On the one hand, the basic idea stipulates that children must be protected against market influences. Media consumption was among the main targets of criticism because of its impact on youth. On the other hand, sporting heroes are used to seduce youth, because of their strong influencing power (Stevens, Lathrop, & Bradish, 2005).

Youth is at the core of the sporting goods markets. Young people[1] from 12 to 25 are a major target group of sports brands.[2] A variety of reasons can be brought forward to explain this youth focus. First, youth are "heavy" sporting goods consumers (e.g., in France, men from 15 to 24 spend 163 euros compared to 102 euros per year for the 25–34 year olds[3]). Second, they rank the sporting brands at the top of their preference list at a very young age, i.e. 6–8 years.[4] Third, youth has increased their autonomy related to leisure expenditures. Their culture is a culture of consumption, which they embody very early (Miles, 1998; Roedder John, 2001). Fourth, attitudes towards sporting goods reveal changes in their course of life. Growing up can be materialised through their appearances by wearing new brands or clothes or by using new objects. Consuming independently is a way to affirm their emancipation against their family. Their autonomy of decision-making in the consumption realm is a way to show that they can be themselves, and exist as an independent person within the family. Finally, children's consumption influences their parents' choices, and more generally, adults' choices. Sport is the territory of youth, it reflects youthfulness, and is considered a "youth culture". Youth has, therefore, become the "pre-conizer" or "prescriptors" for young and old in many different markets.

Parents show very little opposition with regard to the consumption of sporting goods by their children. Two reasons can be identified: (a) sport is associated with positive qualities (e.g., fair-play, performance, health, courage, demeanour and success) and, (b) parents, at least the father, share the sporting culture with their children. In a context of increasing horizontal socialisation among children, i.e., between friends, and weaker vertical socialisation (Pasquier, 2005; Yoh, 2005), sport is one of the few cultural interests and practices that can be shared between parents and children. Most of the other cultural activities are more exclusively shared within each generation. Thus, children increase their autonomy in many cultural practices, including some sports, but in many cases sport reinforces family bonds. For example, a lot of parents and children can share a passion for hockey, football or basketball and may be fans of the same teams and heroes. During key events, such as the World Cup, they often watch TV together.

Despite the narrowing gap in gender differences in some forms of consumption, e.g., women commonly wear pants, and men's cosmetic consumption is increasing, many goods still recall and reinforce gender differences. While the sporting goods industry offers many goods, clothes, shoes or technical equipment specifically for men and women mainly for marketing reasons, it gives the impression that differences in anatomy or physiology require this product diversification. Fowler (1999) discussed some of the major changes in active wear and the sports apparel market, emphasising differences in sport apparel preferences between males and females. Both men and women looked for comfort, quality, durability and style, however, women ranked "fit" significantly higher than men. Thus, sporting goods are signs, which recall and emphasise the boundaries between genders. Objects are used to recall identities and especially gender identities. The success of sport consumption is also related to social uncertainty and identity. In contrast to girls, boys have a stronger affiliation with brands, and with sport heroes, whom they use as identification figures to construct their ideal ego. For young boys having access to, and using goods, referring to their sporting heroes is a way to look like them. Brand marketing and communication try to add value to goods that will assist in building a positive identity, often a typical male one. As for some women, femininity is more often constructed through fashionable clothes, makeup or accessories such as jewellery or shoes with stiletto heels. Sporting brands also communicate through female athletes, very often in a stereotyped fashion, as is the case with Anna Kournikova.

There is a production–consumption complex involving many social actors and the whole process of consumption is gendered. From the conception of goods, design, production, marketing, communication, advertising and retailing, to the uses of sporting goods, most of the stages are gendered. Thus buying and choosing sporting goods are gendered activities, which can, for example, be observed in social interactions between customers and sellers (Ohl & Tribou, 2004). General household consumption studies have stressed the role of mothers as primary socialisation agents in consumption decisions, i.e. women make 80% of the daily household consumption decisions (Carlson, Grossbart, & Walsh, 1990). Falk and Campbell (1997, p. 166) suggested, however, that aesthetical goods are a "female" territory, while technical goods are a "male" territory. The authors suggested that variation in shopping is more correlated with gender than any other variable. Male "technology shopping" is perceived as a serious economical transaction of goods that needs specific knowledge. Female shopping is perceived as a less serious matter because it is more focussed on aesthetics and on goods which are perceived to require less rational choices and driven by pleasure-seeking. This means that most of the organisation of the supply of sporting goods tends to reproduce gender divisions. Even the distribution of jobs in the sporting goods sector, is based on characteristics of the goods. The testimony of Hélène Meillan, a female seller at an outdoor store (Caribou in Lyon, France), reflect this when she talks about a gendered division among sellers "I regret not to be in charge of the equipment in the store. It is true that the "technical ski" is still very macho. When I arrived at Carribou eight months ago, they gave me the men's' clothes section".[5] For the manager of the store, it was difficult to imagine finding a woman with technical skills and/or a man with aesthetical skills.

4. GOODS AND THE MEANING
OF SPORTING STYLES

Styles are social practices through which people create meanings, and consuming goods is a key element in the creation of styles. At least three interpretations can be provided on how material things take on social meanings.

The first interpretation is based on Bourdieu's analysis. One of his main interests was the analysis of the formation and the reproduction of symbolic practices. He focused on consumption because it is among those practices by which social groups try to recall, maintain or change, at least symbolically, their social positions. His frame was a social class approach that helps to observe how social conditions and positions are reflected in consumption. Among others, he studied sport while using field theory. Sport consumption was a way to position oneself in the sporting field and to transform, in euphemistic way, social struggles between agents into symbolic and meaningful relations. Bourdieu used the triptych: social position, habitus and field, to explain the meaning of style. A homology between social position and consumption forms the basic hypothesis. The habitus determines the taste and style that positions a person in various fields. As such, sport consumer styles are supposed to align with social positions. Thus, sports, brands and consumer choices can often be explained by the necessity to "keep a certain position, or to maintain a certain distance" (Bourdieu, 1984[1979], p. 61). Taste and distaste for goods express one's position in a field. This means that distances and proximities are reaffirmed through the uses of the goods. Yet, it is difficult to maintain a hypothesis of homology for all possible configurations. Sport consumption is often more strongly related to age, gender and other specific subcultures than to class differences. Social position plays a role in explaining the diversity of sport subcultures but it is difficult to follow Bourdieu's homology hypothesis to explain sporting goods choices and meanings associated with it. Understanding experiences related to the position in a field seems to be more appropriate. However, despite some insights about luxury goods or cars, Bourdieu gave little attention to the consumption of ordinary goods such as sporting goods.

The second interpretation refers to stylistic choices as a result of a kind of "bricolage" (De Certeau, 1980). Practices, chats and goods are combined to produce new meanings or to transform old ones (Hebdige, 1991). The *Centre for Contemporary Cultural Studies* (CCCS) from Birmingham University produced many studies on musical taste, linking styles with youth subculture. They promoted the idea that new styles were related to working-class youth resisting or adapting to new social contexts. However, it has also been argued that new styles were a way to symbolically escape from traditional class-based identities. Studies often focused on more visible groups such as mods, teddy boys, punk or skin-heads, and less on ordinary people and their ordinary consumptions. Some sporting styles seemed to reflect resistance. Subcultures constituted around sports such as snowboarding, skating, hip-hop or surfing, are expressing an opposition against adults and traditional sport organisations. Their styles are expressed through their specific sporting skills but also through their clothing, their sporting goods (brand, name, look of the object) as well as their language or other lifestyles elements such their music preferences. Thus, while focusing on their specific subculture, they probably neglect ordinary behaviour, and often ignore girls and young women. Brands such as Nike often use figures of resistance, irreverence and rebellion in their commercials to position themselves in the market (Goldman & Papson, 1998). It could also be argued that instead of resistance, consumption can also give the illusion of having access to a new status.

The third line of interpretation is related to subcultures and lifestyles. Goods which people buy are often an expression of their subculture. In many cases, belonging to a group requires material signs. It is impossible to find fans, supporters or hooligans not wearing the signs of deference of their favourite team. Buying top of the line sporting goods, using the most valuable brands or objects, provide the opportunity to endorse recognised styles and identities. Thus, despite commercial uses, there is no evidence of a clear link between sport consumption's styles and resistance. There is no doubt that the meanings of sporting goods are related to specific sporting experiences, but they are not always embedded in strong sporting subcultures. Ordinary sport styles and the consumption of ordinary goods cannot be related to any strong and coherent subculture. According to Maffesoli (1988, 1990), multiple and unstable identifications are characterising the late modern consumer-based society. Sporting goods consumption cannot always be related to a coherent style and subculture. Furthermore, media and marketing play an obvious role in constructing stylistic categories. The unity and coherence of sporting subcultures is needed to market a product. Even if such categories do not exist as a real cultural group, marketing and communication will stage subcultures to catch the consumer's attention and use their wish to be affiliated with some heroes or sport groupings (surfer, skater, snowboarder as tribes are marketing creations). In such case, sporting goods consumption reflects a "tribal" identity which is more transitory compared to subcultural identity. Instead of being related to subcultural groups, which in turn are often connected to classes, style should be understood as a form of late modernity "sociality" in which people are involved. Styles and goods consumption are not expressing consumer's belonging to a class, a family or a community, but allow consumers to switch from one ephemeral group to another (Maffesoli, 1988). Thus, social groupings do not explain styles, but styles, appearances and leisure explain new forms of groupings. They are organised by, and organise, a subjective construction of social reality.

These three orientations seem to be mutually exclusive. Nevertheless, even if we are not particularly sensitive to theoretical ecumenism, all three can be right concerning sporting goods consumption. Some goods recall class divisions, while other goods evoke subcultures and many neo-tribes of mass-consumers. In short, data indicates that sporting goods consumption is influenced by class, age, gender and subcultures (Ohl & Taks, 2007). This can be explained by the fact that sporting goods consumption is also related to personal social experiences, which cannot be exclusively defined through their relation with social groupings. Class, gender, age or specific subcultures constitute a frame in which each social agent builds his/her own experience. The social constraint that imposes one to build and to invent him/her-self in a specific manner (Ehrenberg 1991, 1998), helps to explain that the sensitivity to the self-definition valorises the so-called personal experience. Analyses focusing on objects as extended-selves take into account the role of material culture as a resource of social experiences and emotions.

5. SPORTING GOODS, SELF-IMAGE, IDENTITY AND EXTENDED SELF

More than most products or brands, sporting goods have a symbolic value for the consumer and help define the consumer. Products need to be congruent and consistent with personal pictures or images of one self. Consumer behaviour literature has since long recognised a wide variety of self-images: (a) actual self-image (how consumers in fact see themselves); (b) ideal self-image (how consumers would like to see them selves); (c) social self-image (how consumers feel others see them) and (d) ideal social self-image (how consumers would like others to see them) (Schiffman, Kanuk, & Das, 2006). Schiffman et al. suggest two additional types of self-images, i.e. the expected self-image (how consumers expect to see themselves at some specified future time), and "ought-to" self (traits and characteristics that an individual believes it is his or her duty to possess). Emotions of sport experiences are reflected in consumption, uses and possession of sporting goods which help develop ones self-image and identity. Sometimes we hold on to sporting goods, for example our first pair of ballerinas, which recall, fix and materialise one's first dance experiences and emotions that can be part of one's identity. Sporting goods are often related to specific performances or events, and act to store memories and feelings; they also bring out new experiences and sensations (Ohl & Taks, 2007). In other words "you are what you have, and you have what you are" (e.g., Belk, 1988, p. 137). People buy products, not only for what they do, but also for what they mean. The roles products play in our lives go often well beyond the task they perform (Solomon, Zaichkowsky, & Polegato, 2005). When you buy a Nike Swoosh, you are doing more than buying a shoe; you make a lifestyle statement about the type of person you are or want to be. Interestingly, there is a contradiction between the wish to follow codes and fashion in order to express the bonding with a particular group or subculture, while on the other hand we feel the necessity to create or own self and identity. This is in line with the postmodern perspective of consumer behaviour, which "stresses the symbolic, subjective experience and the idea that meaning is in the mind of a person – that is, individuals construct their own meanings based on their unique and shared cultural experiences, so that there is no single right or wrong answers" (Solomon et al., 2005, p. 29).

The consumption of sporting goods, allows bonding with others who share similar preferences, and facilitates the creation of subcultures or "postmodern tribes" or "pseudo-tribes" when experiences are more fragmented. Data on young people involved in sport indicate that goods consumption is related to their important sport experience. Using goods helps to visualise and exteriorise the identity and core values of sport subcultures and it is difficult to understand sport subcultures without studying the role of the objects within it. So far, marginal groups which threatened society and/or basic sport values, such as hooligans (e.g., Bodin, 1999), urban skating, surfing (Wheaton & Beal, 2003) or snowboarding (Loret, 1995), have received more research attention than ordinary subcultures which represent the main market. In this case, these "postmodern tribes" experiences are more fragmented, less stable, and brands and goods consumption are strongly related to events, fashion and celebrities which are changing over time.

Among people that have a strong sport experience, sport objects can be incorporated into ones life in a way that they become an extension of the self, or the "extended self". Belk (1988) defines the extended self as a multi-layered construct, including the body of the person, external objects and personal possessions, other persons, places and group possessions. The individual's identity is expressed through the object. People cherish possession as they were part of them. Fanatical skiers, for example, will refer to their skis as "my skis", they will take good care of them, and would be devastated if they were lost or stolen, as if they lose a part of themselves. Avid sportspeople transform their goods, making them more personal, and human.

Sport equipment is an integral part of the sports culture, since engagement in sport is strongly related to objects. Sporting goods can be experienced as a resource, a constraint, a motivator and/or facilitator to participate in sport. For example, the wish to posses a certain type of sports equipment can trigger participation. This is especially true for younger kids, where a girl may long for a tutu and therefore picks up ballet; or a boy who loves bokken, jos or tantos (martial arts weapons) and therefore, starts to participate in aikido, or likes swords and starts fencing.

Generally, one of the main goals of sports people is to control their objects; e.g., surfers, skiers, windsurfers, footballers all want to control their respective objects. But sporting goods can also be perceived as barriers or obstacles; for example: balls are difficult to control; skis bring you out of balance; a surf board makes you feel as is you are standing on slippery soap; roller blades make you feel loose motor control; missing carrying the bar at your first weightlifting attempt makes you feel ridiculous. Despite the fact, however, that objects create difficulties, people can have strong relationships with their sports equipment. The weightlifter in Fig. 1, for example, tells her barbells that she loves them despite the difficulties they create. This picture reveals a level of anthropomorphism that can be observed between people and objects, and illustrates the key role specific objects play in sporting subcultures.

Sports objects can make you feel ridiculous at first when you are trying to control them. However, these stages serve as a "rite de passage" within a particular sporting culture. Think, for example, of a child who learns how to ride his or her bike. After numerous attempts, the child will gradually be able to start, stop and ride on his/her own; this new skill level gives him/her a new status in a new age category. The same holds true for snowboarders, surfers or skaters when they learn to perform new tricks or acquire new goods. However, in order to accede to a sport subculture, objects need to be controlled in two ways, i.e. by using them, and by talking about them (Ohl & Taks, 2007). Expertise in sporting goods feeds conversations between sports people, and receives a lot of attention in specialised magazines.

Except for some research on automobiles as a dominant mode of experience in the mid-20th century (Dant, 2004; Urry, 2004), the analysis on the experiences of goods has received little attention. Consumer behaviour literature addresses this topic when discussing the relationship between goods and the creation of so-called peak experiences. In certain sports for example, pieces of equipment can lead to "peak experiences", e.g., mountain bikes, rafting equipment, parachutes. Peak experiences are defined as "highly intense, significant, and fulfilling experiences ... and are often

Fig. 1. "I Still Love You (the Bar) – Even if You Fail Me Sometimes". *Source:*
Quotation and photo are from the Weightlifting International Federation website,
on a page presenting the history by a short text and two photos, see http://
www.iwf.net/iwf/sport_org/weightlifting_sport/history.php

considered turning points which lead to a change in self-concept and
identity" (Dodson, 1996, p. 317). Research on mountain bikers by Dodson,
for example, shows a correlation between the occurrence of a peak
experience and the incorporation of the mountain bike and the activity of
mountain biking in the extended self. The objects associated with the peak
experience become a treasured symbol for the participant.

A previous study by Ohl and Taks (2007) analysed the consumption of
sporting goods in a cross-cultural perspective. First and second year
university students in physical education and/or sport programs from four
different countries, i.e., Belgium, Canada, Germany and France, participated
in the study. The results revealed very little differences between the four
groups of students, indicating that there is a common frame which guides
attitudes and representations towards sporting goods. Some minor cultural
differences appeared in preferences for particular sporting goods, such as
skates for Canadian students, but in essence, the differences were related to

sporting experiences and individual biographies rather than cultural (i.e., country of origin) or socio-cultural backgrounds (i.e., social class). Some minor differences also appeared in the usage of sports apparel (clothing and shoes) outside the sporting context. Belgian and Canadian students, for example, were wearing sports apparel more often at university compared to their French and German counterparts. Canadian students were wearing sporting goods more frequently in other public spaces such as stores, movie theatres, restaurants or bars. In this case the local context does play a role. First, Canadian students showed the highest level of sport participation. Second, sport is strongly embedded in daily life and hyper developed in North America (Westerbeek & Smith, 2003). An abundance of sporting goods is available in a wide variety of stores, and in very wide price ranges. Finally, some gender differences appeared between the countries under investigation. In the French and Belgian sample, men enjoyed talking about sporting goods, giving advice, taking care of sport equipment, more so than the women. Finally, the Germans seemed to receive sporting goods more frequently as a gift, or because of a competition, while the Canadians treasured their sporting goods as memorabilia. Overall, the differences were weak. The role of sporting goods was much more linked to individual sport experiences, and their social frame, to the presentation of self than to other cultural differences. The homogeneity of the sample, all physical education students with a relatively high affinity for sport, may partly explain the outcomes.

6. CONCLUSION

Sporting goods consumption is related to identities, self-image and social bonds; it exteriorises some outlines of culture. Studying this ordinary consumption shows that sporting goods are a way to communicate with others. This can either be "within" or "between" subcultures or in other social groupings such as "neo-tribes" (e.g., Bennett, 1999). Exploring the relation between subcultures and socialisation processes (with age, gender, social class, significant others, etc., as influential factors) brings to question the diffusion of goods. Although sporting goods are in essence products of the global mass culture, produced by trans-national corporations, their consumption is often linked to local and self-identity. In some cases, purchase decision of sporting goods reflects the strong peer socialisation influence on youth (Yoh, 2005). In other cases, parents, sporting heroes, media, advertising, life course events or sport experiences can influence the sensitivity to sporting goods consumption (Jackson & Andrews, 2005; Ohl &

Taks, 2007). Focusing on the purchases, uses and diffusion of sporting goods helps us to understand some important aspects of culture. It allows to focus on the relation between social groups, encompassing the classical view of the dominance of the upper class (the so-called top down) versus the pushing power of popular culture (the so-called bottom up); as well as the effect of globalisation in contemporary society. In the traditional view on the diffusion of sporting goods, the lower classes are believed to mimic the consumption patterns of the upper class to symbolise social success. The upper class is believed to use the goods to distinguish themselves from the middle and lower classes (Bourdieu, 1984 (1979)). However, the ostentatious usage of sport goods is also a common practise for other groups in society, such as urban skaters or black minorities, to express a collective identity (Lamont & Molnar, 2001).

People from different countries, with different cultural backgrounds, consume similar goods. But meanings are always built into the specific social frame in which people behave. Social uses of sporting goods metamorphose them from standardised commodities into personal objects. Thus, analysing sporting goods consumption provides an original gaze to sporting cultures.

NOTES

1. Caution is needed when using "youth" as a category. From a sociological point of view, "it is only a word", and the diversity between young people is important (Bourdieu, 1981). However, there is also mass consumption and youth from different social categories, cultures or countries of origin can buy the same goods and value the same brands, even if they use and value the goods in different ways.

2. Puma, for example, targets the 11–24 years olds as their core market segment (J. F. Jeanne, *Journal du textile*, 1999). Very few brands, such as New Balance have a different positioning, their main target is older, from 23 to 60 (*La lettre de Sports France*, Janvier 1999).

3. Source, Fédération de la Maille, *Du sport compétition au sport loisir et à la mode*, 1999 and Secodip, *étude Consojunior*, 2000.

4. From 6 years old in a study concerning France, Source: ABC+, Disney, *LSA*, *Licence et marques, comment les jeunes les vivent?*, 2001.

5. *Spor-éco*, n 366, 3.12.2001, p. 12

REFERENCES

Appadurai, A. (1986). *The social life of things: Commodities in cultural perspectives.* Cambridge University Press: Cambridge.

Baudrillard, J. (1968). *Le Système des objets.* Gallimard: Paris.

Belk, R. W. (1988). Possessions and the extended self. *The Journal of Consumer Research* (15), 137–168.

Bennett, A. (1999). Subcultures or neo-tribes? Rethinking the relationship between youth, style and musical taste. *Sociology, 33*(3), 599–617.

Birrell, S. (2001). Sport as ritual, interpretations from Durkheim to Goffman. *Social Forces, 60*(2), 354–376.

Bodin, D. (1999). *Hooliganisme: Vérités et mensonges [Hooliganism: Truths and lies].* ESF: Paris.

Boltanski, L., & Chiapello, E. (1999). *Le nouvel esprit du capitalisme.* Gallimard: Paris.

Bourdieu, P. (1981). *Questions de sociologie.* Paris: Minuit.

Bourdieu, P. (1984[1979]). *Distinction: A social critique of the judgement of taste.* Cambridge University Press: Cambridge.

Carlson, L., Grossbart, S., & Walsh, A. (1990). Mothers' communication orientation and consumer-socialization tendencies. *Journal of Advertising, 19*(3), 27–38.

Certeau De, M. (1980). L'invention du quotidien (Vol. 1). Arts de faire, Paris, Union Générale d'Editions, coll. 10/18.

Dant, T. (2004). The driver-car. *Theory, Culture and Society, 21*(4/5), 61–79.

Dodson, K. J. (1996). Peak experiences and mountain biking: incorporating the bike into the extended self. *Advances in Consumer Research, 23*, 317–322.

Douglas, M., & Isherwood, B. (1979). *The world of goods. Toward and anthropology of consumption.* Allen Lane: London.

Ehrenberg, A. (1991). *Le culte de la performance.* Calmann-Lévy: Paris.

Ehrenberg, A. (1998). *La fatigue d'être soi. Dépression et société.* O. Jacob: Paris.

Falk, P., & Campbell, C. (1997). *The shopping experience.* Sage: London.

Fowler, D. (1999). The attributes sought in sports apparel: A ranking. *Journal of Marketing Theory and Practice, 7*(4), 81–88.

Gartman, D. (2004). Three ages of the automobile the cultural logics of the car. *Theory, Culture and Society, 21*(4/5), 169–195.

Goffman, E. (1967). *Interaction ritual: Essays on face to face behavior.* Doubleday, Anchor: New York.

Goldman, R., & Papson, S. (1998). *Nike culture.* Sage: London.

Halbwachs, M. (1933). *L'évolution des besoins dans les classes ouvrières.* Alcan: Paris.

Hebdige, D. (1991). *Subculture: The meaning of style.* Routledge: New York.

Hetzel, P. (2002). *Planète conso. Marketing expérientiel et nouveaux univers de consommation.* Éditions d'Organisation: Paris.

Jackson, S., & Andrews, D. L. (Eds). (2005). *Sport, culture and advertising: Identities, commodities and the politics of representation.* London: Routledge.

Lamont, M., & Molnar, V. (2001). How blacks use consumption to shape their collective identity: Evidence from marketing specialists. *Journal of Consumer Culture, 1*(1), 31–46.

Langer, B. (2002). Commodified enchantment: Children and consumer capitalism. *Thesis Eleven* (69), 67–81.

Loret, A. (1995). *Génération glisse.* Paris: Autrement.

Maffesoli, M. (1988). *Le temps des tribus : le déclin de l'individualisme dans les sociétés postmodernes.* Paris: Méridiens Klincksieck.

Maffesoli, M. (1990). *Au creux des apparences.* Paris: Plon.

Miles, S. (1998). *Consumerism – as a way of life.* London: Sage.

Ohl, F., & Taks, M. (2007). Secondary socialisation and the consumption of sporting goods: Cross cultural dimensions. *International Journal of Sport Management and Marketing*, 2(1/2), 160–174.

Ohl, F., & Tribou, G. (2004). *Les marchés du sport: les consommateurs et la distribution*. Paris: Armand Colin.

Pasquier, D. (2005). *Cultures lycéennes. La tyrannie de la majorité*. Paris: Autrement.

Roedder John, D. (2001). 25 ans de recherche sur la socialisation de l'enfant-consommateur. *Recherche et Applications en Marketing*, 16(1), 87–129.

Schiffman, L. G., Kanuk, L. L., & Das, M. (2006). *Consumer behaviour*. Toronto, Canada: Pearson/Prentice Hall.

Solomon, M. R., Zaichkowsky, J. L., & Polegato, R. (2005). *Consumer behaviour: Buying, having, and being* (3rd ed.). Toronto: Pearson Prentice Hall.

Stevens, John, Lathrop, A., & Bradish, C. (2005). Tracking generation Y: A contemporary sport consumer profile. *Journal of Sport Management*, 19, 254–277.

Urry, J. (2004). The "system" of automobility". *Theory, Culture and Society*, 21(4/5), 25–39.

Veblen, T. (1970[1899]). *Theory of leisure class*. London: Unwin Books.

Westerbeek, H., & Smith, A. (2003). *Sport business in the global marketplace*. MacMillan: New York.

Wheaton, B., & Beal, B. (2003). Keeping it real': Subcultural media and the discourses of authenticity in alternative sport. *International Review for the Sociology of Sport*, 38(2), 155–176.

Yoh, T. (2005). Parent, peer and TV influences on American teens' athletic shoe purchasing. *International Journal of Sport Management and Marketing*, 1(1/2), 180–189.